The Self-directed Teacher

CAMBRIDGE LANGUAGE EDUCATION
Series Editor: Jack C. Richards

This series draws on the best available research, theory, and educational practice to help clarify issues and resolve problems in language teaching, language teacher education, and related areas. Books in the series focus on a wide range of issues and are written in a style that is accessible to classroom teachers, teachers-in-training, and teacher educators.

In this series:

The Self-directed Teacher

Managing the learning process

David Nunan
University of Hong Kong

Clarice Lamb
ATLAS English Learning Center

CAMBRIDGE
UNIVERSITY PRESS

PUBLISHED BY THE PRESS SYNDICATE OF THE UNIVERSITY OF CAMBRIDGE
The Pitt Building, Trumpington Street, Cambridge, United Kingdom

CAMBRIDGE UNIVERSITY PRESS
The Edinburgh Building, Cambridge CB2 2RU, UK   http://www.cup.cam.ac.uk
40 West 20th Street, New York, NY 10011–4211, USA   http://www.cup.org
10 Stamford Road, Oakleigh, Melbourne 3166, Australia

First published 1996
Fourth printing 2000

Typeset in Sabon

Library of Congress Cataloging-in-Publication Data

Nunan, David
The self-directed teacher : managing the learning process / David
Nunan, Clarice Lamb.
p. cm.–(Cambridge language education)
Includes biblioraphical references and index.
ISBN 0-521-49716-7 (hardback).–ISBN 0-521-49773-6 (pbk.)
1. Languages, Modern – Study and teaching. 2. Language teacher-
Training of. I. Lamb, Clarice. II. Title. III. Series.
PB35.N86 1996
418'.007 – dc20   94-49134
                                                       CIP

A catalog record for this book is available from the British Library

ISBN 0 521 49716-7 hardback
ISBN 0 521 49773-6 paperback

Transferred to digital printing 2003

For B.T., Harriet, and José, for teaching us the value of self-direction and for giving us opportunities for learning to make informed choices.

Contents

Series editor's preface

The Self-directed Teacher offers a unique perspective on how language teachers manage the complex array of instructional and interactional decisions they confront in every lesson. Rather than considering teaching from the perspective of methods or methodology, Nunan and Lamb examine the *processes* of teaching, in particular, the decision making used to create effective contexts and conditions for learning in second language classrooms.

The book begins with a consideration of the contextual factors which shape the environments in which teachers work, including the curriculum frameworks, syllabuses, texts, and resources that serve as a backdrop to teaching. From there the authors move to an examination of a rich range of issues that are central to the life and success of every language classroom, such as classroom interaction, classroom dynamics, grouping, resources, monitoring, and evaluation. Each issue is presented through the use of authentic classroom extracts and is followed by tasks which enable readers to explore further the points raised and apply them to their own contexts.

Evident throughout the book is the view that teachers are managers of a complex thinking process, one which involves them in ongoing monitoring, assessment, problem solving, hypothesis testing, and goal-oriented improvisation. Teachers are aided in these processes by their understanding of themselves, their learners, and their classrooms, as well as by information derived from theory and research. Therefore, classroom teachers will find this book to be an excellent resource for examining their teaching and the decision making which underlies it. By examining their own assumptions and practices, teachers will also find ways of becoming more effective managers of their own teaching processes.

Jack C. Richards

Preface

This book is written for teachers and teachers in preparation. It is designed for use in both pre-service and in-service teacher preparation programs in a variety of flexible ways, as well as for use by individual teachers in self-study mode. Moreover, the book complements other volumes in the Cambridge Language Education series, in particular, discussion on reflective teaching in second language classrooms.

The most difficult part of writing a book is formulating a title. In our struggle with this most challenging of tasks, we came up with our own "pet" working title: "Chaos: The Art and Science of Classroom Management." It was born out of late-night phone calls and faxes across several continents, and desperate writing sessions in hotels and airport lounges. It does, however, reflect a central truth of this book: that teaching, while complex and difficult, is, as chaos theory suggests, ultimately capable of being understood, particularly when the understanding comes from the inside, as both an art and a science.

In the final analysis, all teachers have to develop and refine their own teaching style. In a sense, the methods debate is a dead issue because there will be as many methods as there are classroom teachers. It is our hope that the ideas and resources in this book will help less experienced teachers to develop their own distinctive teaching style, and prompt more experienced teachers to reflect on and refine theirs. In this way, all teachers might ultimately be self-directed.

David Nunan
Clarice Lamb

Introduction: The language teaching challenge

Why did we write this book?

This book is intended to fill what we see as a major gap in the language education literature. It covers the central issues and concerns relating to the effective management of teaching and learning processes in second and foreign language classrooms. By "management" we mean the creation of a positive pedagogical environment which facilitates learning. Our focus, therefore, is less on the instructional issues of curriculum planning and methodology, and more on the professional decisions teachers must make to ensure that learning takes place effectively. The ultimate aim of the book is to provide teachers and teachers in training with knowledge and skills that will allow them to take control of teaching processes in their classrooms – help to operationalize the notion of the self-directed teacher. This concept of self-direction on the part of both teachers and learners is one to which we unashamedly adhere.

What is the book about?

This book is basically about decision making. Its aim is to help you make informed decisions as you manage the learning process in your classrooms. According to Wong et al. (1992), effective classroom management has three dimensions:

1. *Planning and preparation*   preventing problems from arising
2. *Classroom strategy*   coping with problems as they arise
3. *Whole-school strategy*   ensuring that the actions and intentions of teachers are in harmony

In this book we deal with all three dimensions, although the principal focus is at the level of classroom strategy. However, it is only with reference to prespecified aims and objectives, within the curricular frameworks estab-

1

lished in this section, that one can predict and develop strategies for dealing with problems which may potentially arise within the classroom. Effective management, then, means taking steps to prevent problems from arising and coping with problems "on line" as they occur in the classroom.

Everard (1986: 127) identifies five key managerial qualities, which are set out in the following list along with examples which we have interpolated from language teaching contexts. The list illustrates the orientation we take here – seeing management, not in terms of budgets, the manipulation of human resources, and so on, but in terms of the managerial skills and knowledge needed for effectively planning, implementing, and evaluating language learning opportunities in both second and foreign language classrooms.

Managerial quality	*Language teaching context*
1. To know what he or she wants to happen and cause it to happen	Developing aims and objectives of a lesson or sequence
2. To exercise responsibility over resources and turn them to purposeful account	Making effective use of resources
3. To promote effectiveness in work and search for continual improvement	Motivating learners toward better learning strategies
4. To be accountable for the performance of the unit he or she is managing	Being accountable to parents, head, and learners
5. To set a climate or tone conducive to enabling people to give of their best	Establishing rapport with learners and maintaining good classroom organization

Biggs and Telfer (1987: 362) suggest that instructional decision making can be located on a continuum that has high-structure decisions at one extreme and low-structure decisions at the other.

Our focus is on the sorts of decisions a teacher must make to be a successful manager of instruction in the here-and-now of the classroom. These decisions fall between two extremes:

1. *high-structure decisions,* which emphasize the teacher's role in setting up the learning environment, and which allow relatively few options and hence require a reactive role from the students;
2. *low-structure decisions,* which provide the pupil with many options and maximum autonomy when in the learning experience (which is not to say that the teacher does not have to work very hard to provide a low-structure environment).

In the pages which follow, we have attempted to deal with both high- and low-structure management decisions, and you will find a synthesis of relevant research and practice in the planning, implementation, and evaluation of language programs in relation to both of these managerial dimensions. In writing the book, we have taken care to present issues and data from a wide range of classroom contexts and situations, while avoiding the temptation to present neatly pre-packaged solutions. Rather than attempt to push a particular line, we invite you to consider the issues, challenges, and options in a reflective way and relate them to the pedagogical contexts with which you are familiar.

How is the book organized?

Because this book is concerned with effectively managing the learning process, its essential concerns are methodological in flavor and deal with issues such as teacher talk, group work, class size, and resources. A basic tenet of the book, however, is that decisions cannot be made in a vacuum. The curricular context determines what is the correct or incorrect decision in most instances. For this reason, Chapter 1 deals with curriculum issues within which methodological issues related to the management of classroom learning can be situated and contextualized. It also articulates our understanding of key terms such as learner-centeredness, learning-centeredness, self-directed teaching, and communicative language teaching. We believe that these concepts are closely related, and we hope to demonstrate these interrelationships as well as the ways in which the appearance of these new concepts in the classroom have increased the managerial demands upon the teacher.

Management decisions can be understood and dealt with in terms of the degree to which particular tasks require the balance of power to be handed from teacher to student. There are times – high-structure situations – when it is appropriate for power and control to be invested in the teacher. Low-structure tasks, however, require student initiative. The learning process is managed appropriately when both the teacher and students acknowledge and have skills to deal with the two situations. In Chapter 2, we illustrate the operation of high- and low-structure decision making through a two-dimensional framework or grid. One dimension consists of planning, implementation, and evaluation – the three essential curricular dimensions. The other dimension consists of the essential management decisions associated with high-structure and low-structure contexts. These concepts are also described in some detail in Chapter 3.

What do we believe?

Learner-centeredness, self-directed teaching, and learning from general education are now being associated with the concepts of communicative language teaching and task-based learning in applied linguistics. In Chapter 1 we present our interpretation of these terms and describe how these concepts have changed language classrooms for those teachers who have embraced them. We argue that learner-centeredness, collaborative learning, and school-based curriculum development, terms which are heard with increasing frequency these days, place greater power and control in the hands of classroom teachers who wish to incorporate them into their teaching. This additional responsibility requires teachers to be effective managers of the teaching/learning process in ways which differ from the challenges posed by systems in which the teacher is the servant of someone else's curriculum. In effect, the emergence of new concepts and ideas about language and learning "destabilizes" the classroom, and presents challenges to the established order. It is therefore impossible to divorce pedagogical issues from managerial ones, and this symbiotic relationship is captured in the following observation:

The press for "responsible self-direction" results in teachers having to help students to take responsibility for their own learning. Such teaching is usually group or individually based, requiring specialist techniques quite different from those of the traditional classroom. (Biggs & Telfer 1987: 367)

We believe that if teachers can give reasoned responses to the questions underpinning the organizational structure of this book, then learning will be successful. This, of course, is a working hypothesis to be contested in individual contexts, rather than a conclusion to be derived from one context and applied to the next. We recognize and acknowledge the challenges posed by emerging concepts of language learning and teaching, but believe that challenges provide opportunities as well as threats. In managerial terms, the greatest challenge is posed by the imperative to shift with greater frequency than hitherto from high-structure (teacher-controlled) to low-structure (student-centered) teaching/learning contexts. There are occasions in which curricular goals are best met by high-structured tasks; in other contexts, low-structured tasks are called for. In the course of the book, we try to indicate those curricular goals and contexts in which one mode is more effective than another.

What would you like to get out of the book?

In keeping with the general philosophy of the Cambridge Language Education series, this book aims to bring together research and practice in the area of language classroom management. Through this integration, we hope that you will be able to see and appreciate how research and indeed theory can both enrich our understanding of the life of the classroom, as well as help answer the questions and address the challenges inherent in all pedagogical encounters.

Apart from the initial contextualizing chapter and the final chapter on evaluating the learning process, we have written this book so that individual chapters can be read in any order. This modular approach will enable you to explore issues in the order of importance to you, and also to skip sections that do not speak to concerns that are salient in your particular context.

What does the book contain?

You will find five different kinds of material integrated into the body of each chapter. These are input, classroom extracts, resources, tasks, and end-of-chapter projects.

Input   Here, we speak directly to you, setting out the issues and challenges relating to the area in question, synthesizing relevant research, and spelling out our attitudes, beliefs, and reactions to the issues at hand.

Classroom extracts   Contained in the book is a substantial number of classroom transcripts which are designed to illustrate the realization of previously discussed issues within the context of the classroom. The transcripts are supplemented with diary extracts, retrospective protocols, and stimulated recalls.

Resources   There are also a wide range of practical resources relating to issues in the management of learning in the classroom. These include observation schedules, lesson plans, questionnaires, and surveys.

Tasks   Within each chapter you will find a series of reflection questions and tasks. Through these the teacher and teacher in preparation can reflect on and relate the issues raised to the context of their own classroom situation.

Projects   At end of each chapter are projects which are longer and more involved than the chapter tasks. They are designed to encourage you to apply some of the ideas presented in the book by observing, recording, and analyzing classroom tasks, and even entire lessons. Because some readers will not be in a position to collect such data, we have provided a lesson and an extended lesson extract as an appendix to the book.

How can the book be used?

The book can be used in a variety of ways. We recommend that you read Chapter 1 first because it provides a curricular framework for making sense of decision making as well as defining key terms. We also suggest that you read the chapters on affective issues and evaluation last. Apart from that, we have tried to present the material so that you can work through the book in any order that suits your own purposes and interests.

As indicated already, the book consists of various elements, including tasks, extracts, and data of various kinds. It is not necessary to do all or even any of the tasks in the book in order to benefit from what it has to offer. The rich array of texts, tasks, and data allow for greater flexibility on the part of teachers and teachers in preparation working in a range of different contexts and situations. Needless to say, it is not mandatory for all tasks and projects to be undertaken by each and every reader; in fact, there may be some contexts and situations in which it is not feasible for all projects to be done. Our aim is to provide resources for further application for those readers who might wish to do so.

You will notice as you work through the book that some tasks suggest the use of video and audiorecorded extracts of classroom interactions. We are aware that many teachers are hesitant to be videotaped or observed. However, we would like to point out that self-observation and, where possible, the observation of other teachers' classes are potentially rewarding forms of professional renewal and reflection on the various aspects of the classroom. Ideally, classroom observation should be a normal part of one's professional practice, providing opportunities for personal and professional growth while not being a threat through which teachers are criticized. Videotaping is an aid to help you reflect on how the issues raised throughout the book can be dealt with more effectively. If you manage to obtain access to a bank of recorded data, this can be used at various points throughout the book. As an additional aid to those who have difficulty obtaining classroom data, we have included lesson transcripts throughout the books as well as a transcript of an entire lesson in the appendix.

Key questions dealt with in the book

In the body of the book are questions related to all aspects of the management of learning — from teacher language to the organization of group work, from the deployment of resources to dealing with affective factors. In concluding this introduction, we would like to invite you to think about and write down the questions you would like answered in some of these key areas.

TASK

Aim To give you an opportunity to think about the questions and issues you would like dealt with in key areas relating to the management of learning.

Procedure Write down questions you would like answered in the following areas.

Area	*Questions*
Lesson preparation	_____
Teacher questions	_____
Lesson pacing	_____
Teaching large classes	_____
Small groups	_____
Teacher roles	_____
Learner roles	_____
Using resources	_____
Motivation	_____
Discipline	_____
Monitoring	_____

1 A context for classroom action

"I dunno," Jimmy said, "I forget what I was taught. I only remember what I've learnt."

(Patrick White)

You are given the experiences you need to understand the world.

(Paulo Coelho)

Introduction

The decisions that teachers are required to make during the instructional process are all driven by the nature of the program, the goals of instruction, and the needs of the individual learners. It is therefore critical for us to consider these issues before turning to the management of the learning process in the classroom. This chapter is a scene-setting exercise, proving a foundation, as well as a point of departure, for the rest of the book.

In the first section we define some of the key concepts that provide a framework for the rest of the book. These concepts include learner-centeredness, learning-centeredness, self-directed teaching, communicative language teaching, and high- and low-structured teaching. We then outline our conception of "curriculum," a broad term that covers the planning, implementation, and evaluation of educational programs.

Concept map of Chapter 1

In this chapter we cover the following issues and concepts:

- *Setting the context and defining terms* key terms defined are "learner-centeredness," "experiential learning," "humanism," "learning-centeredness," "communicative language teaching," "high-structure and low-structure teaching"
- *Curriculum processes* the scope of curriculum development and the importance of curriculum development for the management of learning
- *Needs analysis* definition and examples of needs analysis

– *Setting goals and objectives* from learner needs to learning goals, illustration of goals and objectives, how clearly stated goals and objectives provide a sound basis for managing the learning process

Setting the context and defining terms

In the introduction we asserted that managing the learning process in the language classroom had gradually become more complex with the introduction into pedagogy of new views of language, learning and the role of the learner within the learning process. In this section we examine the key concepts of learner-centeredness, learning-centeredness, self-directed teaching, communicative language teaching and high- and low-structured teaching, and we explain their relevance to the book as a whole.

Learner-centeredness

The concept of learner-centeredness has been invoked with increasing frequency in recent years. What does the term mean? Like many widely used terms, it probably means rather different things to different people (Nunan & Brindley 1986). For us, learner-centered classrooms are those in which learners are actively involved in their own learning processes. The extent to which it is possible or desirable for learners to be involved in their own learning will obviously vary from context to context (and, indeed, from learner to learner). If learners are to learn anything at all, however, ultimately they have to do the learning for themselves. Thus it is a truism to say that they should be involved in their own learning. In an ideal learning-centered context, not only will decisions about what to learn and how to learn be made with reference to the learners, but the learners themselves will be involved in the decision-making process. Each element in the curriculum process will involve the learner, as Table 1 shows.

The philosophy of learner-centeredness has strong links with experiential learning, humanistic psychology and task-based language teaching. These links are evident in the following quotes:

[A learner-centered] curriculum will contain similar elements to those contained in traditional curriculum development, that is, planning (including needs analysis, goal and objective setting), implementation (including methodology and materials development) and evaluation (see for example Hunkins 1980). However, the key difference between learner-centred and traditional curriculum development is that, in the former, the curriculum is a collaborative effort between teachers and learners, since learners are closely involved in the decision-making process regarding the content of the curriculum and how it is taught. This change in orientation has major practical implications for the entire curriculum

Table 1   Learner roles in a learner-centered curriculum

Curriculum stage	Role of learner
Planning	Learners are consulted on what they want to learn and how they want to go about learning. An extensive process of needs analysis facilitates this process. Learners are involved in setting, monitoring, and modifying the goals and objectives of the programs being designed for them.
Implementation	Learners' language skills develop through the learners actively using and reflecting on the language inside and outside the classroom. They are also involved in modifying and creating their own learning tasks and language data.
Assessment and evaluation	Learners monitor and assess their own progress. They are also actively involved in the evaluation and modification of teaching and learning during the course and after it has been completed.

process, since a negotiated curriculum cannot be introduced and managed in the same way as one which is prescribed by the teacher or teaching institutions. In particular, it places the burden for all aspects of curriculum development on the teacher. (Nunan 1988: 2)

The proponents of humanistic education have broadened our concept of learning by emphasizing that meaningful learning has to be self-initiated. Even if the stimulus comes from outside, the sense of discovery, however, and the motivation which that brings has to come from inside driven by the basic human desire for self-realization, well-being and growth. . . . [I]n terms of personal and interpersonal competence the process-oriented classroom revolves around issues of risk and security, cooperation and competition, self-directedness and other-directedness; and meaningful and meaningless activities. We have also tried to make clear that "teachers who claim it is not their job to take these phenomena into account may miss out on some of the most essential ingredients in the management of successful learning" (Underhill 1989, p. 252). (Legutke & Thomas 1991: 269)

We can see from these extracts that learner-centeredness is strongly rooted in traditions derived from general education. Our view is that language pedagogy needs to draw on its general educational roots for sustenance, which it has not not always done. In fact, some language programs seem to have suffered an "educational bypass." During the course of this book, our orientation will become clear, as we have drawn on insights and resources, not only from language pedagogy, but from education in general (Brown 1989; Everard 1986; Everard & Morris 1990).

TASK

Aim To evaluate your own attitude toward the concept of learner-centeredness.

Procedure With reference to a teaching context you are familiar with, indicate your attitude to the concept of learner-centeredness by rating the following statements from 1 (totally disagree) to 5 (totally agree).

1. Learners have a right to be involved in curriculum   1 2 3 4 5
   decision making (e.g., selecting content, selecting
   learning activities and tasks).
2. Learners learn best if the content relates to their   1 2 3 4 5
   own experience and knowledge.
3. Learners have fixed ideas about language learning   1 2 3 4 5
   that need to be taken into account in developing
   language programs.
4. Learners who have developed skills in "learning   1 2 3 4 5
   how to learn" are the most effective students.
5. Learners are less interested in learning for   1 2 3 4 5
   learning's sake than in learning in order to achieve
   immediate or not too far distant life goals.
6. Learners have different learning styles and   1 2 3 4 5
   strategies that need to be taken into consideration
   in developing learning programs.
7. Learners who have developed skills in self-   1 2 3 4 5
   assessment and self-evaluation are the most
   effective students.

In doing this task in workshops with teachers, we have found that teachers will give different answers according to the context and situation in which they are working. This finding serves to underline the essential point that learner-centeredness is not an all-or-nothing concept. It is an attitude, a philosophy, which will be conditioned by the situation and context in which teachers finds themselves.

Learning-centeredness

Table 1, which sets out the role of the learner in relation to curriculum planning, implementation and evaluation, represents the ideal. As teachers

Table 2   Learner-centeredness in the experiential content domain

Level	Learner action	Gloss
1	Awareness	Learners are made aware of the pedagogical goals and content of the course.
2	Involvement	Learners are involved in selecting their own goals and objectives from a range of alternatives on offer.
3	Intervention	Learners are involved in modifying and adapting the goals and content of the learning program.
4	Creation	Learners create their own goals and objectives.
5	Transcendence	Learners go beyond the classroom and make links between the content of the classroom and the world beyond the classroom.

and course designers, we have been in relatively few situations in which learners from an early stage in the learning process have been able to make critically informed decisions about what to learn and how to learn. In our experience, learners need to be systematically taught the skills needed to implement a learner-centered approach to pedagogy. In other words, language programs should have twin goals: language content goals and learning process goals. Such a program, we would characterize as being "learning centered." By systematically educating learners about what it means to be a learner, learners reach a point where they are able to make informed decisions about what they want to learn and how they want to learn. It is at this point that a truly learner-centered curriculum can be implemented. Learning-centeredness is thus designed to lead to learner-centeredness.

The previous discussion underlines the fact that learner-centeredness is not an all-or-nothing process. Rather it is a continuum from relatively less to relatively more learner-centered. Nunan (1995b) has captured this continuum in the following tables, which show that learner-centeredness can be implemented at a number of different levels. The tables also illustrate some of the practical steps that can be taken in implementing a learner-oriented approach to instruction.

Table 2 relates to the experiential content domain. It demonstrates that, all other things being equal, a classroom in which learners are made aware of the pedagogical goals and content of instruction is more learner-centered

Table 3   Learner-centeredness in the learning process domain

Level	Learner action	Gloss
1	Awareness	Learners identify strategy implications of pedagogical tasks and identify their own preferred learning styles/strategies.
2	Involvement	Learners make choices among a range of options.
3	Intervention	Learners modify/adapt tasks.
4	Creation	Learners create their own tasks.
5	Transcendence	Learners become teachers and researchers.

than one in which goals and content are left implicit. We would argue that all learners should, in the first instance, be alerted to goals and content. In collecting data for this book we were surprised at how infrequently this step happened. However, we would go further, and argue that it is just a first step along a path that, given the appropriate context and types of learners, could take the learners through a gradual learning process in which they made selections from a range of alternatives, modified and adapted goals and content, created their own goals and selected their own experiential content areas and finally moved beyond the classroom itself. (For practical descriptions and illustrations of these processes, see Nunan 1995b.) How far one chooses to move along the continuum depends on one's learners and the context and environment of the instructional process.

Table 3 shows how the continuum can apply to the learning process domain. Once again, we see that learner-centeredness is not an all-or-nothing process, but can be implemented in a series of gradual steps.

Communicative language teaching

Communicative language teaching emerged from a number of disparate sources. During the 1970s and 1980s applied linguists and language educators began to re-evaluate pedagogical practice in the light of changed views on the nature of language and learning, and the role of teachers and learners in the light of these changing views. The contrast between what for want of better terms we have called "traditionalism," and communicative language teaching (CLT), is shown in Table 4 in relation to a number of key variables within the curriculum. The table presents contrasts in relation to theories of language and learning, and in relation to objectives, syllabus, classroom activities and the roles of learners, teachers and materials. The views illustrated represent points on a continuum, rather than exclusive categories, and most teachers will move back and forth along the continuum in re-

Table 4 Changing views on the nature of language and learning: Traditionalism and CLT

Teaching	Traditionalism	Communicative language
Theory of language	Language is a system of rule-governed structures hierarchically arranged.	Language is a system for the expression of meaning: primary function – interaction.
Theory of learning	Habit formation; skills are learned more effectively if oral precedes written; analogy not analysis.	Activities involving real communication; carrying out meaningful tasks and using language that is meaningful to the learner promote learning.
Objectives	Control of the structures of sound, form and order, mastery over symbols of the language; goal – native speaker mastery.	Objectives will reflect the needs of the learner; they will include functional skills as well as linguistic objectives.
Syllabus	Graded syllabus of phonology, morphology, and syntax. Contrastive analysis.	Will include some or all of the following: structures, functions, notions, themes and tasks. Ordering will be guided by learner needs.

Activities	Dialogues and drills; repetition and memorization; pattern practice.	Engage learners in communication; involve processes such as information sharing, negotiation of meaning and interaction.
Role of learner	Organisms that can be directed by skilled training techniques to produce correct responses.	Learner as negotiator, interactor, giving as well as taking.
Role of teacher	Central and active; teacher-dominated method. Provides model; controls direction and pace.	Facilitator of the communication process, needs analyst, counselor, process manager.
Role of materials	Primarily teacher oriented. Tapes and visuals; language lab often used.	Primary role of promoting communicative language use; task based, authentic materials.

sponse to the needs of the students and the overall context in which they are teaching. The truth is that language is, at one and the same time, both a system of rule-governed structures and a system for the expression of meaning. Learning is a matter of habit formation as well as a process of activation through the deployment of communicative tasks. The challenge for the teacher, the textbook writer and the curriculum developer is to show how the rule-governed structures enable the language user to make meanings.

We do not believe that many classrooms can be defined exclusively in terms of a particular methodology. Whether a classroom is characterized as "traditional" or "communicative" is therefore determined by the relative emphasis and degree to which the views listed in the table underpin what happens in the classroom rather than on the exclusive adherence to one set of views to the exclusion of any other. The difference lies, not in the rigid adherence to one particular approach rather than another, but in the basic orientation. Some teachers operate out of a traditional paradigm, making occasional forays into CLT, and for others it is the other way around. In the ESL and EFL classrooms we have worked in and studied in recent years, the prevailing trend has been toward CLT, although by no means exclusively so.

High- and low-structure teaching

The insight that communication was an integrated process rather than a set of discrete learning outcomes created a dilemma for language education. It meant that the destination (functioning in another language) and the route (attempting to learn the target language) moved much closer together, and, in some instances (for example, in role plays and simulations), became indistinguishable. The challenge for curriculum developers, syllabus designers, materials writers and classroom teachers revolved around decisions associated with the movements between points on the continua set out in the tables in the preceding section. Questions such as the following therefore appeared with increasing frequency in teacher-training workshops: How do I integrate "traditional" exercises, such as drills, controlled conversations and the like, with communicative tasks such as discussions, debates, role plays, etc.? How do I manage decision making and the learning process effectively in classroom sessions devoted to communicative tasks which, by definition, require me to hand over substantial amounts of decision-making power and control to the learners? How can I equip learners themselves with the skills they will need to make decisions wisely and to embrace power effectively?

For some individuals the solution lay in rejecting the changing views along with their inconvenient pedagogical implications. Others went to the opposite extreme, eschewing "traditional" solutions to their materials development and language-teaching challenges. In most contexts, however, a more balanced view prevailed.

For some time after the rise of CLT, the status of grammar in the curriculum was rather uncertain. Some linguists maintained that it was not necessary to teach grammar, that the ability to use a second language ("knowing how") would develop automatically if the learner were required to focus on meaning in the process of using the language communicate. In recent years, this view has come under serious challenge, and it now seems to be widely accepted that there is value in classroom tasks which require learners to focus on form. It is also accepted that grammar is an essential resource in using language com-municatively. (Nunan 1989a: 13)

In educational terms, a useful way of viewing this emerging dilemma in language education is in terms of high- and low-structure teaching. High-structure tasks are those in which teachers have all the power and control. Low-structure tasks are those in which power and control are devolved to the students. We have borrowed the terms "high-structure" and "low-structure" from Biggs and Telfer. As we pointed out in the introduction, they suggest that the successful management of the learning process de-pends on teachers knowing where to locate themselves on the high- to low-structure continuum in relation to a given task. In a high-structure task, students are placed in reactive roles and accorded relatively little choice. In a low-structure context, students have many options and maximum auton-omy. However, we do not equate high-structure with non-communicative and low-structure with communicative tasks. In certain communicative tasks, learners have relatively little freedom of maneuver. However, we do believe an association exists between low-structure and CLT and that the incorporation of communicative tasks with low-structure implications into the classroom increases the complexity of the decision-making process for the teacher.

We would argue that the kinds of managerial issues that arise and the sorts of decisions that teachers are required to make will be largely driven by the degree of structure implied. This concept is illustrated in Table 5, which provides exemplary questions relating to high- and low-structure contexts as these apply to key elements at the levels of curriculum planning, implementation, and evaluation. This schema will be referred to constantly in the pages that follow, as it is one of the key organizational frameworks underpinning the work as a whole. It allows us to deal coherently with the following key managerial questions and to demonstrate that the answers will vary according to the degree of structuring called for by the instruc-tional goals guiding the interaction at that particular time.

Table 5 Curriculum decision-making in high-structure and low-structure contexts

Curricular elements	Management issues	
	High-structure contexts	*Low-structure contexts*
At the planning stage		
Course design	What does the institution tell me to teach? What are the managerial decisions entailed in the teacher's manual?	How do I design/adapt my own my own content/goals/tasks?
Needs analysis	How can I identify the learning preferences of my students?	How can I involve my learners in identifying and articulating their own needs?
Collegial	How can I cooperate with colleagues in course planning? How can I get the most out of staff meetings? How can staff meetings contribute to effective planning?	What opportunities exist for team teaching?
Resources	How do I manage use of set text?	How do I modify/adapt the text? How do I create my own resources? How do I design split information tasks that will be effective in my context?

At the implementation stage		
Talk/interaction	What are effective strategies for direct instruction? How do I give feedback on high-structure tasks?	What questioning strategies facilitate learner contributions to low-structure tasks? How do I give feedback in low-structure tasks? What types of teacher questions maximize student output?
Learner language	How do I correct learner errors?	How can I provide language models in small group role plays in which the principal focus is on the exchange of meanings?
Learner attitude		How do I deal with group conflicts? How do I deal with student resistance to learner initiated tasks?
Group configuration	How do I organize controlled practice? How do I manage teacher-fronted instruction effectively?	How do I set up small group learning? What strategies exist for setting communicative tasks in which students work independently?
At the evaluation stage		
Learner assessment	What techniques will help me to assess the achievement of my learners?	How can I help my learners develop effective techniques for self-assessment?
Self-evaluation of the learning process		
Formal evaluation		How can learners be involved in providing input to the evaluation process?

What aspects of teacher talk (direct instruction, feedback, instructions, and questioning strategies) facilitate or impair effective learning?

What issues need to be taken into consideration in lesson planning and preparation?

How can the teacher most effectively exploit resources in the classroom?

What strategies exist for setting up different modes of classroom interaction, from teacher-fronted through small group, pair and individual work?

What are the implications of affective attitudes (e.g., motivation, attitude and aptitude) for the effective management of learning?

What tools, techniques, and strategies exist for the ongoing monitoring and evaluation of classroom interaction and acquisition?

(All of these questions can be explored through the investigative procedures suggested in Nunan 1990, 1992a).

The curriculum in outline

Implicit in the foregoing discussion is the fact that classroom decision-making and the effective management of the learning process cannot be made without reference to the larger context within which instruction takes place. The context and environment of the learning process, including the curriculum plans that should drive the pedagogical action, are critically important here. In other words, classroom decisions cannot be made without reference to structures operating outside of the classroom. For this reason, we have included in this initial framing chapter a section in which we set out our understanding of key concepts associated with "curriculum."

Language curriculum development has been greatly influenced by changing views on the nature of teaching and learning. These changing views are reflected in the objectives and content of language programs, as well as activities, materials, and teacher/learner roles. The influence of these different views was made clear in the Table 4, which contrasted traditionalism with CLT.

As we can see from Table 5, communicative language teaching has had a major influence on language curriculum development. First, curriculum development has become much more complex. Whereas twenty or thirty years ago, the point of departure for curriculum development tended to be restricted to the identification of the learner's current level of proficiency, with the development of communicative language teaching and the insight that curricula should reflect learners' communicative needs and learning preferences, much more information about and by learners came to be incorporated into the curriculum process. The other major modification occurred with the emergence of the communicative task as a central build-

Table 6   Key curriculum questions, procedures, and areas

Questions	Procedures	Areas
Content		
What?	Selecting	
Why?	Justifying	} Syllabus design
When?	Grading	
Processes		
How?	Enacting	
When?	Sequencing	} Methodology
Outcomes		
How well?	Assessing	Assessment
How effective?	Evaluating	Evaluation

ing block within the curriculum. Instead of being designed to teach a particular lexical, phonological or morphosyntactic point, tasks were designed to reflect learners' communicative needs. Language focus exercises were developed as a second-order activity.

In summary, we can say that curriculum development represents a delicate juggling act involving the incorporation of information about the learner, about the language, and about the learning process. Language content questions include what are we teaching, why are we teaching it, and when we are teaching it. Learning process questions, which are methodological in character, include how are we arranging the learning environment. Among other things, when we focus on the learner, we must ask how well the learner has done and how well the curriculum has done in serving the needs of the learner.

We can relate these key questions to each other in terms of the central curricular elements of syllabus design, which has to do with the selection, sequencing and grading of content; methodology, which is concerned with task selection and sequencing; and assessment and evaluation, which are concerned with determining how well students have done, as well as evaluating how well the instructional process has met curricular goals. These relationships are set out schematically in Table 6.

One view of "curriculum" has it that curriculum processes have to do with the development of tactical plans for action. In this view, "curriculum" is taken to refer to statements about what should happen in the teaching and learning situation. According to this view, the curriculum specialist's task ends when the ink is dry on the various documents that have been produced to guide teaching and learning. We believe that this view is simplistic and naive, that while "curriculum" includes the planning process, it also in-

Phase I:	Planning (initial needs analysis, goals and objectives, content, and process)
Phase II:	Implementation (ongoing needs analysis, monitoring, action research)
Phase III:	Evaluation (assessment, self-assessment, program evaluation

Figure 1   Three phases or perspectives on the curriculum process

cludes the processes of implementation and evaluation. These three phases
are captured in Figure 1.

The final point we wish to make in this preliminary overview is that the
language curriculum should concern itself, not only with language content
goals, but also with learning process goals. Learners should be focused on
the processes through which learning takes place as well as on the target
language they are learning. It is our contention that learners who have
developed skills in identifying their own preferred learning skills and strategies will be more effective language learners.

| Curriculum goals | Language content | For example, to develop the ability to obtain goods and services in the target language |
| | Learning process | For example, to develop skills in learning how to learn |

TASK

Aim To familiarize you with some of the key tasks concerned with curriculum development and to provide an opportunity for you to relate these
to your own teaching situation.

Procedure

1. The following list contains some of the tasks that need to be carried
   out in the course of designing and implementing a curriculum. Study
   the activities and decide which of them, in relation to a context with
   which you are familiar, should be carried out by a teacher, a curriculum specialist, a counselor, a director of studies, etc. Write these
   down in the spaces provided.

2. Select those areas for which the teacher has primary responsibility. What are some of the decisions that need to be made? Express these as questions.

Data

Interview students _____
Conduct needs analysis _____
Assign students to class groups _____
Carry out diagnostic test _____
Assess students' current level of English _____
Diagnose individual learning difficulties _____
Identify individual learning styles _____
Select and grade linguistic content (grammar, vocabulary, functions, notions) _____
Select experiential content (topics, themes, situations, settings, etc.) _____

Set out course goals _____
Write performance objectives _____
Select, adapt or develop learning tasks and materials _____
Monitor student progress _____
Assess learning outcomes _____
Evaluate language program(s) _____

In some teaching contexts, teachers will be responsible for all these tasks. In others, they will have little control. Some of the questions raised by teachers in relation to interviews, needs analysis, and assigning students to groups include the following:

— *Student interviews*   Should these be carried out before, during, or after the course has begun? Should the learners be forced to respond in the target language? How do I get information from low-proficiency learners when I don't speak their language?
— *Needs analysis*   What techniques exist for doing needs analysis? How can the resulting information be used for writing course goals and objectives? What if my learners have conflicting needs?
— *Assigning students to groups*   What criteria, other than proficiency level, can be used to assign students to groups? Is it possible to have different configurations at different times during the teaching day?

Needs analysis

In the course of designing a teaching program from scratch or modifying an existing one, it is generally desirable to collect and interpret data about the learners and the institutional context in which they learn. This information may be collected formally or informally before the course and once the course has begun. A variety of different types of information can be collected. Such information might include biographical information about the learners, data on the types of communicative tasks that learners might want or need to carry out in the target language, information on the ways in which the learners prefer to learn, and so on. A wide range of information can be collected through needs analysis procedures of various kinds, as will be seen in the sample instruments provided in this section. In the initial planning stages, the extent to which learners' subjective needs can be canvassed depends on the range and extent of learners' previous experiences. (It would be unrealistic, for example, to ask learners whether they like to learn through role play and simulations if they have never experienced such activities.)

In attempting to obtain information from learners, as well as about learners, additional limitations and constraints will apply with young learners, or with low-proficiency learners if the teacher does not speak the learners' first language and does not have the benefit of bilingual assistants or other first language resources.

Brindley (1989) suggests that there are basically three different approaches to needs analysis. He calls these the language proficiency orientation, the psychological/humanistic orientation and the specific purpose orientation. The three approaches are differentiated according to their educational rationale, the type of information collected, the method of data collection and the purposes for which the data are collected. The salient characteristics of the three approaches are set out in Table 7.

In learner-oriented contexts, the types of information required and the purposes to which the information will be put will vary somewhat from programs developed without reference to the learners themselves, and those for which any preliminary analysis will be largely restricted to the needs of the institution or the educational system that the curriculum is intended to serve. Within a second, rather than foreign, language context, Brindley suggests types of information and purposes that are important (see Table 8 on page 26).

A major purpose for conducting needs analyses is to categorize and group learners. This grouping process facilitates the specification of content and learning procedures that are consonant with some aspect of the learner data that has been gathered. Figure 2 on page 27 exemplifies some ways in which data can be used for grouping purposes.

Table 7 Approaches to needs analysis

	Language proficiency orientation	Psychological/humanistic orientation	Specific purpose orientation
Educational rationale	Learners learn more effectively if grouped according to proficiency.	Learners learn more effectively if involved in the learning process.	Learners learn more effectively if content is relevant to their specific areas of need/interest.
Type of information	Language proficiency/language difficulties	Attitudes, motivation, learning strategy preferences	Information on native speaker use of language in learners' target communication situation
Method of collection	Standardized forms/tests Observation	Standardized forms Observation, interviews and surveys	Language analysis Surveys of learners' patterns of language use
Purpose	So learners can be placed in groups of homogeneous language proficiency	So learners' individual characteristics as learners can be given due consideration	So that learners will be presented with langauge data relevant to their communication goals
	So teachers can plan language content relevant to learners' proficiency level	So learners can be helped to become self-directing by being involved in decision making about their learning	So motivation will be enhanced by relativeness of language content

Source: After Brindley 1989: pp. 67–69. Used by permission.

Table 8   Types of information required in a learner-centered system

Type of information required	Purpose
1. Learners' life goals	So that teachers have a basis on which to determine or predict learners' language goals, communicative networks and social roles
2. Language goals, communicative networks and social roles	So learners may be placed in a group based on common social roles, and teachers may make preliminary decisions about course content appropriate to learners' social roles
3. Objective needs, patterns of language use, personal resources (including time)	So learners can be grouped according to their needs and/or interests
4. Language proficiency and language difficulties	So learners can be grouped according to their language proficiency
5. Subjective needs including learning strategy preferences, affective needs, learning activity preferences, pace of learning, attitude toward correction	So that teachers may adapt learning activities to learning strategy preferences, individual needs
6. Information about learners' attainment of objectives	So that the teacher can monitor performance and modify program accordingly
7. Information about developmental processes in second language learning, including learners' communicative strategies	So that teacher can gear language content and materials to learners' stage of development

Source: Adapted from Brindley 1984. Used by permission.

I. Language proficiency profile
   1. Students with oral skills, but with few or no literacy skills in L1
   2. Students who belong in a new arrivals program
   3. Students who require general support in the mainstream
   4. Students with specific affective, language and communication needs
   5. Students who are approximating nativelike proficiency

   (Adapted from S.A. ESL Guidelines)

II. Learning strategy profile
   1. *"Concrete" learners*   These learners tend to like games, pictures, films, video, using cassettes, talking in pairs and practicing English outside class.
   2. *"Analytical" learners*   These learners like to study grammar, study English books, and read newspapers; they also like to study alone, find their own mistakes, and work on problems set by the teacher.
   3. *"Communicative" learners*   These students like to learn by watching, listening to native speakers, talking to friends in English and watching television in English, using English out of class in shops, trains, etc., learning new words by hearing them and learning by conversations.
   4. *"Authority-oriented" learners*   These learners prefer the teacher to explain everything; they also like to have their own textbook, to write everything in a notebook, to study grammar, learn by reading, and learn new words by seeing them.

   (Adapted from Willing 1988)

III. Learning purpose
   1. New arrivals
   2. English in the workplace
   3. English for further study
   4. English for professional employment
   5. English for access to vocational training and employment

Figure 2   Three alternative ways of grouping learners

Setting goals and objectives

In the content domain, needs analysis provides a basis for setting goals and objectives. Goal and objective setting are important tasks in most educational contexts, because they provide a rationale for selecting and integrating pedagogical tasks, as well providing a point of reference for the decision-making process. Goals are broad statements that provide general signposts for course development. The following sample goals have been extracted from a variety of second and foreign language programs. They are expressed in the broadest possible terms.

– To develop sufficient oral and written skills to obtain promotion from unskilled worker to site supervisor
– To establish and maintain social relationships through exchanging information, ideas, opinions, attitudes, feelings, and plans

- To develop communicative skills in order to acquire, record and use information from a variety of aural sources
- To develop the academic listening skills in order to extract key information from university lectures
- To develop basic communicative skills in order to obtain basic goods and services as a tourist

More limited goals, couched in functional terms, can be found in teaching materials of various sorts. The following have been taken from an intermediate-level textbook.

In this book you will:
Make comparisons
Ask for and give advice
Express obligation
Talk about past experiences
Express opinions about entertainment.

(Nunan 1995a)

These goal statements are very general in nature and can encompass numerous subsidiary objectives. Most curriculum documents based on a goal and objectives approach contain a limited number of goals (perhaps five or six) that provide a basis for the development of objectives. Formal performance objectives specify what learners should be able to do as a result of instruction. Formal objectives should contain a performance (which sets out what learners are to do), conditions (specifying the conditions and circumstances under which the learners should perform) and standards (setting out how well they should perform). The three objectives that follow illustrate the three components of performance, conditions, and standards.

- Working in pairs, learners will provide enough information for their partner to draw their family tree. They will provide enough information for a three-generation family tree to be drawn.
- Students will extract and record estimated minimum and maximum temperatures from a taped radio weather forecast. They must accurately record four of the six regions covered by the forecast.
- While watching a videotaped conversation between two native speakers, students will identify the various topics discussed and points at which they are changed. All topics and change points are to be identified.

The use of an objectives approach has been criticized in general education on the grounds that precise statements of what the learner should be able to do at the end of a course is somehow undemocratic and needlessly restricting on both the student and the teacher. Others argue that such precise specification greatly facilitates other steps in the design process. It forces

Table 9   Communication and learning-how-to-learn goals

Broad goal	*Specific goals*
Communication By participating in activities organized around use of the target language, learners will acquire communication skills in the target language, in order that they may widen their networks of interpersonal relations, have direct access to information and use their language skills for study, vocational and leisure-based purposes	To be able to use the target language to: − establish and maintain relationships and discuss topics of interest (e.g., through exchange of information, ideas, opinions, attitudes, feelings, experiences, plans) − participate in social interaction related to solving a problem, making arrangements making decisions with others, and transacting to obtain goods, services, and public information − obtain information by searching for specific details in a spoken or written text and then process and use the information obtained. − obtain information by listening to or reading a spoken or written text as a whole, and then process and use the information obtained

continued

the designer to be realistic about what learners can achieve and helps guide the selection of appropriate materials and classroom activities. It is also an essential prerequisite for devising appropriate forms of learner assessment.

Some years ago, an interesting set of specifications was developed in Australia. Called the Australian Language Levels (ALL) guidelines, these specifications were intended to be general enough to help materials writers and teachers working in a range of second and foreign languages. The ALL guidelines take as their point of departure a number of broad goals that are refined into specific goals, as shown in Table 9.

Table 9   *continued*

Broad goal	Specific goals
	— give information in spoken or written form (e.g., give a talk, write an essay or a set of instructions) — listen to, read or view, and respond personally to a stimulus (e.g., a story, play film, song, poem, picture, play)
Learning-how-to-learn Learners will be able to take a growing responsibility for the management of their own learning so that they learn how to learn, and how to learn a language	To develop: — cognitive processing skills (to enable them to understand values, attitudes and feelings to process information, and to think and respond creatively) — learning-how-to-learn skills — communication strategies (to enable them to sustain communication in the target language)

Source: Adapted from Scarino et al. 1988.

You can get some idea from this further example of the breadth of the goal-setting exercise. You can also see how numerous subsidiary objectives could be formulated from each of the goal statements. Interestingly, the designers of the ALL guidelines chose to move directly from goals to the specification of task or activity types without elaborating detailed sets of objectives. We also have employed this procedure in some of our work. Although we do not feel it necessary to develop formal three-part objectives for everything we wish to teach our learners, we do believe that a sample set of objectives can greatly assist in managing the learning process. They can be particularly useful in the ongoing monitoring and assessment of the learning process.

The latest manifestations of the goals and objective approach to curriculum development have appeared in competency statements that attempt to specify what learners should be able to do at different levels. The following are core competencies designed for an adult immigrant program. Once again, you can see they are formulated in terms of what the learners should be able to do as a result of instruction.

English for study

1. Can understand the context of further education/training in Australia
2. Can utilise a range of learning strategies relevant to further education/ training contexts

---

3. Can understand an oral presentation relevant to further education/training contexts
4. Can negotiate complex/problematic spoken exchanges related to further educational/training contexts
5. Can participate in group discussions relevant to further educational/training contexts
6. Can deliver short oral presentations relevant to further educational/training contexts

---

7. Can read diagrammatic/graphic texts relevant to further educational/training contexts
8. Can read procedural texts relevant to further educational/training contexts
9. Can read informational texts relevant to further educational/training contexts

---

10. Can write short reports relevant to further educational/training contexts
11. Can write short essays relevant to further educational/training contexts
12. Can write procedural texts relevant to further educational/training contexts
13. Can take notes from oral and written texts

Vocational English

1. Can understand the context of work in Australia
2. Can utilise a range of learning strategies relevant to employment contexts

---

3. Can understand an oral presentation relevant to workplace contexts
4. Can negotiate complex/problematic spoken exchanges relevant to employment contexts
5. Can participate in group discussions/meetings
6. Can participate in casual conversations

---

7. Can read diagrammatic/graphic texts relevant to the workplace
8. Can read procedural texts relevant to workplace contexts
9. Can read informational texts relevant to employment/workplace contexts

---

10. Can write short reports relevant to the workplace context
11. Can write procedural texts relevant to the workplace context
12. Can complete formatted texts relevant to employment/workplace contexts
13. Can write letters of application for employment
14. Can write a resume

_____

English for community access

1. Can understand the context of welfare/community services in Australia
2. Can utilise a range of learning strategies relevant to the local community context

_____

3. Can understand an oral report relevant to the local community context
4. Can negotiate complex/problematic spoken exchanges for personal business and community purposes
5. Can participate in casual conversation

_____

6. Can read common diagrammatic/graphic texts
7. Can read procedural texts (e.g., appliance instructions)
8. Can read relevant informational texts (e.g., formatted, short reports and other texts)
9. Can read formal letters/notes from agencies

_____

10. Can write short informal letters/notes from agencies
11. Can write short formal letters/notes
12. Can complete formatted texts e.g. library forms, agency forms for personal business

(NSW Adult Migrant Education Service Draft Competencies)

Another useful tool is the curriculum-planning grid. Planning grids such as the following can be used to relate goal and objective statements with other curricular elements (such as grammar, functions, or topics). In Figure 3 the task or performance elements from a set of objectives are cross-referenced with settings. The grid was developed for a general English speaking course.

TASK

Aim To apply the planning grid described in this section to your own teaching situation.

Data The planning grid above.

Procedure Develop a planning grid, similar to the one in Figure 3, to a course of your choosing.

TASKS	SETTINGS									
	1	2	3	4	5	6	7	8	9	10
Identify people										
Talk about past events										
Give and receive messages										
Talk about future ability										
Report what someone says										
Talk about where things are located										
Make excuses										
Express regrets										
Talk about personal qualities										
Give reasons										
Give opinions and advice										
Express preferences										
Make a complaint										

Key to settings
1 At work   3 Using public transport   5 On holiday   7 At the market   9 At a dinner party
2 At home   4 In bar/coffee shop   6 In a store   8 At school   10 In a government office

Figure 3   Planning grid for general English course

In this section we have tried to illustrate a range of ways in which goals and objectives can be expressed. Despite their differences, all of these goals and objectives share something in common; they all describe what learners should be able to do as a result of instruction. We believe that all language programs should take as their point of departure goals and objectives, however couched, that have been derived from an analysis of learner needs.

Summary and conclusions

The basic theme of this chapter is that a firm basis for effective classroom decision making and management must be laid well before the teacher sets foot in the classroom. As we shall see in the rest of this book, it is difficult, if not impossible, to say whether many managerial decisions are either good or bad without reference to the needs of the learners or the goals and objectives of the curriculum. Because the decisions that teachers are required to make during the instructional process are driven by the nature of the program, the goals of instruction and the needs of the individual learners, we include a detailed description and discussion of these issues and procedures in the chapter.

We also define several key concepts that we believe are currently having an influence on the field and that have changed the nature of language classrooms around the world. These concepts include learner-centeredness, learning-centeredness, self-directed teaching, communicative language teaching, and high- and low-structured teaching. In setting out our understanding of these terms, we tried to indicate how the introduction of these concepts has changed the nature of the decision-making process in the classroom. In the rest of this book we shall explore challenges and solutions to the management of the learning process posed by the realization of these concepts within the language classroom.

PROJECT

1. Study the needs analysis instruments provided in the following samples and evaluate the usefulness of the information solicited in each instance.
2. Drawing on one or more of the instruments, devise your own questionnaire. Administer it to a sample of learners.
3. Evaluate the results. How useful is the information you obtained? How might it be used for course planning purposes?

Sample 1   General learner needs survey

Name _____
Age _____
Language learning history _____
Intended occupation _____
Purposes for English _____
People with whom learner will interact _____
Target variety or dialect _____
Current proficiency level _____
Educational background _____
Other languages _____
Aptitude _____
Where language will be used _____
Degree of mastery required _____
Language genres required _____

Sample 2   Language contact survey

We would like you to tell us which of the following uses of English are important for you. Please put an X for each under the column "Very Useful," "Useful," or "Not Useful."

	Very useful	Useful	Not useful

Do you want to improve your English so
that you can
1. Tell people about yourself
2. Tell people about your family
3. Tell people about your job
4. Tell people about your education
5. Tell people about your interests
6. Use buses, trains, ferries
7. Find new places in the city
8. Speak to tradespeople
9. Speak to landlord/real estate agent
10. Buy furniture/appliances for your
    home
11. Deal with door-to-door salesmen
12. Communicate with your friends
13. Receive phone calls
14. Make telephone calls
15. Do further study
16. Get information about courses,
    schools, etc.
17. Enroll in courses
18. Get information about the
    educational system
19. Help children with schoolwork
20. Apply for a job
21. Get information about a job
22. Go to the Commonwealth
    Employment Service
23. Attend interviews
24. Join sporting or social clubs
25. Join hobby or interest groups
26. Watch TV
27. Listen to the radio
28. Read newspapers, books,
    magazines
29. Give, accept, refuse invitations
30. Make travel arrangements
31. Talk to your boss
32. Talk to doctors/hospital staff
33. Talk to neighbors
34. Talk to children's teachers
35. Talk to government officials

	Very useful	Useful	Not useful

36. Talk to English-speaking friends
37. Get information about goods and
    services
38. Complain about, or return goods
39. Arrange credit/hire-purchase/lay-by

From this list, choose five you want to learn first.

1. _____   4. _____
2. _____   5. _____
3. _____

Sample 3 Methodological preferences

How do you like learning? Circle your answer.

1. In class do you like learning
   a. Individually?   YES/NO
   b. In pairs?   YES/NO
   c. In small groups?   YES/NO
   d. In one large group?   YES/NO

2. Do you want to do homework?   YES/NO
   If so, how much time do you have for   _____ hours a day
     homework outside class hours?   _____ hours a week
   How would you like to spend the time?
   a. Preparing for the next class?   YES/NO
   b. Reviewing the day's work   YES/NO
   c. Doing some kind of activity based on your per-   YES/NO
      sonal experience, work experience or interests?

3. Do you want to
   a. Spend all your learning time in the classroom?   YES/NO
   b. Spend some time in the classroom and some   YES/NO
      time practicing your English with people
      outside?
   c. Spend some time in the classroom and some   YES/NO
      time in an individualized language center?

4. Do you like learning
   a. By memory?   YES/NO
   b. By problem solving?   YES/NO
   c. By getting information for yourself?   YES/NO
   d. By listening?   YES/NO

e. By reading?	YES/NO
f. By copying from the board?	YES/NO
g. By listening and taking notes?	YES/NO
h. By reading and making notes?	YES/NO
i. By repeating what you hear?	YES/NO

Put a check mark next to the three things that you find most useful.

5. When you speak do you want to be corrected

a. Immediately, in front of everyone?	YES/NO
b. Later, at the end of the activity, in front of everyone?	YES/NO
c. Later, in private?	YES/NO

6.

Do you mind if other students sometimes correct your written work?	YES/NO
Do you mind if the teacher sometimes asks you to correct your own work?	YES/NO

7. Do you like learning from

a. Television/video/films?	YES/NO
b. Radio?	YES/NO
c. Tapes/cassettes?	YES/NO
d. Written material?	YES/NO
e. The blackboard?	YES/NO
f. Pictures/posters?	YES/NO

8. Do you find these activities useful?

a. Role play	YES/NO
b. Language games	YES/NO
c. Songs	YES/NO
d. Talking with and listening to other students	YES/NO
e. Memorizing conversations/dialogues	YES/NO
f. Getting information from guest speakers	YES/NO
g. Getting information from planned visits	YES/NO

9. How do you like to find out how much your English is improving?

a. Written tasks set by the teacher?	YES/NO
b. Oral language samples taken and assessed by the teacher?	YES/NO
c. Checking your own progress by making tapes, listening to them critically and comparing?	YES/NO
d. Devising your own written tasks for completion by yourself and other students?	YES/NO
e. Seeing if you can use the language you have learnt in real-life situations?	YES/NO

10. Do you get a sense of satisfaction from
     a. Having your work graded?   YES/NO
     b. Being told that you have made progress?   YES/NO
     c. Feeling more confident in situations that you   YES/NO
        found difficult before?

Sample 4   Subjective experiences of the learner

Dear Student,

We are currently looking at what students think about learning another language and would like to find out what you think. We would be very grateful if you could take a little time to complete this questionnaire.

Part I   Information about yourself
1. I am in year _____.
2. I am _____ years of age.
3. Are you a good language learner compared with other students? Circle the response that describes you best.

   Compared with other students, I am
   a. Better than average
   b. About average
   c. Below average

Part II   Your feelings about language learning
Indicate your attitude to the following statements by circling the appropriate number.
     1 – This is never, or almost never true of me.
     2 – This is generally not true of me.
     3 – This is somewhat true of me.
     4 – This is generally true of me.
     5 – This is always or almost always true of me.

1. I feel embarrassed when the teacher asks me to   1 2 3 4 5
   speak in front of the other students.
2. I like to learn by reading.   1 2 3 4 5
3. I like to learn by listening to and using cassettes. 1 2 3 4 5
4. I like to learn through games.   1 2 3 4 5
5. I like to write everything down.   1 2 3 4 5
6. I like the teacher to explain rules of grammar to 1 2 3 4 5
   me.
7. I like to figure out rules of grammar myself.   1 2 3 4 5
8. I like the teacher to explain the meaning of new   1 2 3 4 5
   words.

9. I like to figure out the meanings of words by myself.   1 2 3 4 5

10. I like the teacher to tell me all my mistakes.   1 2 3 4 5

11. I like the teacher to let me find my own mistakes.   1 2 3 4 5

12. I like to study by myself.   1 2 3 4 5

13. I like to work in pairs.   1 2 3 4 5

14. I like to work in small groups.   1 2 3 4 5

15. I like to work with the whole class.   1 2 3 4 5

16. I like to practice outside of the classroom.   1 2 3 4 5

17. I like to be part of the decision-making process about what we will learn (that is, the content of the lessons).   1 2 3 4 5

18. I like the teacher to make all the decisions about what we will learn (that is, the content of the lessons).   1 2 3 4 5

19. I like to be part of the decision-making process about how we will learn (that is, the classroom tasks and activities we will take part in).   1 2 3 4 5

20. I like the teacher to make all the decisions about how we will learn (that is, the classroom tasks and activities we will take part in).   1 2 3 4 5

21. I like to be responsible for my own learning.   1 2 3 4 5

22. I like the teacher to explain the objectives of the lesson to me.   1 2 3 4 5

23. I like the teacher to give reasons for what we are learning and how we are learning.   1 2 3 4 5

24. I like to assess my own progress.   1 2 3 4 5

25. I like the teacher to assess my progress for me.   1 2 3 4 5

Part III   What happens in your situation?
Indicate what happens in your situation by circling the appropriate number.

     1 – This is never or almost never true.
     2 – This is generally not true.
     3 – This is somewhat true.
     4 – This is generally true.
     5 – This is always or almost always true.

1. The objectives of the lesson or unit of work are explained to us.   1 2 3 4 5

2. We are helped to set our own objectives.   1 2 3 4 5

3. The reasons we are learning certain things are explained to us.   1 2 3 4 5

4. We are given opportunities to choose the content of the lessons.   1 2 3 4 5

5. The reasons we are learning in certain ways (for example, through group work) are explained to us.   1 2 3 4 5

6. We are given opportunities to make choices about how we will learn.   1 2 3 4 5

7. We are given opportunities to assess our own progress.   1 2 3 4 5

8. We are encouraged us to practice and learn outside the classroom.   1 2 3 4 5

Part IV
Please write down three things you like best about learning another language.

1. _____
2. _____
3. _____

Please write down three things you like least about learning another language.

1. _____
2. _____
3. _____

Thank you very much for taking the time to complete this survey.

Sample 5   Prospective course survey

Dear Student,

We are developing a new course for teaching English to Japanese students, and I would like your help. Can you take a little time to complete this survey?

Part I   What do you like to learn?
Indicate your attitude toward the following topic areas by circling the appropriate numbers.

    1 – I don't like this at all.
    2 – I don't like this very much.
    3 – This is OK.
    4 – I quite like this.
    5 – I like this very much.

1. Giving personal information (e.g., name, address, etc.)   1 2 3 4 5
2. Talking about families and friends.   1 2 3 4 5
3. Describing occupations, jobs and work.   1 2 3 4 5
4. Talking about music, movies, TV programs.   1 2 3 4 5
5. Talking about sports and hobbies.   1 2 3 4 5

6. Finding out about/talking about education.   1 2 3 4 5
7. Finding out about/talking about housing and accommodation.   1 2 3 4 5
8. Describing people's dress and appearance.   1 2 3 4 5
9. Finding out about how other young people spend their time.   1 2 3 4 5
10. Finding out about customs and habits of people from other countries.   1 2 3 4 5
11. Finding out about/talking about other cities and countries.   1 2 3 4 5
12. Making complaints/giving advice.   1 2 3 4 5
13. Using the telephone.   1 2 3 4 5
14. Listening to the radio.   1 2 3 4 5
15. Talking about pop stars, film stars and other famous people.   1 2 3 4 5
16. Talking about holidays, festivals, etc.   1 2 3 4 5

Part II   How do you like to learn?
Indicate your attitude to the following statements by circling the appropriate number:

    1 – This is never or almost never true of me.
    2 – This is generally not true of me.
    3 – This is somewhat true of me.
    4 – This is generally true of me.
    5 – This is always or almost always true of me.

1. I don't like to speak in front of the other students.   1 2 3 4 5
2. I like to learn by reading.   1 2 3 4 5
3. I like to learn by listening to and using cassettes.   1 2 3 4 5
4. I like to learn through games.   1 2 3 4 5
5. I like to write everything down.   1 2 3 4 5
6. I like the teacher to explain rules of grammar to me.   1 2 3 4 5
7. I like to work out rules of grammar myself.   1 2 3 4 5
8. I like the teacher to explain the meaning of new words.   1 2 3 4 5
9. I like to work out the meanings of words by myself.   1 2 3 4 5
10. I like the teacher to tell me all my mistakes.   1 2 3 4 5
11. I like the teacher to let me find my own mistakes.   1 2 3 4 5
12. I like to study by myself.   1 2 3 4 5
13. I like to work in pairs.   1 2 3 4 5
14. I like to work in small groups.   1 2 3 4 5
15. I like to work with the whole class.   1 2 3 4 5

16. I like to practice outside of the classroom.   1 2 3 4 5
17. I like to listen and repeat.   1 2 3 4 5
18. I like to memorize conversations and practice   1 2 3 4 5
    them with another student.
19. I like the teacher to give reasons for what we are   1 2 3 4 5
    learning and how we are learning.

Part III

Work with another student. Write down three other things you like to learn about and three other things you like to do to learn English.

We like to learn about:

1. _____
2. _____
3. _____

We like to learn by doing the following things:

1. _____
2. _____
3. _____

Part IV

Is there any other information that you would like to give me to help me plan this course?

_____
_____
_____

2 The planning process

"The best-laid schemes o' mice an' men . . ."

(Robert Burns; "To a Mouse")

Introduction

As we saw in Chapter 1, the ingredients for an effective language class must be assembled long before teachers and students come together in the classroom. The potential success or relative failure of a lesson will often be determined by the amount of planning and preparation the teacher is able to devote to the lesson, class or unit of work, and the extent to which the preparation of lessons and units of work is tied in to teacher's overall pedagogical goals. In a sense, "lessons" are artifacts, which dissolve against the larger context within which teaching and learning take place (see, for example, Nunan forthcoming). That said, classroom management problems can often be traced to poor or ineffective preparation for teaching. We are not suggesting that good preparation is a sufficient condition for effective classroom management and instruction; however we would argue that it is a necessary one. This preparation need not be a formal process that results in detailed lesson plans, but may simply be the development of expectations based on program goals and the reflective monitoring of those expectations during the teaching process. (Devon Woods, personal communication, uses an illuminating image: "the course is the trail that the decision-making process leaves behind.") In this chapter, then, we shall argue that teaching effectiveness will be enhanced if teachers spend part of their planning time in creating mental pictures of how the students should be spending their time and devising an action plan of what to do if reality does not match expectations.

We also look at some of the elements of planning that provide a solid basis for the effective management of the classroom. In the first substantive section of the chapter, we look at options for lesson preparation. This section is followed by a discussion of the pre-instructional decisions that can facilitate the instructional process. The chapter concludes with a section on professional collaboration with colleagues, focusing in particular on planning and staff meetings.

Concept map of Chapter 2

In this chapter we deal with the following concepts and issues:

- *Lesson preparation*   formal and informal program planning and lesson preparation, describing and illustrating frameworks for lesson planning
- *Pre-instructional decision making*   exploration of the decisions which teachers make before going into the classroom
- *Collaborating with colleagues: planning and staff meetings*   the value of opportunities for professional contact with colleagues, collaboration with colleagues for more effective teaching

Lesson preparation

In many pre-service teacher education programs, the importance of program planning and lesson preparation is generally given a great deal of weight. However, when teachers actually begin teaching, it quickly become apparent that effective teaching is much more than simply implementing a pre-determined plan. The mechanistic model, with its assumption that planning equals teaching equals learning simply does not match the reality, which is that planning, teaching and learning are complex, multidimensional activities, and that the relationships between them are organic rather than linear. In other words, the process of helping students to learn is more like growing a garden than building a brick wall.

Over time, as teachers gain experience, planning tends become more informal and internalized, reflecting the essentially organic nature of the process. Although studies of teachers' planning procedures are not particularly common, those that exist reinforce the organic nature of planning, implementing and monitoring learning. In an early study, Taylor (1970) investigated the curriculum planning procedures of 261 secondary teachers. He found that, in planning their programs, teachers gave greatest prominence to the needs, interests and abilities of their students, followed by subject matter, goals and teaching methods. Evaluation was seen as a relatively low priority, as was establishing links between the teacher's own program and the wider curriculum. Taylor concluded that planning was unsystematic and that most teachers were not adequately prepared for or skilled in program planning. This interpretation reflected the prevailing rhetoric of the time, that planning and implementation ought to be logical, and "linear." It was consistent with the "rational" curriculum model established twenty years earlier by Tyler (1949), who argued that curriculum development ought to be a linear process of establishing goals and objectives, selecting content and instructional opportunities, and determining evaluation. In recent years, this linear view, which focuses on learning products, has been challenged by those who have embraced the organic metaphor (Nunan 1988) and those who focus on instructional processes rather than products (Woods 1993).

Woods has been particularly important in helping to reshape our understanding of the planning process. In a detailed study of the role that planning plays in the practice of TESOL, he has this to say about planning and decision making:

Clearly, the structure of events in a course is the result of a decision-making process. Decisions are made about what will be done when in order to accomplish the course. Decisions result in actions, which when carried out result in classroom events—ultimately in the form of verbal and non-verbal events among students and teacher in the classroom, which over the period of a term, we call a course. Decision-making is thus the cognitive work which culminates in a course. Decisions are based on knowledge and beliefs about the current state of the world (such as students' knowledge and abilities, the content of the curriculum, and what is happening in the classroom), and about what is good and bad about this current state. Part of understanding a course therefore is understanding the decisions which create it. . . . (Woods 1993: 111–112)

In this section we look at the pre-teaching planning decisions that play an important part in creating the patterns and fibers that give texture to a course. We believe that planning for teaching includes at least three elements:

– a knowledge of the students and their needs
– a set of goals and objectives
– a personal view of the nature of language and learning

We also believe that, although teachers have views on the nature of language and learning, these views are often implicit. The self-directed teacher, however, is one who is able to make these things explicit to themselves and others.

In observing teaching and learning in many different contexts, we have found that, as relationships develop between teachers and students, a "culture" begins to emerge with its own norms and rules of interaction. This "culture" is influenced and can be enhanced by careful thought and preparation.

Wong et al. (1992) provide a set of questions to guide the pre-course planning process. Although the questions were devised with younger learners in mind, they provide a useful checklist for teachers working with

Table 1   Elements of the standard planning tool

	Presentation	*Practice*	*Production*
Role of teacher	Model	Conductor	Monitor
Role of students	Listener	Performer	Interactor
Activity type	Lecture	Substitution drill	Role play
Class arrangement	Whole class	Pair	Small group

students at any age level. (The question guide is included as a project at the end of this chapter.)

In relation to younger learners, Wong et al. (1992: 47) comment that

these pre-lesson preparations are very useful. They can help the teacher to have a good start with the students and thus establish a good relationship with them. Thinking them through helps the teacher to anticipate problems. As usual there are no absolute 'right answers', but it is best to greet the students rather than ignoring them. . . . When they are at their seats, it helps to call for attention – make sure you have obtained it from everyone – and tell pupils what they should do with schoolbags, what to get out and put on the desk and so on.

Twenty years ago, the standard planning tool (which is still widely used today) was the three-stage presentation/practice/production procedure. This procedure was based on the psychological model that viewed learning as a linear process of understanding, internalizing, and activating knowledge. At the presentation stage, the teacher makes explicit and illustrates the target language item or items. At the practice stage, the students develop control over the item(s) through various sorts of manipulation drill. At the production stage they are involved in actively using the target item(s) in meaningful situations. These three stages represent a gradual movement from high- to relative low-structure interactions (although many production tasks give the illusion of student control.)

Teachers make numerous managerial decisions as they plan each of these stages in a teaching cycle. These decisions include the content and procedure (what is to be taught and how it is to be taught), roles of teacher and students, type of class arrangement for each phase (pair work, group work, individual work), how students will demonstrate mastery. Some of these elements are illustrated in Table 1.

Despite its simplicity, and the fact that it has been around for many years, this planning model is effective and useful for meeting many discrete language objectives. These may be lexical (for example, "to learn key vocabulary associated with employment"), grammatical ("to practice the distinction between the present perfect and the simple past") or functional ("to ask for directions"). Its continued presence, in various guises, in classrooms and materials around the world is a testamony to its value, particularly in those language schools where the only qualification for employment is that a teacher is a native speaker of the language being taught. However, for more contextualized and integrated objectives, more sophisticated models are required.

Although the next model contains elements of presentation, practice and transfer, it is more elaborate and is based on very different assumptions about the nature of language and learning from those of the preceding model. It was developed by Estaire and Zanón (1994) for planning units of work within a foreign language system based on a thematic task-based approach that integrates objectives, content, methodology and evaluation. It is interesting as an approach, because it suggests that the teacher should design the final task or series of tasks and then work backward, from the target task, identifying objectives, content, procedures, and means of assessment and evaluation.

1. Determine theme or area of interest.
2. Plan final task or series of tasks (to be done at the *end* of the unit).
3. Determine unit objectives.
4. Specify contents that are necessary or desirable to carry out final task(s): thematic aspects to be dealt with, which will determine (a) linguistic content and (b) other content.
5. Plan the process: determine communication and enabling tasks that will lead to final tasks(s); select/adapt/produce appropriate materials for them; structure the tasks and sequence them to fit into class hours.
6. Plan instruments and procedure for evaluation of process and product (built in as part of the learning process).

The following example is a partly completed first draft. It shows how one teacher used the framework to begin planning a unit of work for a group of elementary students.

1. *Theme*   Describing people (physical characteristics)
2. *Final task: (for END of unit)*   Mingle or work in groups of 8–10 students. Through question and answer, students find out what their mothers look like and check if there are any similarities among them. Finally they listen to the teacher describing his or her mother and do a task to show understanding.

3. *Objectives*   During the unit, students will develop ability and knowledge necessary to:
   a. Write a simple description of a person.
   b. Give information orally describing a person.
   c. Ask questions necessary to find out about physical characteristics of a person.
   d. Understand a simple written or spoken description of a person.

} covering aspects specified in 4

4. *Content*
   a. *Thematic aspects*   (N = new, R = recycled)

Physical characteristics

color of eyes (ND)	height and weight (N)
color and length of hair (N)	glasses (N)
age (R)	beard and mustache (N)

   b. *Linguistic content*
   Grammar: *be, have,* possessive adj., questions (Yes/No and Wh . . .)
   Vocabulary: eyes, hair, beard, mustache, glasses, adjectives to refer to thematic aspects specified in (a)

   c. *Other content*   (to be added later as the planning advances)

5. *The process: Tasks for day 1, day 2, day 3, etc, [leading to the final task(s)]*

   Discussion of plans for the unit, perhaps eliciting in L1, aspects normally included in descriptions of people and circling those planned to be covered.
   Special attention to final task and objectives: presented to students.
   Students write objectives in their notebooks (+poster?).
   Presentation of new items, using visuals and students as examples.
   Reading, listening, speaking, writing tasks; form–focus tasks; from textbook and supplementary materials. Tasks based on song and video.

   Final task(s) as specified in 2.
6. *Evaluation (procedure/instruments)*
   Carried out by students ⎤ find instruments and procedures during
   Carried out by teacher ⎦ the course we're doing
                              (Estaire and Zanón 1994: 5; used by permission)

The next planning model is more sophisticated than either of the two already presented. It is also more explicit in the way it relates classroom action to learner needs, program goals and the nature of language and learning. This explicitness is important because, as we suggested at the beginning of the section, effective planning takes as its point of departure:

– a detailed knowledge of the students and their needs
– a clearly formulated set of goals and objectives
– a firm view of the nature of language and learning

Chapter 1 provides detailed guidance on how to identify students' needs and establish goals and objectives. In the following discussion, we shall illustrate how these three elements can provide a solid foundation for lesson preparation, and therefore the effective management of the learning process by presenting a case study of the planning process at work. This case study is taken from a language class for adult immigrant students, which is described in Hammond, Burns, Joyce, Brosnan and Gerot (1992; used by permission). In presenting their case study, the authors begin with their philosophy of language. The three core principles, which are derived from the theory of systemic-functional linguistics, are as follows:

– Language is functional, that is, language is the way it is because of the meaning it makes. The theory suggests that resources available within the systems of discourse, grammar and vocabulary are utilized in specific ways to make specific meanings.
– It is a theory of language in context, and suggests that language can only be understood in relation to the context in which it is used. The different purposes for using language and different contexts result in different language texts. The construction of language texts in turn impacts on the context. There is thus a two-way relationship between text and context.
– The theory focuses on language at the level of the whole text. By text is meant any connected stretch of language that is doing a job within a social context. Thus the term 'text' is used to refer to stretches of spoken and written language. Text may be as short as one word, e.g., EXIT, may be as long as a book such as a training manual. This theory differs from most other approaches to language study, notably traditional grammar, which offers systematic analyses of language only up to the level of the sentence, and provides little guidance to the language learner, who needs to know about structure, organization and development in connected oral discourse and written texts.

(Hammond et al. 1992: 1)

The proponents of this approach to language education have developed a curriculum model, which they call the "teaching-learning" cycle. This cycle has four recursive phases. They are as follows:

1. *Building control of the field*   This initial phase is designed to provide learners with the background content knowledge that they will need in order to carry out the tasks and achieve the goals of the curriculum.
2. *Modeling*   Here learners are provided with examples, in the form of models, of how native speakers or competent users of the language would use the language.
3. *Joint construction*   Teacher and student work collaboratively to create a text following the model provided in the preceding state in the teaching-learning cycle.
4. *Independent construction*   Learners, working independently, construct their own texts.

The following example shows how the teaching-learning cycle was used to develop a unit of work for low-intermediate learners to help them learn about and act upon their rights in regard to tenancy laws.

Stage	*Commentary*
1. *Building control of field* Discussion of houses in poor repair. Spoken request What to do?	Here the teacher activates students' background knowledge, including key vocabulary and grammatical structures
2. *Modeling* Spoken request — analysis of structure and vocabulary — grammatical patterns	At this stage, learners are presented with a native speaker model of the target interaction for discussion and analysis. In some ways, this stage is similar to the "presentation" stage in the model discussed above. It differs in that learners are presented with whole language in context rather than discrete language items.
3. *Joint construction* — role play	Following the model already presented, teacher and learners create their own version of the interaction.
4. *Independent construction* — role play	Working individually, in pairs, or in small groups, students create their own interaction.
5. *Building control of field* What to do if spoken request ignored? (Need for written texts.)	A second cycle is initiated, this time focusing on written rather than spoken language.
6. *Modeling* Analysis of model of written texts	
7. *Joint construction* Joint construction of written texts	
8. *Independent construction* Independent construction of written texts	

(Hammond et al. 1992)

How was this cycle made to work in practice? The following lesson plan shows the tasks that were actually used for the first four steps in the cycle. As you read, you might like to consider how closely the tasks "mesh" with the description provided of the cycle.

1. *Building the field for spoken request*

Task	Purpose	Task characteristics
1. Discuss picture of house in poor repair	To begin building a repertoire of shared experience of context and field To begin developing the language needed to state the nature of any problems with houses	− Whole class activity − Teacher focus − Spoken language focus
2. Discuss what to do should such a problem arise	To alert students to what they should do if a problem arises − using appropriate modality (e.g., *should, must, can*) Naming type of tradesmen who could help	− Whole class activity − Teacher focus − Spoken language focus
3. Produce grammatically well-formed sentences	To ensure students have a record of independent activity To practice sentence construction using modals and names of tradesmen (e.g., "What should you do? *The toilet is blocked. I must call a plumber.*")	− What to do if a problem arises − Learner focus − Spoken and language focus

2. *Modeling*

Task	Purpose	Task characteristics
4. Listen to model of spoken (telephone) request for service of real estate agent	To identify text-type To discuss purpose of such a text	− Whole class activity − Teacher focus − Spoken language focus
5. Practice dialogic re-quest for service	To ensure students un-derstand the stages of this genre To practice using the language of service requests	− Whole class activity − Teacher focus − Spoken language focus

| 6. Role play request for service | To develop students' understanding of the stages and language used in spoken (telephoned) requests for service through use of structure role play | – Student pairs
– Learner focus
– Spoken language focus |

3. *Joint construction*

Task	*Purpose*	*Task characteristics*
7. Role play telephoning real estate agent requesting service	To consolidate individual learners' ability To request service of a real estate agent through use of less structured role play	– Teacher-student pairs – Teacher-learner focus – Spoken language focus

4. *Independent construction*

Task	*Purpose*	*Task characteristics*
8. Students independently construct a telephone request for service to a real estate agent and role play	To consolidate individual learners' ability to request service of a real estate agent through independent construction and use of role play	– Student pair activity – Learner focus – Spoken language focus

(Hammond et al. 1992)

We selected these three models because, despite some similarities, they represent contrasting approaches to instructional design. The appropriacy of one model over another will depend on the needs of the learners, the goals of the curriculum, the institutional context within which the instruction takes place and the professional background of the teacher.

This "generic" planning model has several notable strengths. It is based on an explicit theory of language, a theory that is particularly suitable for language education. It is also underpinned by a model of language learning, although this model is rather naive in some respects. Nevertheless, we like the fact that the planning approach outlined here provides explicit support and instruction for the learner as well as clear models of the language which they are expected to produce. It also provides practical exemplification of the way in which the teacher can shift from high-structure to low-structure teaching within a given lesson or unit of work. In addition, the collaborative nature of the first three steps in the instructional process articulates nicely with recent work in experiential learning. Finally, the model can be adapted to a wide range of language teaching contexts and environments, from elementary second language classrooms to college-level foreign language classrooms. In relation to the high-structure, low-structure continuum presented in Chapter 1, we can see that the model allows for a gradual movement from high-structure, teacher-controlled interaction, through to relatively low-structure tasks, in which students have the initiative. It is worth noting, however, the amount of careful preparation and support given to the students before the initiative is handed over to them.

TASK

Aim To apply one of the described approaches to your own teaching situation.

Data One of the planning models presented earlier.

Procedure Plan a unit of work following the selected model.

In our discussions with and observations of teachers working in many different contexts over many years, we have noted that the greatest impediment to effective planning is lack of time. Many educational establishments and (regrettably) many administrators are either ignorant of or simply unprepared to bear the financial burden of giving teachers time for adequate preparation. In many places the view seems to be that time spent by teachers away from the teaching "coal-face" is time wasted. Although we have a certain amount of sympathy for those who have to manage tight budgets, we are just as firm in our belief that time invested in careful planning and preparation will pay off in terms of enhanced student outcomes.

Because of constraints of space, we have only been able to describe three lesson preparation models, one relatively simple, the others quite sophisticated. In a number of respects the third is an elaboration of the first. If you can evolve your own planning model, it will greatly enhance the quality of your teaching as well as helping to save time.

Pre-instructional decision making

As we have already pointed out, many decisions need to be made before the teacher actually steps into the classroom. We have also argued that these decisions should be made with reference to what we know and believe about language and language learning, an understanding of the learners and their needs and a curriculum framework which contains explicit and achieveable goals and objectives. Decision making, informal and otherwise, is referenced against these factors, along with the exigencies of the situation we are in. Although we all have beliefs about language and learning, they are not always easy to express. Our own ideas can often be revealed by considering the views of others.

TASK

Aim   To identify views on the nature of language and learning implicit in teachers' statements about the instructional process.

Procedure

1. Compare the following statements and note similarities in the pre-instructional decision-making process of these teachers.
2. Rank the teacher from most to least similar to you.

Data

1. ". . . first one of the things I try and do is try and figure out the components that should make up the course/that I want to teach . . . for example, I wrote down the normal/the reading, listening, speaking, writing, vocabulary, grammar/all six main areas and then I just brainstormed on what I thought should go in and what kind of activities that I possibly could do in those areas." (Woods 1993: 177)
2. "Using what I hear from the students on the first day as some kind of guideline to what I expect to see in writing I think is a bit of a faliacy and trap that one can fall into . . . and I try to disregard that as much as possible and concentrate on their writing." (Ibid.)
3. "Well, I always analyze the whole unit to see the main ideas to be taught. As I teach mostly the more advanced levels, and as at this stage students have been introduced formally to many aspects of the language, but still make mistakes of form and use, and their receptive skills (listening and reading) exceed their productive ones (speaking and writing), I worry about directing students to review and analyze grammar points and discuss written texts. I think this way I'll be offering them the opportunity for more practice of the target language." (Authors' data)
4. "When I plan, the main things I consider are age, nationality, type of course, the aims of the course (for example, whether it's exam based, or whether it's to complete a set book), and the time – how much, and at what time of day. Then, on a day to day basis, I think about the lesson aims and the problems I anticipate the students might have. For example, today I'm revising and practicing the concept and use of the present perfect. I anticipate that there will be confusion in students' minds between a completed action in the past, and an action within the structure of the present perfect." (Authors' data)
5. "I'm team teaching a course for academic purposes, so I have two points of departure in planning what I'm going to teach – the ideas of my co-teacher and the subject matter of the course. Both of these things put constraints on what I do (and sometimes what I'd like to do). While I generally agree with the ideas of my co-teacher, there are times when I disagree and have to compromise. The major difference

between us, and the thing that makes me rather uncomfortable from time to time, is the fact that I like to be well prepared (probably over-prepared), with an entire program mapped out and tied to course goals and objectives while she's much inclined to "go with the flow." (Authors' data)

These statements all reveal views on the nature of language and the language learning enterprise. It is interesting to note that, in the case of our own data, several teachers stated that they do not have a "theory of language or learning," that they just get on with the practical business of teaching. However, we would maintain that it is not possible to "get on with the practical business" without a "theory." What we found encouraging was the realization that all teachers are able to provide a rationale for what they do. Often the very invitation to reflect on and report what they do was a stimulus for teachers to articulate their rationale for the first time. In at least one instance, this came as something of a revelation.

Another interesting aspect of the interviews we conducted with teachers was that the discussions were largely couched in terms of learner needs ("When I plan, the main things I consider are age, nationality. . . ."), linguistic objectives (". . . today I'm revising and practicing the concept and use of the present perfect") and classroom tasks (". . . I just brainstormed on what I thought should go in and what kind of activities that I possibly could do in those areas. . . .'). There were virtually no references to the kinds of planning models presented in the preceding section. As we have already pointed out, with models such as those presented in this section, we believe that the planning process will be more effective.

Collaborating with colleagues: Planning and staff meetings

Most of us have experienced the frustration of the staff meeting that seems to go on and on while there are pressing matters to be dealt with elsewhere, such as assignments to mark, students to consult, lesson plans to prepare, materials to write, and students to teach. Despite this, we believe that the professional growth potential of collegial collaboration is enormous and deserves to be taken seriously. Unfortunately, when professional development push comes to administrative shove, it is the professional development items which tend to disappear off the end of the staff-meeting agenda.

This is unfortunate as staff meetings are an essential strand in the fabric of any educational institution, and, although attention to administrative matters is important, opportunities to build and strengthen professional relationships with colleagues should not be missed. Just as the effectiveness of the language classroom can be enhanced with careful planning and preparation, so, too, can staff meetings. We have found that meetings can be enhanced if procedures such as the following are adhered to:

- Meetings should have a chairperson who allocates speaking turns, determining who should speak and for how long. This position need not be held by the head of department or director of studies. In fact, it can often be a disadvantage if such a person chairs a meeting. Such persons should not contribute to the debate. Their function is to manage the meeting. The position can, in fact, be one which is rotated among colleagues.
- Meetings should also have an agenda. All colleagues should have the opportunity of contributing to the agenda, which should be circulated in advance of the meeting. During the meeting the agenda should be adhered to. It is one of the functions of the chair to ensure that this happens.
- Staff meetings should have their own regularly scheduled time. Ideally, these meetings be at a time when all members of staff can attend (that is, it should not conflict with teaching time), and it should also be in teachers' paid time. (Staff meetings can be a problem for part-time teachers, who are generally not paid to attend them.)

Not all readers will be in a position to carry out the following task, which will require a degree of sensitivity on the part of the recorder. For those who are able to negotiate with colleagues to record a staff meeting, it should provide interesting data.

TASK

Aim To explore the ways in which issues are raised and dealt with in staff meetings.

Procedure

1. Record a staff meeting.
2. Review the issues dealt with and calculate the relative amounts of time devoted to administrative, managerial and professional issues.
3. Decide whether the mix of issues is adequate or appropriate.
4. Recall how the meeting was conducted. Think of any ways in which the meeting might have been more effectively managed (for example, having a chair who allocates speaking time, having an agenda that has been agreed to beforehand).

Opportunities for professional contact with colleagues do not (and should not) be quarantined to formal staff meetings of course. In fact, in many places, particularly those in which the focus of the staff meetings is on the administrative and managerial issues, most of the professional contact will occur outside of formally constituted meetings. The frequency and formality of such meetings will be partly determined by the predilections of those involved, and partly by the context and situation in which the teachers are working. Teachers who are team teaching or sharing a class, for example, will need more frequent and systematic contact than those who are teaching in isolation. In Chapter 8, we discuss the use of peer observation as a professional development tool of some potency. All teachers who took part in the exercise of observing the teaching of colleagues, and being observed in turn, found the experience an enriching one.

The focus of collegial discussions can vary greatly, from general issues in language education, through to specific problems which are peculiar to the particular institution in which the individuals are working. Discussion might center on problem students, timetable clashes, examinations, materials or any of the myriad issues that preoccupy teachers in their daily professional lives.

TASK

Aim To identify contexts in which opportunities for consideration of professional issues occur in the workplace.

Procedure Interview several colleagues and identify patterns of professional contact. Find out who they tend to talk to/work with on professional issues, the sorts of things they talk about, when the discussions tend to occur, and the amount of time devoted to such discussions.

When we kept records of our own professional contact, we discovered that most exchanges were relatively informal and tended to occur spontaneously over coffee, in staff rooms and during meetings called for other reasons. We also found that the amount of time we spent discussing professional issues was much more extensive than we had thought. The preceding task illustrates the fact that professional development does not happen only in formally constituted seminars and workshops, but is an ongoing facet of professional interaction.

Summary and conclusions

In this chapter we looked at some of the work that needs to be carried out before one steps into the classroom. We argued that planning and pre-instructional decision making should be firmly based on a curriculum framework, a knowledge of learner needs and explicit beliefs about the nature of language and learning. Although we advocate the advantage of planning and making plans explicit, we ackowledge the value of the relatively informal planning and thinking that occurs before and during the teaching process. We also reject the simplistic notion that there is a linear relationship between planning, teaching, and learning.

In the final section we looked briefly at the professional contact that teachers have with colleagues. Here we saw that collegial discussions and relationships vary greatly in style, substance and formality, and that they often entail conflict. We would like to conclude by stating that, despite the occasional conflict and the fact that professional contact with colleagues can be time-consuming, the rewards, in terms of professional growth, can be great.

In the next chapter, we step into the classroom and take a detailed look at the ways in which language itself is used and misused in managing the learning process. Although the bias will necessarily be toward teacher talk, this view will be within the context of teacher-student interaction and will necessarily involve learner language as well.

PROJECT 1

Aim The very first lesson is important in setting the tone and establishing an initial relationship between teacher and students. The aim of this project is to help you reflect on your first meeting with a class of students.

Procedure Choose a class you will meet, and complete the following questionnaire.

Data Questionnaire for evaluating the planning and implementation of the first lesson with a class (adapted from Wong et al. 1992: 46–47).

Before lessons begin:

1. What do you already know about the class you are going to teach (including what students already know)?

   _____

   _____

   _____

2. What will be your objective(s) in the first lesson? Where have they come from?

   _____

   _____

   _____

3. If the students are to wait outside the classroom before you arrive, what will you do:
   a. Before the class enters the room?

   _____

   _____

   _____

   b. After they have entered the room?

   _____

   _____

   _____

During the first lesson:

1. How will you begin the lesson:
   a. If the class is restless and slow to settle down?

   _____
   _____
   _____

   b. If the class settles down quickly and rather quietly?

   _____
   _____

2. Will you tell them your expectations and requirements for the subject? How will you begin? Write down the precise points you want to
   make in the first five or ten minutes of your lesson.

   _____
   _____
   _____

3. What teaching strategies will you employ in your first lesson, and
   why?

   _____
   _____
   _____

PROJECT 2

Aim To compare and evaluate the pre-course preparation procedures of
several practicing teachers.

Procedure

1. Record interviews with a number of teachers about their pre-course
   preparation.
2. Review the recordings and make a note of the similarities and
   differences in their practices. Do these mainly seem to result from the
   background of the teacher (e.g., personality factors, experience,
   training) or the context and situational constraints under which they
   work?
3. Decide which procedures seem to be most effective.

3 Classroom talk

Introduction

Talk is the essential tool of the teacher's trade. Needless to say, talk is critical to the learning process. For second language teachers, there is the additional fact that the medium is the message. In other words, the tool (that is, the language through which the learning process is managed) is also the artifact that teachers and learners are trying to construct with the tool.

All dimensions of pedagogical processes in the classroom, from the provision of feedback, through monitoring, the establishment of small groups, giving instructions and explanations, disciplining and questioning students involve language. In this chapter we shall look at the role of classroom talk, with a particular focus on teacher talk, in all of these areas.

Concept map of Chapter 3

In this chapter the following ground is covered:

- *Direct instruction* "teaching" defined, the role of direct instruction in the learning process, a presentation of grammatical explanations, the attitude of the learner toward teacher explanations
- *Error correction and feedback* the importance of errors in the learning process; error gravity; key questions: how, when, where, and why to correct errors; strategies for providing effective feedback; error correction: the preferences of the learner; the importance of positive feedback to learning
- *Teacher questions* multiple functions of questions, advantages and disadvantages of increasing wait time, distribution of questions: who gets the goodies?, display and referential questions, questions as elicitation devices
- *Instructions* the effect on task work of giving poor instructions, techniques for giving clear instructions
- *The use of the first language* the grammar-translation approach, advantages and disadvantages of using the first language

Because there are many issues to be dealt with in this chapter, we have provided a preliminary task, which we hope will act as an "advance organizer" to make more meaningful the content covered in the body of the chapter.

TASK

Aim To explore, in a preliminary way, some of the language functions fulfilled by teacher talk.

Procedure

1. Study the following extract. Is it from the beginning, middle or end of the lesson? What is it about the extract that helps you to guess?
2. Now look at the extract again, and identify examples of the following:
   a. Teacher question/student response/teacher followup
   b. Orientation to lesson
   c. Explanation of lesson objective
   d. Check to confirm student understanding
   e. Solicitation of information from student
   f. Student interjection
   g. Direct instruction from teacher

Data

T: OK, now we're going to take a slightly new approach. You've all been in language classes because English is not your native language. It's not my native language either so. English is my third language. Um, as you can tell I have an accent here because I'm not Australian, I'm Canadian – I come from er Western Canada. Um if you have any problems understanding me, tell me and I can still go [*laughs*]. . . .

S: Not at the moment.

T: Not at the moment. Good. Now when you've done language classes, you've gone through the traditional grammar right? You've all done English language classes at some place?

S: Yeah.

T: Turkey?

S: [Inaudible]

T: Where?

S: In. . . .

T: In China?

S: . . . Vietnam.

T: Vietnam – you're Vietnamese. Yuri?

S: In . . . university.

T: But where?

S: In China.

T: In China. . . . Where are you from Lee?

S: I come from Vietnam.

T: From Vietnam, OK. OK now, the approach we're gonna take here — there will be some traditional grammar in this, but what I'm going to try to give you is some analytical skills. Of how to analyze your own writing. Skills that you can take away from here and use them. OK? It's not just grammar we're looking at. What we're looking at is how do I make myself understood to somebody else? Right? And how can I work on this on my own all of the time? Now some of you gave me some examples of writing in the beginning, and I've looked at that to see exactly what kind of writing is it that you want to do and that you have to do. OK. And we've we've called this course scientific writing and the type of writing you do is what we call [writes on board] "report writing." Whether it's report writing for your supervisor, for the department or for a journal. Report research writing. And this is what we call the [writes on board] genre, the type. Genre means the type of writing you do. And each type of writing has its own conventions, its own rules, right? Now, where's . . . here it is. You'll have to excuse the printer of my computer. It went crazy, so the printouts are not the same. The first part we're looking at in any type of writing you do is the introduction — right? So, if you look at — if I go back to the report, you would have what? The introduction. What would come after the introduction? You first introduce your topic. What comes next?

(Authors' data)

This extract is either from the beginning of a lesson or a lesson sequence. This phase is signaled by the phrase "now we're going to take a slightly new approach." The various phases in a lesson, including transitions from one part of the lesson to another, are signaled by phrases such as these, and students quickly learn to identify and respond appropriately to such expressions, even though these are rarely explicitly taught.

Here are examples of the functions we asked you to identify in the second part of the task.

Teacher question/student response/teacher followup
T: Where are you from Lee?
S: I come from Vietnam.
T: From Vietnam, OK.

Orientation to lesson
"OK, now we're going to take a slightly new approach."

Explanation of lesson objective
"I'm going to try to give you is some analytical skills. Of how to analyze your own writing."

Checks to confirm student understanding
"The first part we're looking at in any type of writing you do is the introduction — right?"

Solicitation of information from student

"You've all done English language classes at some place?"

"What would come after the introduction? You first introduce your topic. What comes next?"

Student interjection

T: Um if you have any problems understanding me, tell me and I can still go [laughs]. . . .

S: Not at the moment.

Teacher provides direct instruction

"Genre means the type of writing you do. And each type of writing has its own conventions, its own rules, right?"

From this brief excursion into the world of the classroom, it is possible to see that within even the most circumscribed piece of interaction, many things are going on. In the piece of high-structure interaction in the preceding task, the teacher uses language, among other things, to set up the lesson and prepare learners for what is to come, give explanations, and obtain output from students. The piece of interaction also contains numerous instance of the basic patterns of interaction in the classroom, namely, teacher question, student response, teacher followup.

Direct instruction

If you ask a layperson what teachers do, you will most likely receive the unsurprising response that they "teach." If you pursue your line of inquiry, you will probably find that your interlocutor conceives of the act of teaching as one in which knowers impart what they know through a process of direct instruction, that is, by telling what they know. This particular view of teaching has been called the "good news" approach to instruction. This approach to teaching involves explicit instruction by textbook or teacher on specific features of the language. In language classrooms, this approach is generally used to explain unfamiliar words. Less frequently, it is employed to explain points of grammar. In most instances where the teacher engages in this explicit instruction, the instruction is unplanned and occurs spontaneously as a result of a student query, or the teacher becomes aware that the students have not understood. These impromptu inquiries can, of course, provide unexpected pitfalls for the unwary teacher, although the wary teacher will generally have a way out as the second extract that follows demonstrates.

It is worth noting that research into classroom interaction shows that this particular concept of teaching is a very narrow one. There are many different types of pedagogical action, and the good news approach is only one of them. Telling somebody something they do not know is only one way of bringing about learning (and, some would argue, not a particularly effective one). Other modes of instruction include modeling, eliciting, demonstrating and exemplifying.

Here are examples of what we have called direct instruction. (Another example can be found in the classroom extract in the preceding section.)

T: Now, another job that you will need to know about is this – this is a book, OK, now when we're putting the words on a book, we call that, when we make the book with ink, we call that . . . [Students murmur hesitantly] . . . printing. OK, to put the words on the book and to make the book. Now a person who reads the book and checks for mistakes is called a printer's reader. Printer's reader. [Pauses to write on board].

(Authors' unpublished data.)

T: OK, he's looking for a house with three bedrooms, or, what do we say? We don't, in English we don't usually say a house with three bedrooms. . . . What do we usually say?
S: Three-bedroom house.
T: A three-bedroom house, a three-bedroom house, a three-bedroom house. So, what's he looking for?
S: For three-bedroom house.
T: What's he looking for?
S: [Inaudible]
   [Laughter]
T: What's he looking for?
S: House.
T: What's he looking for?
S: Three-bedroom house.
T: All right.
S: Why three bed, er, three bedroom? Why we don't say three bedrooms?

TASK

Aim To consider the way in which you would deal with a request for a grammatical explanation.

Data The preceding classroom extract.

Procedure

1. How would you respond to this request for an explanation?
2. Do you know the answer to the student's query?
3. If not, what would you do?
   a. Change the subject
   b. Admit that you don't know
   c. Say that you will give a lesson on the point tomorrow
   d. Have students look for an answer in a grammar book
4. Now look at the continuation of the exchange to see what the teacher did. Do you think that this is an appropriate way to respond?

T: Ahh, oh . . . I don't know, um.
S: Is not right.
T: We don't say it. We don't say it. There's no explanation. But we often do that in English. Three bedroom house.
S: Don't ask for it.
S: Yes.
T: Well, do ask why. Ask why, and 99 per cent of the time I know the answer. One per cent of the time, nobody knows the answer. If I don't know it, nobody knows. [Laughter] Ah, no, I don't know the answer, sorry.

(Nunan 1989b: 27)

The critical incident in this piece of classroom interaction occurs when a student asks the teacher for a grammatical explanation. In most instances the teacher would know the grammar point and would be able to provide an explanation of sorts. (Whether the students are able to understand or appreciate the explanation is quite another matter, of course.) In this interaction, the teacher did not know the explanation, that "bedroom" is used as an adjective and that we do not mark it for plurality. In some varieties of English, the word would be marked as an adjective by the addition of "-ed" to the root word. The problem occurred because the question was a by-product of the input in a low-structure task, not a pre-planned instructional objective. The basic mistake was probably placing the grammatical item on the pedagogical agenda in the first place.

Having been led off target by raising an issue that had not been planned, and then being confronted with a question to which he did not know the answer, the teacher admits his ignorance. This admission takes a certain amount of courage and a good deal of confidence. However, it is probably the best course of action to take in the long run. Being able to admit that they do not know everything is a mark of mature teachers. Ultimately, of course, it is the teachers who must decide whether they can afford to run the risk of losing face and credibility by admitting ignorance.

This particular teacher, in our view, made the correct managerial decision in the circumstances. The sensible next step would be to tell the students that he would promise to find out the answer between classes and deliver on the promise at the next opportunity. (It is also worth noting, in passing, that the incident is a piece of high-structure interaction embedded within a low-structure task.)

Keith Johnson (personal communication) points out that whether the correct word is "bedroom" or "bedroomed" is an interesting question and raises issues of general principle. What are the options for decision making here? Should teachers become involved in a detailed discussion of the options? Should they present their own (perhaps highly idiosyncratic) interpretation of the grammatical point in question? In our opinion, the simpler choice is the better when two competing forms are generally considered acceptable.

One of the things that the classroom extracts presented in this section highlight is the importance of teachers being aware of what is happening on a moment-by-moment basis within the classroom. Such awareness does not come automatically, but needs to be worked on. By the same token, students need to develop skills in identifying and evaluating their own preferred styles and strategies and the options presented to them within the classroom. One way of developing connections between learner preferences and the pedagogical plans of the teacher is through the administration of questionnaires and surveys inviting students to provide their own attitudes and reactions. This sort of needs analysis illustrates one of our basic arguments, namely, that there is a symbiotic relationship between the self-directed teacher and the learning-centered classroom.

The following data were provided by learners who were surveyed on their attitude to teacher explanations of unknown vocabulary. The results provide some illuminative insights into the attitude of one group of learners at least to the issue of direct instruction.

Student Survey on Teacher Explanations

We would like to know how you feel about new words which come up in class and if you have preferences on how teachers should explain them. (Figures are a percentage of total rank.)

1. When you hear or read a new word do you:
   a. Always want the teacher to explain it   75
   b. Look it up after class   15
   c. Ask a classmate first   10
   d. Other   N/A

2. If you ask a teacher and he/she says it isn't important do you:
   a. Forget about it and wait until you can look it up later   40
   b. Feel the teacher should explain it straight away   50
   c. Try to find out by asking a classmate   10
   d. Other   N/A

3. If your teacher asks you to ask a classmate for the explanation do you:
   a. Think it's a good idea (he/she might know the meaning).   55
   b. Think it's the teacher's job to do this   15
   c. Wait until after the class to check in your dictionary   20
   d. Other   10

4. If the teacher explains but you don't really understand do you:
   a. Tell the teacher than you don't understand   60
   b. Pretend you understand   10
   c. Forget about it, look it up later or ask someone later   25
   d. Other   5

5. If the teacher spends a long time explaining something to you and
   you can see the class becoming annoyed do you feel:

a. Embarrassed and wish you hadn't asked	20
b. Happy that the teacher has made you understand	50
c. A little embarrassed, but you know it's important	30
d. Other	N/A

(Baker 1990: 109; used by permission)

These data show that learners want to know what their learning targets are,
and they want to be told the answers to problems when they arise, not left in
the dark. Although we generally favor the provision of explanations when
students ask for them, we realize that there are occasions when this interrupts the flow of the task and is probably best left until later in the lesson.

TASK

Aim To consider ways of dealing with explanations in the classroom and
the attitudes and reactions of other teachers and learners to
explanations.

Data The preceding survey.

Procedure

1. Administer the survey to a group of language learners and compare
   the results with Baker's. Are they basically similar or different? If they
   are different, how do you account for this?
2. Modify the survey so that it relates to grammar rather than vocabulary. Administer it to a group of students, and, if possible, compare
   results with a colleague.
3. Imagine that you are learning another language. Complete the survey and compare the results, either with your students or with one or
   two colleagues.

Administering surveys such as this has the effect, not only of sensitizing
students to their own preferred learning styles and strategies, but also of
helping them see what it is that the teacher is trying to achieve. Additionally, by doing Part 3 of the survey (effectively putting yourself in the
place of your students), you will deepen your own appreciation of the
different possibilities that inhere in various modes of pedagogical intervention (in this case, teacher explanation).

If the teacher is aware of learner preferences in relation to things such as
instructions and feedback, it is easier to negotiate a common pathway
through the language program, and to overcome potential problems and
blockages within the learning process.

Error correction and feedback

If the layperson sees direct instruction as the primary task for the teacher, then the provision of error correction and feedback runs it a close second. The place of errors in foreign language learning has been controversial. During the heady days of audiolingualism, a great deal of effort was spent trying to ensure that learners did not make mistakes. It was believed that they would learn any mistakes they made and would have to endure a subsequently painful period of "unlearning." More recently, the view has emerged that making mistakes is a healthy part of the learning process, and that mistakes and subsequent correction can provide the learner with valuable information on the target language.

It is now accepted that a very important factor in learning a new language, both for babies learning an L1, and all students of an L2, is that of hypothesis-forming. What is this? Basically, the sequence of events is as follows: The baby or L2 learner:

– Is exposed to a lot of language
– Subconsciously forms ideas – or hypotheses – about how the language works
– Puts these ideas into practice by trying out the new language
– Receives new information, that is, is exposed to more language
– Changes the original ideas to fit the new information
– Tries out the new ideas

(Bartram & Walton 1991: 12)

The way teachers deal with students' errors depends basically on their own beliefs on the nature of the learning process, an awareness of students' needs, and the objectives of the course. Developing sensitivity to students' needs and expectations is crucial. An ability to develop rapport and create a positive classroom atmosphere also guide the foreign language teacher in dealing with students' errors. Different students react differently to being corrected, and it is therefore important to take into consideration the different types of students in the classroom. Another relevant issue concerns the phase of the lesson in which the error occurs. Does the teacher correct only when the focus is on rules of usage, or also when the focus is on the message not the form? We know that the seriousness of the error and the kind of correction strategy to be used depends on the objective of the lesson and the context in which the instruction takes place. If the focus is on accuracy, the teacher should monitor and provide feedback on the relationship between the accuracy of the structure and the meaning conveyed within the discourse. For example, if the teacher is conducting an accuracy-oriented exercise contrasting the active and passive voice, the teacher should, in the course of correcting learners' errors demonstrate, not only the correct formation of the structure, but also the way in which using the passive voice enables the speaker or writer to topicalize a particular entity and maintain that entity as the topic of the discourse. On the other hand, if the focus is on fluency, there are many alternatives that we shall outline.

From the perspective of classroom management, then, providing corrective feedback can be a complicated business. The teacher has to decide:

— Which errors to correct (phonological, lexical, grammatical? only those that interfere with communication?)
— When to correct (at all times? only during form-focused exercises? immediately after the error occurs?)
— How to correct (providing the correct model? asking for repetition? asking another student for the answer?)
— Which students to correct

(Chaudron 1988; Cole 1994)

In the following task, you are invited to examine some learner errors and decide how you would react to them. In particular, we would like you to consider the gravity of the errors and how you would deal with them.

TASK

Aim To evaluate your own attitude toward the treatment of error correction.

Procedure

1. Study the following learner errors, and grade them from most to least serious.
2. Make a note of the contexts in which you would correct these errors and the contexts in which you would leave them uncorrected.
3. What criteria did you use to decide on the gravity of the errors?
4. Discuss how you would correct the errors.

Data

a. "Before I came here, I was knowing all the English language tenses."
b. "He thinks we should all give money to the poor and I'm agree."
c. "Well, it's depend on the situation."
d. "She don't like to read."
e. "I like very much to play tennis."
g. "Are you understanding me?"
h. "I don't know where is my purse."
i. "I'm going to Rio where live my parents."
j. "I visited many differents countries."
k. "I'm doctor."
l. "He explained me why he was late."

Having decided which errors to correct, and when, the teacher must decide how to correct. Here are some options:

— Interrupt students before they have completed their turns.
— Wait for the student to finish speaking and then correct.
— Provide the correct answer.
— Give a non-specific indication that something is wrong with the utterance.
— Repeat the student's utterance with a rising inflection.
— Expand on the student's utterance.
— Call on another student to respond.

The kind of correction strategy will depend on the context and the pedagogical focus at that particular point in the lesson. In addition, in a learner-centered classroom, the teacher will want to know what the students think. In an investigation of teacher behaviors and student responses, Cole (1994) posed the question: Do students' attitudes about the types of error treatments used by their teachers in the classroom during oral classroom tasks influence their motivation? The researcher carried out observations of foreign language and ESL classes to identify the types of errors committed by learners and the correctional techniques of their instructors. The observations were used to create an attitudinal questionnaire to probe the reaction of students to hypothetical teacher responses to oral errors. A sample questionnaire item follows.

In your class you are giving an oral report about your family. You spent a long time preparing for this assignment. You are in front of the class. You say, "My brothers, he always teased me." How would you feel if the teacher interrupted you to say,

a. There is a mistake in your sentence.
b. That's too bad. Are they older than you?
c. My brothers. . . .
d. The teacher says nothing.
e. He always teased me . . . or . . . *they* always teased me?
f. The teacher waves a finger to say "no."
g. Try again, please.
h. Very good.
i. *They* always made fun of me.
j. The pronoun has to reflect the same number as the noun.
k. My brothers, he always teased me. No.

The researcher found that students do hold attitudes about the different ways that teachers treat their errors. In general, they preferred being prompted, given a choice or told that there was a mistake in their utterance. As the researcher noted, these strategies allow the learner some independence in correcting their error. They did not like non-verbal signals of disapproval such as the teacher waving a finger or the teacher saying "no." The researcher came up with the following list of needs:

- Learner training so that learners understand how and why teachers make decisions about correction
- Strategy training so that learners develop ways to be involved in the correction process at appropriate times and in appropriate ways
- Individualized attention during oral practice so that the public threat of correction does not loom over students
- Teacher observations of self and others to see what types of correction are available and appropriate in different settings and to gain an awareness of which strategies an individual tends to use
- Carefully marked transitions during the lesson so that students and teachers know when correction might occur, when it will be appropriate and why it will be used or not for different activities

According to Crichton (1990: 59), difficulties in the treatment of error constitute some of the most unpleasant classroom experiences of many language teachers. He says that many teachers can recall situations in which error correction has been "particularly difficult, or even traumatic." Crichton looked at how teachers deal with potential "crisis points" involving error. (A crisis point was defined as "a breakdown of communication between student(s) and teacher which results from inadequacy of either teacher or student strategies for coping with the treatment of student error.") The following correction episode is taken from Crichton. It incorporates classroom transcripts and data from a post-lesson interview with the teacher.

Transcript	*Teacher's interpretation*
T: Who can think of another word that would describe teenage mother or that you would associate with teenage mothers?	
S: Conversation, conversation.	I was unsure of what she actually had in mind, I didn't want to put her off straight away by showing that I was puzzled by her response, so I wrote "conversation" on the board and then I turned to her and said "conversation" as a suggestion trying to elicit a little more information.
T: Conversation.	
S: Teenage mother must talk, have conversation.	

T: Conversation, speaking? A teenage mother must have long conversations with . . .

S: Their family.

When she explained, it was quite obvious that she was talking about a "discussion."

T: Or else . . . that's good. What would be another way you could describe "conversation" in this situation?

S2:   Or . . . (unclear) or . . . (unclear)

T: Could you spell that again?

T: Oh . . . (writing on board)

S2:   Orchard.

T: Orchard?

S2:   Orchard.

T: What does "orchard" mean?

S2:   Er . . . some boy not have father or mother.

I was trying to build confidence in the students, trying to give them opportunities to be really involved in the lesson. I didn't want to correct him and tell him straight away that what he said was entirely inappropriate.

T: Orphan. Thank you Albert. The word you want is "orphan." What does "orchard" mean? What is "orchard?" Kim, you're a farmer.

S3:   Ah . . . farmer.

T: Yes, what kind of a farm is it? Do you know? (Pause)

T: An orchard is a farm where you have fruit trees. Where you have grow oranges and peaches and . . .

S3:   Oh, yeah, yeah.

T: Back to the word "conversation." What would be another phrase that could describe this kind of conversation? Maybe something like this. "Family conference" or "family discussion."

(Crichton 1990: 59; used by permission)

This piece of interaction contains what Crichton calls a "crisis point." In the following task, we would like you to consider the factors that make this particular piece of interaction a potential crisis point.

TASK

Aim To evaluate a piece of classroom interaction involving error correction.

Data The classroom extract from the Crichton study.

Procedure Crichton argues that the following factors make the preceding interaction a potential crisis point:

1. The presence of ambiguity
2. Lack of clarity in teacher explanation
3. The inability of students to clarify their understanding

Do you agree with him? Can you find evidence of these factors in the data?

The major problem in this piece of interaction is that the teacher has no clear idea of the objective of the interaction, or how the interaction fits into the overall fabric of the lesson at this point in time. The result is one of confusion and uncertainty. The first student to respond obviously does not understand the teachers question. Rather than keeping the lesson on track, the teacher allows the agenda to be taken over by the student. The problem is compounded by the second inappropriate response "orchard." Despite the risk of alienating the students concerned, the teacher would probably have been better off ignoring the initial inappropriate response.

Despite the salience of error correction in the classroom, the role of error correction in the development of oral proficiency is unclear, as McPherson (1992) points out. McPherson investigated error correction from the perspective of the learner. Using questionnaires, interviews, diaries, and video-recorded error correction episodes, she sought to determine how learners respond to and use corrective feedback.

Through the questionnaire, students were asked to report on their preferences in terms of:

— Whether or not students wanted the teacher to correct their errors when speaking
— When they would prefer their errors to be corrected
— The kinds of errors they wanted corrected (that is, word order, grammar, vocabulary, pronunciation, or body language)
— How the student felt when corrected in front of the class
— Whether they ever corrected, or were corrected by classmates
— What they did ask a result of being corrected (for example, repeated the correction orally, wrote the correction down, asked a question about the correction)

When making diary entries, learners were encouraged to respond to questions such as the following:

How do you respond to questions asked by the teacher?
How do you respond to questions by your classmates?
Are you an active participant in most class activities? Why?/Why not?
What improvements have you noticed in your performance?
Have you been confused by anything recently?
How have you felt about any errors you have made in class?
What did you do when your error was corrected?
What did you do when other students made mistakes?
Which activities have been particularly useful for you?

(McPherson 1992: 102)

Students made comments such as the following about the method of correction:

Teacher's utterance	Student's comment	Proficiency level*
Mmmm	I don't understand what the teacher wants me to say.	1
	I want to understand why I was wrong.	2
	It will make me embarrassed and afraid to try again.	3
	I might not find out what kind of mistake I made.	4
	This is not friendly!	5
Don't say *go,* say *went.*	Sounds impolite.	1
	I wish my teacher tell me where my mistake is and explain reason.	2
	This way can't give me think time.	3
	I will forget that quickly.	4
	This is saying "You are wrong! You are definitely wrong." I know I am wrong. A little bit softer is better.	5
	If the student really can't make the correction, as the final one, sometimes this one is OK.	5
I went to the Gold Coast.	Corrects my error without explanation.	1
	This example is very easy for me so I can recognize my mistake. But it depends on the level, I think.	5

Teacher's	*Student's*	*Proficiency*
utterance	*comment*	*level**
Go is in the present tense. You need to use the past tense here.	I don't need this method first time. If I can't understand when the teacher says "I went to the Gold Coast," then the teacher had better explain the tense.	2
Please repeat the sentence.	I can't notice my error.	4
	If I say the sentence again, I would probably realize by myself. I can be suspicious about what I've said.	5
Where did you go?	This one would remind me of my mistake.	5

*1 = elementary; 5 = advanced

McPherson's major findings are set out in Table 1. She summarizes her research findings in terms of the following principles:

Principle 1: Correction methods which are compatible with the learners' current language proficiency facilitate learning.
According to this principle, not only the correction methods used, but also the language areas targeted for correction and the frequency of correction, need to be informed by careful consideration of the language learners concerned.
Principle 2: Correction methods which encourage purposeful learner involvement by allowing opportunities to self-correct or analyze the errors facilitate learning.
According to this principle, the learners' attention needs to be fully focused on the task in order for a memorable impression of the desired behavior to be made. If correction is provided in an off-hand fashion, it is not likely to register in any meaningful way with the learners.
Principle 3: Correction which is provided in a positive manner and is directed at providing information or clarification facilitates learning.
According to this principle, correction should not be used as a form of punishment or expression of frustration or anger. It is important to maintain a focus on errors which interprets them in terms of learning rather than in terms of failure.

(McPherson 1992: 92–93)

These principles can be used to evaluate our own error correction practices. In the task on page 77, you are invited to inspect a discussion on error correction and use the views of the students to identify your own principles.

Table 1   The perspective of the learner on error correction

Question posed	Major findings
How do learners respond to the correction of their spoken errors in the classroom?	*Correction by the teacher:* — Generally positive response — Some frustrations at higher levels — Want to be corrected *Correction by peers:* — Not such a positive response — For some, basis for negative comparisons and feelings of inadequacy
Do beginner and advanced learners respond differently to error correction?	— They tend to, partly because they appear to prefer different correction methods
What other factors, besides proficiency, influence learners' responses to error correction?	— Complexity of the error itself — Timing of the correction — Manner in which correction was given — Readiness to accept the correction — Ability to accept the correction — Preoccupation with reactions/ thoughts of peers
How do learners themselves interpret the responses to error correction?	— Common to all levels is an ability, to varying degrees, to explain and rationalize their responses — Some learners view their responses in terms of what they see as their own inadequacies
". . . which correction methods do actually facilitate language learning?" (Cathcart & Olsen 1976: 41)	— Those methods which are compatible with the learner's current stage of interlanguage development — Those methods which give the learner an opportunity to self-correct and/or provide some explanation of the error

Source: McPherson 1992: 88. Used by permission.

TASK

Aim To derive principles for error correction from the views and attitudes of students.

Procedure Study the following transcribed discussion between a teacher and some students about error correction.

1. What attitudes toward error correction are revealed by the students?
2. What principles would you derive from the discussion?
3. Do you see any potential problems in teaching a class with students holding this range of views?

Data

T: How do you feel when you're corrected?

S1: I expect to be corrected but when I am . . . for instance, when I'm trying to report a long story or something – like a movie I've seen – and I'm interrupted step by step I don't like.

T: It interrupts your flow of ideas.

S1: Yeah, I don't have a very good flow, so . . . Usually I like to be corrected, usually I write them, the good answers. If another student makes a mistake and it's also something I also have doubts or usually I make this kind of mistake I write.

T: What about you, Silvia?

S2: I like to be corrected every time. It's something good to me. I think that learning any foreign language is like a play and every time you are making a mistake and being corrected. I don't feel bad. When the other students make mistakes I write and try to pay attention not to make the same mistake another time. I think it's important.

T: Lucio?

S3: I like to be corrected at the moment that I make the mistake. It's no problem. If I'm interrupted – no problem. It's more important to correct the mistake. Later, if the mistake is written in the board, I mean when the teacher interrupts only a second to correct a word, I can't memorize the error.

T: So you mean that you like to be corrected and you want to have time to visualize and correct it?

S3: Exactly.

T: Ana, the other day you were telling me. . . .

S4: Yeah, in my case I like to talk a lot because I think it's making errors that I will learn. So I try to talk about everything. I think this class you're doing is very important because you just speak in English and we have the opportunity to speak in English. It's a different class and it's very important for us to think in English, to speak English and I try to think in English everything I have to do and when I get to dream in English I think I'll be happy. But I think it's important to make errors.

S5: I feel very well when I'm corrected. . . . [Laughs] It's true! I like to speak. I try to communicate something, it's wrong or not, I try to communicate, I think this is the most important.

T: What about you, Grace? How do you feel about correction?

S6: Well, I like it here because the group is homogeneous. Once I was in a French class and my colleagues were more fluent than me, so I felt embarrassed when I made a mistake. Here it is good 'cause no one seems to ridicule – everyone is in the same boat.

Despite the fact that there is some diversity in the viewpoints of the students, most of those contributing to this discussion wanted to be corrected. With advanced students such as these, it helps to encourage students to reflect on and articulate their views on key aspects of language learning and teaching such as error correction. If feasible, it is also useful to videotape segments of a lesson and review the treatment of errors. In low-structure tasks, where errors may be left uncorrected, these discussions can help to develop more flexible attitudes on the part of students who want to be corrected all of the time.

So far, we have focused on error correction, or negative feedback. However, there is also positive feedback. We give such feedback when we want to praise a student, or reinforce a particular response. Similar factors have to be considered here as were discussed in relation to negative feedback; that is, when, how, and what should receive positive feedback?

Another management issue relating to feedback concerns *which* learners should be corrected and/or praised. In general, we may feel that all learners should be corrected. However, it may well be that certain learners respond negatively to negative feedback. The important thing is that we be aware of our feedback practices and also to whom we direct that feedback. Research in content classrooms has shown that:

When high-achieving students gave a right answer, they were praised 12 percent of the time. Low-achieving students were praised only 6 percent of the time following a right answer. Even though they gave fewer correct answers, low achieving students received proportionately less praise. Similarly, low achievers were more likely to be criticized for wrong answers. They were criticized 18 percent of the time, and high achievers were criticized 6 percent of the time. Furthermore, teachers were twice as likely to stay with high achieving students (repeat the question, provide a clue, ask a new question) when they made no response, said "I don't know," or answered incorrectly. (Good & Brophy 1987: 32)

TASK

Aim To identify positive and negative feedback in classroom interactions.

Procedure Identify the instances of positive and negative feedback in the following classroom extracts.

Data

1. T: Do you remember this guy? [Points to a picture in the book]
   Ss: Alan!
   T: Alan, yeah!
   S: He's more older.
   T: He's older. Do you think? I don't think so.
   S: A little bit.
   T: A little bit. So. OK.

2. T: Give me a sentence with the simple present tense, girls.
   Ss: I speak English.
   T: Very good. I speak English. Now put this sentence in the nega-
        ·tive.
   S: I don't speak English.
   T: Very good. Now give me a question. . . .

3. S: When I opened the door, the cat run out.
   T: Ran out.
   S: Ran out.
   T: Ran.
   S: Ran.
   T: Run, ran, run.
   S: She run downstairs to open the door.
   T: She . . . ?
   S: Ran. She ran downstairs to open the door, but it was too late.
        The postman had gone.
   T: Yes!!

In the first extract, the teacher subtly corrects the student by repeating the student's utterance using the correct form of the comparative. She also goes on to encourage the student to give her opinion, and confirms her response in a positive way, thus encouraging her to make further contributions. In the second extract, the teacher gives positive feedback in the form of an affirmation of the student's response. However, the lack of contextualization makes the interaction rather ritualistic. In the third extract, at the end of the interaction, the teacher acknowledges the student's correct use of the form. However, in the course of the interaction, she confuses the student by having her parrot the two different forms of the verb.

Wajnryb (1992) makes the point that if teachers attempted to correct every error that occurred in class, there would very little time to do anything else. Hypercorrection can also create a negative classroom atmosphere, discouraging learners from risk-taking and experimentation. Again, the extent of error correction will depend on the aim of the lesson, whether it occurs in the context of a high- or low-structure instructional sequence and whether it interferes with communication.

In summary, then, the answer to the question of when a teacher should correct a student's error must be "it depends." In many contexts, when the focus is on meaning, it is probably inappropriate to interrupt the flow of interaction. In these situations, the teacher can make a note of errors for follow-up treatment later. (Of course, if the error interferes with communication, then the teacher may have to intervene.) In other contexts, when the focus is on form, then the teacher might well interrupt before the students have finished their turn.

Teacher questions

Teachers ask a lot of questions. In fact, the standard interactional pattern in the classroom is one in which the teacher asks a question, one or more students respond to the question, and the teacher evaluates the response. It has been pointed out that the classroom is one of the few places where the persons asking the questions already know (or thinks they know) the answers. In terms of the management of learning, questions fulfill numerous functions in the classroom. They can be used to elicit information, to check understanding, and also to control behavior. In the task that follows, you are given an opportunity to identify the functions performed by teacher questions in the classroom.

TASK

Aim To identify the range of functions performed by teacher questions in the classroom

Procedure Which of the following questions are used to elicit information/check understanding and which to control and manage behavior? Identify whether the questions asked belong to the beginning, middle, or end of a lesson. What could you have done differently if you were the teacher? How could you maximize class time and ask more meaningful questions? What other way(s) are there to help students remember what was done in the previous class?

Data

T: Remember. What was happening last week? What just started last week in the video? There was a race, right?

S: Yes.

T: And where was the race?

S: Qu . . . quarry

T: In the quarry, that's right. There was a race in the quarry. Between two people. A race between . . . which two people?

S: Between Mike

T: Between Mike and . . . remember?

S: And the college student

T: And the college student. Remember?

S: Rod.

T: Rod. Remember Catherine's old boyfriend. So Mike and Rod have started a race. You made a prediction. Who did you think would win the race?

S: [Inaudible]

T: You thought Mike? Who did you think?

The complexity of the teaching context is illustrated in the preceding task. Questions do not necessarily serve one function. A question to elicit information many be directed (for purposes of control) to a student whose attention is wandering and only an extended context would show whether a question was designed to elicit information or check understanding. Johnson (personal communication) points out that the list of questions in the task illustrates both the range of types of information that can be elicited (linguistic factual) and perhaps the very low level of cognitive response that language teachers tend to require. This idea raises an interesting question: Is this low level of cognitive demand an unavoidable consequence of the aims of language teaching and the low proficiency levels of the students, or is it a consequence of this type of activity, in which there is no time for students to give a considered response to a demanding question and therefore it is necessary for the teacher to avoid raising that type of question? (You might like to consider your own response to this question in light of the classroom extract that follows.)

The questions teachers ask have been of interest to researchers in both content classrooms and language classrooms. This interest is not unusual, given the fact that questions are basic instructional tools. They are also relatively easy to identify and count, which may account for their popularity among certain researchers. Teachers' use of questions has been criticized by researchers such as Good and Brophy (1987), who argue that in too many classrooms discussions resemble a game of verbal "Ping-Pong": the teacher asks a question, one or more students respond, the teacher evaluates the response and then asks another question. This basic initiation/response/evaluation sequence is illustrated in the following extract, which has been adapted from Cazden (1988: 32–33). The extract is interesting, because it shows how the teacher uses questions, not only to elicit information and evaluate students' responses, but also to control the interaction.

Initiation	Response	Evaluation	Comments
T: Uh, Prenda, ah, let's see if you can find, here's your name. Where were you born, Prenda?	P: San Diego	T: You were born in San Diego, all right	Individual nomination of Prenda.
			Teacher acknowledges answers, even to questions for which only Prenda knows the answer.
T: Um, can you come up and find San Diego on the map?	P: [goes to board and points]	T: Right there okay.	
T: So we will put you right there [pins paper on map]			
T: Now, where where did, where was your mother born, where did your mother come from?	Wallace [raises hand]		W bids nonverbally at end of basic sequence but does not get the floor. Instead Prenda's turn continues.
	P: Oh Arkansas	T: Okay	
T: Prenda's mother [writes on paper].			
T: Um, now we [pause] I did point out Arkansas on the map yesterday.			A two-part IR sequence.
	P: I know where Arkansas is.		
T: Can you, do you know where it is Prenda?	W: [points from his seat towards Arkansas on the map]		
	P: [goes to board and points].	T: Yeah, good for you.	

Initiation	Response	Evaluation	Comments
T: How did, how did, how did you come, how did you know that?			A metaprocess question that asks child to reflect on the basis of knowl-
	P: Cause I – C: – This morning	T: Wait a minute, wait a minute. I didn't, couldn't hear what Prenda said.	edge. T's evaluation is simultaneously a negative sanction of C for interrupting, and a request to Prenda to
T: What?	P: [turns head away]		repeat, though neither is explicit in the words of her ut-
T: Who told you? Who told you?	P: Carolyn did she told me where it was, where Arkansas was.		terance.
T: And Carolyn, how did you remember where it was? It's kind of in the middle of the country and hard to find out.	C: Oh, cuz, cuz, all three of the grandmothers [pause] cuz, cuz, Miss Coles told us to find it and she said it started with an A and I said there [pointing] and it was right there.		
P: Little Rock		T: Uh hum. T: Yes, and I thought maybe you remembered, because, Carolyn, you mentioned Little Rock yesterday.	
T: Okay, well so this is green for your mother or your father and we'll put that [pins card to map].		P: My father wasn't born in there.	Prenda's evaluation also functions to initiate sequence of talk about father, the logical next topic.

Table 2   Examples of closed and open questions

Closed	Open
Did you finish your assignment?	What kinds of issues came up when you did your assignment?
Did you like the move?	What were the most interesting issues that came out of the movie?
How did your parents enjoy the trip?	What happened to your parents on their trip to Australia?

Classroom research has also shown that certain types of questioning behavior have persisted over many years despite the fact that teaching materials, curricula and methods have changed over the years. Borg et al. (1970) show that factual questions to determine whether or not students know basic information are far more frequent than higher-order questions that encourage students to reflect on their knowledge, attitudes and beliefs or that require them to follow through and justify a particular line of reasoning. Another distinction that is commonly drawn is that between "open" and "closed" questions. Open questions are those that encourage extended student responses. Examples of both closed and open questions are set out in Table 2. The table demonstrates how, with a little thought, closed questions can be made relatively open.

We do not mean to ascribe any moral superiority to open questions here. The purposes of open and closed questions are clearly different, and the kind of activity (whether it is part of a high- or low-structure activity), the time allocated to answering them and the amount of language support students are going to need in order to answer them are all going to be radically different.

One of the on-line decisions that teachers need to make is what to do when students fail to respond to questions. In both content classrooms and language classrooms, it has been found that teachers seem to become anxious if their questions are followed by silence. Rowe (1974, 1986) found that teachers, on average, waited less than a second before calling on a student to respond, and that only a further second was then allowed for the student to answer before the teacher intervened, either supplying the required response themselves, rephrasing the question, or calling on some other student to respond. This "wait time" research shows that in many classrooms students are given insufficient time to process the question before being called upon to respond.

We believe that it is particularly important for second language students to have sufficient time to think about questions before being required to answer them. However, we also acknowledge the fact that, from the perspective of managing the learning process, silence tends to break up the flow of the lesson; students' attention gets distracted and it is hard to pick up the pace again once it is lost. Maintaining interest through appropriate pacing is a real problem, which is rarely acknowledged by commentators on wait time. In low-level interactions, pacing should have priority. When the answers deserve real consideration, students should be given the time to answer them. In fact, in some cases it may even be worth having them write answers and then take four or five of them before moving on.

Even after explicit training, some teachers never managed to extend their wait time beyond one or two seconds. In those classrooms in which teachers did manage to wait from three to five seconds after asking a question, there was more participation by more students. In particular, the following effects were observed:

1. The average length of student responses increased.
2. Unsolicited, but appropriate, student responses increased.
3. Failures to respond decreased.
4. There was an increase in speculative responses.
5. There was an increase in student-to-student comparisons of data.
6. Inferential statements increased.
7. Student-initiated questions increased.
8. Students generally made a greater variety of verbal contributions to the lesson.

The two classroom extracts that follow illustrate the points we have been making on the importance of context and purpose. The length of time the teachers pause after asking a question is indicated in brackets ("−1" indicates that they wait less than one second). In both extracts, the teachers give the students relatively little "processing" space to formulate and produce extended utterances. In the first example, the interaction is a relatively low-level "social" exchange, and the students have little difficulty in responding appropriately. In the second, the students do not have enough time to process the questions, most of which are answered by the teacher herself.

T: Do you believe in astrology?
F: More or less. [−1]
T: More or less? Do you usually read the horoscope?
F: No. [−1]
T: Never, ever?
F: No. [−1]
T: In *Zero Hora* [the local newspaper]? No? [−1] What about you, Lucio?
L: I read when, um, eventually, but only for. . . . [−1]
T: When you don't have anything to do?

L: Yeah, yeah. [1]

T: All right. When's your birthday, Fabi?

F: Um, 16, May 16.

T: May 16. You are, um, Taurus? [0] What about you?

L: I'm September 23. [−1]

T: 23 . . . Libra. Libra, um. . . .

F: What about you?

T: I'm a Sagittarius, November 26. And, um, Do you know any adjectives that you could use to describe your signs? What do people say about Libra? Libra is a great sign. . . . It's my boyfriend's sign.

F: My relatives . . . [−1]

T: My parents?

F: My parents are both Libra.

T: So, they're nice people.

F: Yeah, they are nice people. But they are so difficult to deal with.

T: Now-what time . . . what time does the train leave?

Ss: Nine. Nine o'clock. Nine p.m. Nine p.m. Nine a.m.

T: [leans over a student and checks the timetable] OK. Depart nine a.m. So . . . [she returns to the board] . . . what can I write here? What time
 . . .
 [She writes, "What time" on the board] What comes next? [−1] What time . . . ? [−1]
 Does . . . does . . . [she writes, "does the train"] . . . does the train . . . yes?

S: [inaudible comment]

T: No. What time does the train . . . ? What's another word for "depart"? [−1] Leave. What time does the train . . . leave." [She writes, "leave" on the board.] OK, you, you tell me. . . . [−1] It leaves at nine a.m. OK. What time does it arrive?

S: Er, eleven fifty-eight a.m.

T: [Leans over his shoulder and checks his timetable] OK. Now − where does it arrive at eleven fifty-eight? At Victor Harbour?

Ss: No. Goolwa.

T: No.

Ss: Goolwa. Goolwa.

T: Goolwa. Have a look at your map and see if you can find Goolwa. See if you can find Goolwa on this map.

S: Near, er, near the Victor Harbour.

T: Near Victor Harbour, yeah. [She writes, "What time"] OK, what comes next? . . . [−1] What time. . . ? [−1] What's the question? [−1] What time . . . ? . . . [−1] does (does) . . .

S: . . . the train arrive . . .

T: Arrive. [She writes, "Does the train arrive at Goolwa?"] All right, so what time does the train arrive at Goolwa? OK. What time?
S: Eleven. Eleven. Eleven fifty.
T: Eleven fifty . . . eight. What's another way of saying eleven fifty eight? [−1] Two minutes to . . . twelve. Yeah, two minutes to twelve. OK.

The issue of wait time is obviously important in language classrooms, not only because of the greater processing time required to comprehend and interpret questions in a second or foreign language, but also because of the findings by Rowe. However, as we will argue, in terms of the management of learning the issue is more complicated than it is sometimes presented to be. It certainly involves more than simply increasing the length of time between asking a question and answering it.

The limited amount of research on wait time in language classrooms has yielded mixed results. Shrum and Tech (1985) investigated French and German high school classes and came to conclusions similar to those of Rowe concerning the average length of wait time following questions. Specifically, they found that wait time following questions was less than two seconds. Long and Crookes (1986) report a similar finding in an investigation of ESL teachers in Hawaii. Holley and King (1971) found that when teachers of German were trained to increase their wait time, the length and complexity of student responses increased. The study by Long and Crookes found that increased wait time did not lead to greater mastery of content by ESL pupils, although this may have been because of the time scale of the study. If it had been conducted over a longer period of time, a significant result may have been yielded. Long and Crookes do not report whether increased wait time led to more participation or more complex language by students.

What are the pedagogical implications of this research? If we believe that acquisition will be maximally facilitated when learners are pushed to the limits of their competence, then, on the evidence of Rowe, wait time should be increased in many contexts and teaching situations. However, as we saw in the case of the two extracts above, sometimes it is unnecessary to prolong wait time.

The researchers and writers on wait time tend to present the issue in a rather simplistic manner, suggesting that less wait time is bad. Although we generally go along with the argument that learners should be given the mental space to process the question and respond, we also accept that there are certain high-structure situations in which pace and momentum are at a premium, and in which prolonged wait time will be ultimately detrimental to the dynamics of the classroom interaction.

Another issue relevant to the management of learning concerns the distribution of questions. It is generally considered desirable to distribute questions among all students rather than restricting them to a select few.

[S]tudents will learn more if they are actively engaged in discussions than if they sit passively day after day without participating. We all know reticent students who rarely participate in discussions but still get excellent grades, but most students benefit from opportunities to practice oral communication skills, and distributing response opportunities helps keep students attentive and accountable. (Good & Brophy 1987: 495)

Although most of us probably imagine that we are even-handed in our treatment of students, we might find, if we obtain an objective record of our teaching, that we favor certain students over others with our questions. Research shows that there is a great deal of variation in the chances afforded to different pupils to speak in class. Jackson and Lahaderne (1967), for example, found that some students were up to twenty-five times more likely to be called to speak than others. Furthermore, it is generally the more able students who get called upon. If we accept that students learn to speak by speaking, this means that those most in need of the opportunity to speak are probably given the least amount of classroom talking time. (Of course, in relation to affective issues, it may well be that less proficient students are "ignored" by the teacher more out of a desire to save them the possible embarrassment of not being able to respond than out of any malicious motivation to prevent them gaining access to the interactional "action.")

One way of monitoring this aspect of our teaching is to audiotape or videotape our teaching over several lessons or get a friend or colleague to observe us and note down the number of questions we direct to each student. These techniques, using seating chart observation records, are set out in Nunan (1989b). Such techniques can reveal tendencies for teachers to restrict their questions to certain students and particular "action zones" in the classroom (not surprisingly, these are usually toward the front). The observation chart in Figure 1 shows the number and direction of questions directed by a teacher to his class.

Another aspect of questioning behavior which has received considerable attention in recent years is the use of display and referential questions. Display questions are those to which we know the answer (for example, when we hold up a book and ask, "Is this a book?") Referential questions, on the other hand, are those to which the asker does not know the answer.

In classrooms of all kinds, display questions are by far the most common For example, in Figure 1, the teacher asks twenty-two display questions, and only four referential questions. In contrast, display questions are hardly ever asked in genuine communication outside the classroom (to begin asking display questions in social situations outside the classroom could lead to highly undesirable consequences).

Several investigations have been carried out into the use of display and referential questions in language classrooms. Brock (1986) discovered that

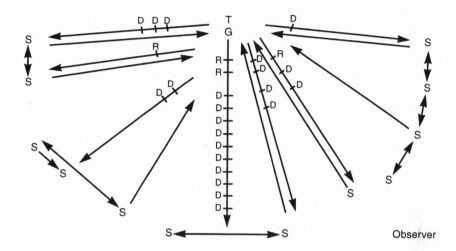

Figure 1   An example of a seating chart for an ESL class (Reproduced from Understanding Language Classrooms *by David Nunan (1989), published by Prentice Hall International)*

teachers could be trained to increase the number of referential questions they ask and that this increase prompted students to provide significantly longer and syntactically more complex responses. Nunan (1987) found also that the use of referential questions by the teacher resulted in more complex language by students. Student interaction was also more like natural discourse (that is, the type of discourse typical of out-of-class encounters).

[T]he following features, which are characteristic of genuine communication, appear in the data: content-based topic nominations by learners; student-student interactions; an increase in the length and complexity of student turns; the negotiation of meaning by students and teacher, with a concomitant increase in the number of clarification requests and comprehension checks. There is even an instance of a student disagreeing with the teacher. (Nunan 1987: 143)

The extract which follows illustrates what can happen when the teacher switches from asking display questions (sequence 1) to referential questions (sequence 2). As you read the extract, you might like to note the differences in learner output between the two interactions.

Sequence 1
[The teacher is working with a small group of students. She stands at the front of the classroom, while the students sit at desks. They are working with six pictures which show the following road accident. A milk van, swerving to avoid a dog which has run across the road, knocks a boy off his bicycle. A passer-by runs to a public telephone and calls an ambulance. Each student has a set of pictures which have been shuffled up so they are out of sequence.]

T: Can you put the pictures . . . number one, number two . . . ?
     [She demonstrates that she wants to students to put the pictures in the sequence in which they think the incidents occur. The students do this quickly.]

T: Finished? Good, good, that was quick. Let me have a look.
     [One student looks at the sequence which has been arranged by the person on his left.]
S: No, this one, you know, hospital, this one first, telephone, hospital, car.
T: [trying to get the student to self correct] This the same, same this? Look at picture number one.
S: Number one.
T: Yes, can you see, Hing? Where are they? Where is this?
Ss: Where are, where are, um, bicycle, bicycle.
T: The man's on a bicycle, mmm.
S: And a man behind, behind a car. Bicycle behind a car. Behind a car.
T: What's the name of this? What's the name? Not in Chinese.
Ss: Van. Van.
T: Van. What's in the back of the van?
Ss: Milk, milk.
T: Milk.
Ss: Milk. Milk.
T: A milk van.
S: Milk van.
T: What's this man? . . . Driver.
S: Driver.
T: The driver.
S: The driver.
T: The milkman.
S: Millman.
T: Milkman.
Ss: Milkman.
T: Milkman.
Ss: Milkman.
T: [pointing to one of the pictures] Where are they?
S: Where are they?.
T: Where are they? Inside, outside?
S: Department.
T: Department?
S: Department store.
T: Mmmm [her intonation indicating that the answer is not quite what she expects]. Supermarket. They're in the street. In the street. They're in the street. Outside. They're in the street. The bicycle and the van – where are they? Where are they? What's this?
Ss: Street.
T: In the street. [She indicates to one of the pictures.] OK, is this a man or a woman?
Ss: Man.
T: A man?

Ss: Woman. Woman. Man. No man.
T: She's a woman there.
Ss: Woman. Woman. Man. Woman.

Sequence 2
[The students and teacher are sitting in a circle.]

T: Da Sheng, have you been in an accident?
S: No.
T: No? Good! Lucky.
S: Lucky.
    [The other students laugh.]
T: Seng?
S: No.
T: No? Little?
S: No.
T: No? You must be a good driver.
    [There is more laughter from the students.]
S: No good driver!
T: No? May Yu?
S: No.
T: No? Heng?
S: No.
T: No? I have. I have been in one, two, three.
    [There is a short pause.]
S: My mother is by bicycle . . . by bicycle, yes, many, many water."
T: She had an accident?
S: In China, my mother is a teacher, my father is a teacher. Oh, she go finish by
    bicycle, er, go to . . .
S: House?
S: No house, go to . . .
S: School?
S: No school. My mother . . .
T: Mmm.
S: Go to her mother.
T: Oh, your grandmother.
S: Grandmother. On, yes, by bicycle . . . By bicycle, oh, is um, accident. [She
    gestures.]
T: In water?
S: In water, yeah.
T: In a river?
S: [Nods] River, yeah, river. . . . Oh, yes, um dead.
Ss: Dead! Dear! Oh!
T: Dead? Your mother?

                                                                    (Nunan 1989b)

The basic difference between the two sequences is that the first is driven by
a series of display questions, whereas the second is initiated by questions

from the teacher to which she does not know the answer. This difference has a marked effect on the language produced by the students. In general, the length and complexity of the responses increases. In interactional and discourse terms there are also notable differences: students initiate interactions, nominate topics, disagree with the teacher, and generally use a greater range of language functions.

Not all researchers agree that the distinction between display and referential questions is a useful one. Van Lier (1988), for example, argues that the distinction is irrelevant, as the function of teacher questions is to elicit learner language, and from this perspective whether or not teachers already know the answer to the question is irrelevant. The following extract illustrates the fact that not all referentially driven interactions are potent when it comes to stimulating student output. Our own view is that both display and referential questions are critical to the management of the learning process. Choice of question should depend on the objectives of the lesson, the task within the lesson (where the task resides on the high-structure/low-structure continuum), the size of the class, and the particular pedagogical imperative driving the management of the learning process at that particular time. It is up to the teacher to be alive to the possibility of switching from a display to a referentially driven interaction (and vice versa) at any particular time in the teaching-learning cycle.

In the following task, you are given an opportunity to evaluate the quality of student responses to display and referential questions. The task will also give you an opportunity to consider the extent to which it is possible to distinguish unambiguously between these two question types.

TASK

Aim To explore possible differences in the student responses prompted by display versus referential questions.

Procedure

1. Read the following extract and identify the display and referential questions.
2. Is there any difference in the quality of the students' responses on these different types of question?
3. Were there any instances in which you found it difficult to identify whether the questions were display or referential?

Data

T: What is your favorite breakfast? What do you usually like to eat for breakfast?
S: Fruit.
T: Which ones?

S: Banana, papaya.
T: Don't you drink anything?
S: Milk.
T: Pure milk?
S: Yes, very cold. I love it.
T: And no bread? You don't like bread?
S: Bread makes you fat.
T: What's your favorite meat?
S: All kinds.
T: Do you like chicken?
S: Yes.
T: What kinds of meat do you know?
S: Chicken, beef.
T: Fish.
S: Pork.
T: And which is your favorite restaurant?
S: I like sea food. I like Chiwawa.
T: OK, open your book – page 82. we talked about this. Just read this part.
[Ss listen to an aural text on making reservations.]
S: OK, I just didn't get the name of the first caller. It's P–A . . . ?
T: It's Parker. And what's her special request?
S: She wants a quick service.
T: Why?
S: Because she was . . . no, she had an appointment.
T: Where was she going?
S: To the theater.

In this extract, the majority of questions are referential. However, they are relatively low level and, judging from the reactions of the students, not very interesting. The result is a series of largely monosyllabic responses from the students. In fact, the display questions at the end of the interaction stimulate rather more extended responses. This extract illustrates a central theme of the chapter (and, indeed, the book), that the context and situation, including student needs and curricular objectives need to be taken into consideration in managing the learning process. Blanket statements such as "increase wait time" and "avoid display questions" are simplistic, misleading, and just plain wrong in many situations.

Elicitation is another common function of classroom teacher questions. Elicitation methods are designed to extract from students information that might otherwise have been provided by the teacher. In the following extract, the teacher misses few opportunities to extract information from the learners rather than giving it to them. Although this can be an effective technique for engaging learners productively in the lesson, it can be overdone, as we see in the following task.

TASK

Aim To identify and evaluate elicitation techniques in classroom interaction.

Procedure

1. Identify the instances of elicitation in the following extract.
2. How do students respond to the elicitations?
3. How successful are the elicitations?

Data

T: OK. Give me a sentence. For example, tell me something about her, in the present.
S: She . . . [one-second pause]
T: In the negative, please.
S: Negative?
T: No, sorry. Positive. [one-second] She . . .
S: She is . . . [one-second]
T: OK, not with the verb to be. Sorry. Except with the verb to be.
S: She work in . . .
T: She . . . ?
S: . . . work . . .
T: She . . . ?
S: . . . works . . .
T: . . . works — it's very important. She works at home. Now put the same sentence, Tati, in the negative.
S: She don't work.
T: She . . . ?
S: . . . doesn't . . .
T: . . . doesn't. Very important. She doesn't work at home. And the question?
S: Does she . . . ?
T: Very good.

In this extract, the teacher misses important opportunities for stimulating meaningful communication. Although he wants to ensure that students know the rule, this type of forced elicitation, in which the language is decontextualized, fails to help students identify the communicative functions which might possibly be served by the particular structures in question.

The final task in this section of the chapter is designed to give you the opportunity of synthesizing the input we have provided on questions. As you do the task, you might like to think about your own use of questioning techniques and how these fit in with your particular teaching style.

TASK

Aim To synthesize the input on teacher questions provided in the section.

Procedure Analyze the questions in the following extract, using the ideas presented in this section (e.g., identify display versus referential questions, open versus closed questions and the effects of the types of questions on student output).

Data

T: What about the thing you mentioned, Daisy, about love?
S: I believe love is necessary.
T: To fall in love, you mean?
S: Yes. Love is the most important thing in a relationship.
T: [Describes a famous person who has lived in an arranged marriage for twenty years.] If this person was to enter this room, what kind of questions would you like to ask her?
S: Do you agree with this? Are you happy? What did you think of your arranged marriage at that time?
T: What else?
S: What would you do if you could go back in time?
T: And advice? Do you have any advice?
   [Students listen to an interview with the person.]
T: How many of our questions she answers in her conversation? . . . What does she say when the woman asked her if she were happy?
S: Of course. . . .
S: Of course, like, "what a silly question."
T: What about the future husband? Did he want this arranged marriage?
S: He showed badly dressed.
T: What's her first impression about him? Do you know what she felt? What was her reaction? . . . Do you remember the second man? Do you remember what she meant when she mentioned about his background?
S: She mentioned that the family owned a village. His family must have been very rich.

This extract contains a nice mixture of display and referential questions. It is based on a topic of obvious interest to the students and results in extended responses from them. This extract illustrates the central point, that questions will "drive" the learning process forward when they are consistent with the lesson objectives and when the objectives are consistent with the learners' needs. To a large extent, the way that teachers use questions defines their teaching style. It is an interesting exercise to examine the relationship between your teaching style as revealed in the questions you ask, and your beliefs, attitudes, and aspirations in relation to teaching.

Instructions

The ability to provide clear instructions is an essential management skill for all teachers. In second and foreign language classrooms where the teacher chooses to give instructions in the target language, clear instructions are critical to the success of classroom tasks and exercises. In the following task, the teacher attempts to set up a reasonably complicated vocabulary task. However, because the instructions given by the teacher are unclear, the students are forced simultaneously to try to do the task and to work out what the teacher had in mind.

TASK

Aim To evaluate the effectiveness of teacher instructions, and the effect of instructions on the effectiveness of small group tasks.

Procedure and data

1. Imagine that you are going to have your students do the following vocabulary task. (This context enrichment exercise is designed to be carried out in small groups.) How would you set up the task for students who are unfamiliar with such a task? What instructions would you give?

Instructions: This exercise will help to direct your attention to the kind of information that a context may give you. In the exercise, there are three sentences, each one adding a little more information. Each sentence has three possible definitions of the italicized word. On the basis of information in the sentence, decide if the definition is improbable, possible, or probable. Write one of these words on the line for each definition.

1. We had a *whoosis.*
   a. a tropical fish   _____
   b. an egg beater   _____
   c. a leather suitcase   _____
2. We had a *whoosis* but the handle broke.
   a. a tropical fish   _____
   b. an egg beater   _____
   c. a leather suitcase   _____
3. We had a *whoosis,* but the handle broke, so we had to beat the egg with a fork.
   a. a tropical fish   _____
   b. an egg beater   _____
   c. a leather suitcase   _____

(Yorkey 1970: 67)

2. Now study the following classroom extract, in which a small group of students is involved in doing the task. How effective are the teacher's instructions? What could/should the teacher have done?

T: This exercise is basically looking at how you can use context to find the meaning of a word. And what I want you to do is discuss among yourselves and decide – if you look down at the first exercise I want you to decide which of these might be a definition for this – whether it's improbable, possible, probable. OK?

S: Oh, we have to put here, after the a b c . . . [yeah] which one is improbable, which one is possible or is probable?

T: Yeah. What you've got here is a nonsense word – a nonsense word. Imagine it's a word you don't know in English. You just discuss among yourselves.

S: OK, we had a – what is this. . . . a tropical fish . . . an egg beater . . . a leather suitcase.

S: OK I'm sure the c, a leather suitcase, is improbable.

T: Why?

S: Doesn't have anything to do with that name.

T: If you had a sentence "We had a leather suitcase." Is that possible?

S: What? We had a . . . ?

T: We had a leather suitcase. Is that, is that good English? Does that make sense?

S: Yes. Yes.

S: [We have . . . *whoosis*] that means . . . is improbable [but if] is improbable and impossible is more or less the same?

T: Improbable . . .

S: and impossible

T: Improbable and probable. . . .

S: No. . . .

T: . . . but possible. . . .

S: And impossible. Means improbable is more or less like impossible?

T: [pause] Yes . . . unlikely, unlikely, unlikely.

S: For me . . . for me . . . I don't know for you. . . . leather suitcase doesn't have anything to do with this word.
[The students begin working by themselves. There is considerable negotiation as they attempt simultaneously to work out what they are supposed to be doing, and at the same time actually doing the task.]

S1: But for me put here improbable.

S2: But it . . . . the . . . the instruction, the instruction say something different . . . we have to . . . we have to change this word and make sentence with a, b and c. For instance, "We had a leather suitcase," "We had an egg beater," and "We had a tropical fish." [Is that it?] That's the instruction. [Mmm] OK. So we have to decide if, if this sentence is . . . if those sentence are good English or not. [You mean each one?] Uhuh.

S1: What sentence? We had a . . .

S2: We had a tropical fish.

S3: Yes. Possible. [Yes]

S1: Improbable, I think. [Why not? Why not?]

S2: We had, er, a tropical fish.
S3: We had an egg beater.
S2: We had an egg beater.
S1: That's, that's probable [yes].
S2: Is it probable, why not? [Possible, probable]
S1: We had a leather suitcase. Yes, possible. I think all of them's possible. Why not?
S3: All synonym [?]
S2: Why not probable?
S1: OK, the first one, it's possible, but not probable, no?
S2: You can't prove that.
S1: OK, the first one is possible – write possible, no? [I think so.]

(Nunan 1991: 125)

Not surprisingly, when the teacher involved in the preceding interaction listened to a recording of the interaction, he was horrified by the quality of the instructions he had given. He felt that they had been unclear, and, as a result, the students were required simultaneously to decide what was required of them and also do the task. (Of course, they could have worked out the task requirements before actually embarking on the task, but they did not do this.) Interestingly, the unclear instructions, which reduced the effectiveness of the task as a vocabulary exercise, probably led to an increase in the communicative interactions between the students.

The validity of this interpretation must be tempered by the aims of the instructional sequence. If the aim were interaction for its own sake, the ambiguity and procedural difficulties apparent in the preceding extract may well be constructive. If the intention were to draw students' attention to the contextual constraints on word meaning, the effect is definitely counterproductive. If the intention were to teach learners about meaning and context, the teacher should have read through the detailed instructions with the students and then modeled the task by doing the first task as a whole class activity. The remainder could then have been done as a group activity.

The use of the first language

The approach to language teaching that has dominated the field for most of its existence is the grammar-translation approach. This approach is characterized by the explicit teaching of grammatical rules and extensive practice in translating written passages from one language to another. It involved the extensive (and in some cases almost exclusive) use of the learners' first language and usually resulted in learners who had a detailed knowledge of the language but a limited ability to put their knowledge to communicative effect. According to Richards and Rodgers (1986: 4), a key feature of grammar-translation was that the students' native language was employed as the medium of instruction, used to explain new items and to draw comparisons between the foreign language and the student's native language.

During the second half of the nineteenth century, however, several scholars criticized the grammar-translation method and proposed their own alternatives for foreign language instruction. These alternative approaches gave much greater prominence to spoken language development and encouraged teachers to avoid using the native language of the learners. For example, proponents of the "Natural Method," argued that

a foreign language could be taught without translation or the use of the learner's native tongue if meaning was conveyed directly through demonstration and action. The German scholar F. Franke wrote on the psychological principles of direct association between forms and meanings in the target language (1884) and provided a theoretical justification for a monolingual approach to teaching. According to Franke, a language could best be taught by using it actively in the classroom. Rather than using analytical procedures that focus on explanation of grammar rules in classroom teaching, teachers must encourage direct and spontaneous use of the foreign language in the classroom. Learners would then be able to induce rules of grammar. . . . Known words could be used to teach new vocabulary, using mime, demonstration, and pictures. (Richards & Rodgers 1986: 9)

In the twentieth century, methods such as the audiolingual method reinforced the primacy of the spoken language and the importance of avoiding the use of the first language in the classroom. Learners were encouraged to operate in the target language from the beginning rather than translating from the mother tongue. Another argument had it that when teachers used the first language, they encouraged students to avoid using the target language. This exhortation not to use the student's first language was the rhetoric, at least. The extent to which teachers eschewed the use of the first language when working with monolingual groups in foreign language contexts is open to question. More recently, certain variants of communicative language teaching and "natural" approaches to instruction have also downplayed the role of the first language.

Despite these trends, the use of the first language has been defended by some language teaching specialists. It has been argued that judicious use of the first language can greatly facilitate the management of the learning process, particularly where grammatical and lexical explanations are concerned. This use is illustrated in the following extract.

S: Teacher, what is the meaning of "lettuce"?
T: If you go to a snackbar, you're very hungry, and then you ask for something to eat – a cheeseburger. But you don't like some of the things

they put inside it, like vegetables, so lettuce is one of the things inside the cheeseburger, the big leaf inside it. It's part of the cheeseburger, OK?

S: I think so.

T: OK, now I want you to get in pairs and prepare a dialogue where you go to a restaurant or a snack bar and you have to say what you want to eat.

S: Please can you give me a lettuce and a Coke?

(Authors' data)

This extract illustrates some of the problems that arise when teachers try to avoid using the first language in class. The explanation is clumsy, consumes valuable class time and, judging by the student's attempt to use it, not understood. A quick translation would have short-circuited the rather tortuous process.

As with other aspects of the management of learning, knowing how, when, and how frequently to use the students' first language cannot be reduced to an algorithm. We believe that in foreign language contexts, for teachers who speak the students' first language, attempting to adhere rigidly to the target language at lower proficiency levels is probably unrealistic and counterproductive. In most foreign language contexts, using the learners' first language to give brief explanations of grammar and lexis, as well as for explaining procedures and routines, can greatly facilitate the management of learning.

Summary and conclusions

In this chapter we have looked at the critically important role played by language in mediating between pedagogy and behavior. We have tried to show that teacher talk occupies a special place in language classrooms because it is both the medium and the message. Language teachers should therefore monitor and evaluate their use of the target language, not only as essential input for their learners, but also as the social lubricant that keeps the pedagogical wheels turning smoothly. To this end, the following questions act as an end-of-chapter summary and a checklist for such monitoring and evaluation.

How much talking do I do?

Is there an appropriate balance between my use of the learners' first and target language?

Do I give students adequate opportunities to talk?

What are the basic interactional and discourse patterns in my classroom? Are these appropriate, given my pedagogical goals and the managerial imperatives of the classroom?

What kinds of questions do I ask, what are their functions, and how do my
learners respond to them?

How do I manage learner errors?

In the body of the chapter we tried to indicate our position on the key issues
raised. We also provided our own personal reactions to the tasks and extracts included in the chapter. However, we must reiterate the fact that these
reactions are contingent upon the aims of the lesson and the context within
which the instruction is taking place. Because aims and contexts are so
important, this book is not a set of recipes for successful practice. Ultimately, you will need to make your own managerial decisions based on a
knowledge of your learners, your own pedagogical objectives, and the
moment-by-moment exigencies of the teaching context and situation you
are in. The teacher who is able to make informed decisions in this way can
be said to be truly self-directed.

In the next chapter we remain in the classroom and look at issues associated with the management of time. Once again, we have found that effective time management is important for the professional health of the language classroom. It is also something to which the self-directed teacher will
devote time and attention.

PROJECT

Aim To raise awareness of the issues involved in error management.

Procedure and data

Before the lesson:
1. Arrange to observe a low-level lesson with an oral/aural objective.
2. Make yourself familiar with the chart on page 102.

During the lesson:
Use the chart to help you record some instances of learner error and
teacher response. Try to capture about eight such instances.

1. Script the instance of learner error, which this might be inaccurate or
   inappropriate language.
2. Note whether the teacher responded and, if so, a brief note as to what
   was said or signaled.
3. Note down where roughly in the lesson it occurred. This prompt is to
   help you recall it later.
4. Note any particular focus at that point in the lesson, for example, on
   accuracy or fluency (A/F).

Learner error	Teacher response	Lesson phase	A/F

After the lesson:

1. Did you observe any pattern in the teacher's way of responding to learner error? Discuss with the teacher their rationale for managing error.
2. Looking over the eight instances you collected, is it possible to *distinguish* among them or perhaps *rank* them in order of importance? Which were very important to correct and which perhaps might have been overlooked?
3. How did *other students* respond to a student's error and (where relevant) to the teacher's response? Was there any peer correction, peer interaction or discussion of the error? If so, what did the teacher do or say to encourage it?
4. Were there any opportunities for the students to *self-correct*? If so, do you recall anything the teacher said or did to encourage self-correction?
5. Was there a link between the *amount* of error correction and the *focus* of the phase of the lesson?
6. When the focus of the lesson is on *fluency,* there may be ways in which a teacher can avoid interrupting the flow of the students' language. Is error correction necessary at such times in a lesson? Is it possible to correct in a non-obtrusive way?
7. Was there any evidence in the lesson of students' *processing information*? For example, in committing an error, having it pointed out, hearing the correct version and trying it out, learners might simply be echoing what they think is required of them or they might be *processing,* that is, adjusting existing notions or hypotheses about language to accommodate newly received information.
8. Focus on the *teacher's language* in response to an error. Were there any occasions when the teacher responded to the error without attending to the *student's intended meaning,* that is, attended exclusively to the form of the language?

What effect did this have: on the student? on other students? on the lesson?

(Adapted from Wajnryb 1992: 103–104)

Commentary: Perhaps the most interesting question in the Wajnryb questionnaire is number 7, relating to student uptake. "Was there any evidence in the lesson of students' processing information?" Wajnryb points out that in having errors pointed out and trying the correct versions, learners might simply be echoing what they think is required of them or they might be actually processing the information. This processing, which is evidence of active learning, is one of the most interesting things to look for in classroom data. In reviewing the data we assembled for this book, we found some fascinating examples of learner uptake, although the uptake was not always of the type intended by the teacher. In the following example, the learner demonstrates learning through being corrected on prepositional phrases of time. Unfortunately, the learner overgeneralizes and commits another error (which this time goes uncorrected).

T: Now, where does the train go after Goolwa?

S: Victor Harbour.

T: Victor Harbour. OK. What time does it arrive at Victor Harbour?
[There is some inaudible muttering from the students. The teacher frowns and inclines her head toward one of the students.]

T: Twenty-two minutes past twelve – OK. Then . . . What time does the train leave to come back?

S: Four thirty. Four thirty.

T: Four forty . . . ?

Ss: Four thirty.

T: Four thirty, OK.

S: Half-past four p.m.

T: [shakes her head] Half past four, yeah. Not half past four p.m. – Half past four in the afternoon . . . yeah. OK. Now, what time does it get back to Keswick?

S: Er, eight p.m.

S: Eight o'clock in afternoon.

T: OK, so how long does it take to come . . . from Victor Harbour to Keswick?

4 Classroom dynamics

We were doing spellings, English ones. Henno had his book out on the desk. He put all our scores and marks into the book and added them up on Fridays, and made us change our places. The best marks sat in the desks along the windows and the worst were put down the back beside the coats. I was usually in the middle somewhere, sometimes near the front. The ones at the back got the hardest spellings . . . If you got into the last row after the marks were added up it was very hard to get out again, and you were never sent on messages.

(Roddy Doyle. 1993. *Paddy Clarke Ha Ha Ha.*
London: Secker & Warburg)

Introduction

In this chapter we consider the dynamics of interaction. First we look at the issue of lesson pacing. Then we turn to an area that has recently caught the attention of a number of researchers, that of on-line monitoring and decision-making within the classroom. This discussion provides a basis for exploring the notions of "effective" and "reflective" classroom practice. In the final part of the chapter, we look at behavior problems in the classroom and ways of dealing with these.

Concept map of Chapter 4

This chapter deals with the following issues:

— *Pacing* deciding how long tasks and activities should last, making pacing decisions in the light of course goals and available resources
— *Classroom monitoring* relationship between preteaching plans/decisions and interactive decisions, interactive decisions: what makes teachers change their minds?
— *Cross-cultural aspects of classroom management* culturally based mismatches between teacher and learner roles
— *The "effective" teaching movement* classroom practices typical of effective teachers, teaching behavior and learner achievement

- *Reflective teaching* describing and justifying reflective teaching, knowledge and skill requirements for reflective teaching
- *Dealing with behavior problems* challenges posed by low-structure tasks, preempting discipline problems, causes of disruptive behavior, strategies for dealing with problems arising during the course of instruction, behavior modification

Pacing

Having decided which tasks and activities to introduce in a lesson, teachers need to determine how long each task and activity should last. Of course, this does not mean that they will stick rigidly to the times determined outside of the classroom. Once a lesson begins, a teacher will use experience, intuition, and gut feeling to decide whether to curtail a task prematurely, either because the learners get through the material more quickly than the teacher had anticipated or because the task simply does not engage the learners. On the other hand, the teacher may decide to prolong an activity because the learners become highly involved or because the material takes them longer to work through than initially predicted.

Planning decisions relating to pacing can be determined through questions such as the following:

What do I hope to get out of a given lesson or unit of work?
How much time do I have?
How many different tasks or activities can I reasonably expect to complete in the time available? (This number will vary from group to group, as some students will progress through material more quickly than others.)
Am I using commercial materials, and if so, does the teacher's guide give advice on pacing?
If I have varying levels of ability within the class, should I try and pace activities differently for different subgroups within the class?

Pacing is an elusive thing, which probably explains why intuition is so important in making decisions in this area. Predetermined rules for deciding how long to prolong an activity simply do not work. In our teacher-training work, we have found that the ability to pace a lesson is one of the key factors distinguishing experienced from inexperienced teachers. Experienced teachers are able to pick up cues from students that indicate their levels of interest or boredom and evaluate these cues against the objective of the lesson. At times a teacher may want to prolong a task, despite the possible disaffection of the students, because it is important for students to master the content and skills being worked on before the focus of the lesson is changed.

Classroom monitoring

Despite an increasing interest in what happens in language classrooms (as opposed to what some say *should* happen), we still know comparatively little about what does or does not go on there. This is particularly true of the relationship between what teachers believe about the nature of language and learning and the adjustments they make to their classroom plans in the course of teaching. In this section we shall look at several key aspects of the monitoring and decision making that go on during the instructional process. These aspects are important, because, as Grosse (1991) points out, a key challenge confronting the profession at present is the development of the teacher as decision maker and problem solver. In addition, Woods (1993) has made the point that in order for new teachers to improve their effectiveness, they need to know what experienced teachers do in the course of planning, implementing and modifying their instruction. They also need a repertoire of techniques for some of the less visible aspects of on-line monitoring and decision making. We concur wholeheartedly with Woods, and we also subscribe to the belief that monitoring and adjusting what a teacher does in the course of instruction is not something that can be reduced to a set of techniques or algorithmic procedures. Making appropriate decisions on the spot is a skill that develops over time as a result of self-monitoring and reflection. Suggestions for such self-monitoring are made in the final chapter of this book. We would also recommend the companion volume on reflective teaching in the series by Richards and Lockhart (1994).

Most of the research on teachers' decision making has focused on pre-teaching planning decisions. Early research is also product oriented and behavioral in its orientation. Zahoric (1986), for example, studied the planning decisions of 194 teachers, asking them to note down the decisions they made prior to teaching. He found that decisionmaking relating to learner activities was the most frequently cited (81 percent of teachers). Only 28 percent of teachers made planning decisions relating to behavioral objectives.

One of the first studies to examine decision making as it actually occurred, rather than as a retrospective activity, was carried out by Peterson, Marx, and Clark (1978). They asked twelve teachers to plan a new unit of work for a group of students with whom they had had no previous contact. As they planned their lessons, the teachers were asked to verbalize their thought processes. These "think aloud" protocols were then coded and analyzed. The researchers found that teachers spent most of their planning time dealing with the subject matter to be taught. The next most frequent category was instructional processes. The least amount of time was spent on objectives. In other words, the teachers taking part in the study spent comparatively little time in determining what learners would be able to do as a result of instruction.

Studies of interactive decision making, that is, of decisions made in the course of teaching, are comparatively rare. No doubt, this rarity is partly because of the difficulty of obtaining data. Researchers can hardly ask teachers to explain what they are doing and why the teachers are doing it while they are actually teaching. Most studies of interactive decision making are aimed at determining the extent to which decisions are reflective or reactive (Clark & Yinger 1979). Twelve teachers taught a social studies unit to three different groups of eight junior high school students. The lessons were videotaped, and teachers were shown brief segments and asked to talk about what they were doing during the segment. The researchers found that alternative teaching strategies were considered only when the teachers thought that the lesson was going poorly, the inference being that teachers would prefer to adopt a "steady as she goes" attitude rather than trying to optimize learning opportunities. Learner behavior was the primary cue used by teachers in determining how well the lesson was going. Perhaps most significantly, it was found that even when things were not going well, teachers rarely departed from their teaching plan.

An investigation of the interactive decisions of forty elementary teachers by Morine and Valence (also cited in Clark & Yinger) used a stimulated recall task to identify types of decisions. Decisions were categorized as either interchanges (decisions relating to instantaneous verbal interaction), planned activities (decisions related to preactive decisions) and unplanned activities (activities that teachers decided to initiate spontaneously, which were not part of the original lesson plan). The great majority of decisions were either interchange or planned, and there were no significant differences between the decisions of more or less effective teachers. In their review of the study, Clark and Yinger (1979: 249) note, "A general pattern observed in all responses was that teachers focused more on the instructional processes than on students' characteristics or behavior when commenting on the substance (focus) of their decisions. When the considerations and bases for the teachers' decisions were referred to, however, the focus changed. In these instances, the characteristics of students carried more weight than the instructional process."

Marland (1977) also examined interactive thoughts through the use of stimulated recall. He found four principal functions for such thoughts. There were (1) modifying the lesson when it was deemed to be going poorly, (2) modifying behavior with reference to certain principles of teaching, (3) dealing with unpredictable student behavior (4) modifying instruction in response to individual student differences. According to Marland, there was little or no evidence that teachers self-monitored, verified

interpretations of student behavior, considered alternative teaching behavior or sought to optimize instruction. They rarely considered their own
teaching style or its effect on learners, and tended to act on intuition, rather
than direct evidence.

Despite some variations, a number of common themes emerge from this
research. In the first place, teachers appear not to be guided by the traditional curriculum model, which argues that they should begin the planning
process by specifying objectives and use these as the basis for developing
learning tasks. Most teachers tend to think in terms of task rather than
objective, and the instructional task is the basic unit of planning and instruction. Another general finding is that teachers tended to modify their
behavior only in the face of the most severe disruptions. Finally, there do
not appear to be any major differences between the interactive decisions of
experienced and inexperienced teachers, nor of effective versus ineffective
teachers. The problem with most of this work, however, is that it views
teaching from a purely behavioral perspective. More recent work has
adopted more interpretive perspectives and has attempted to reconceptual-
ize the work on decision making by exploring the links between teaching
processes and the conceptual bases upon which the decision making rests.
Shulman (1987: 1) for instance, explores the following questions: What are
the sources of the knowledge base for teaching? In what terms can these
sources be conceptualized? What are the processes of pedagogical reasoning and action? What are the implications for teaching policy and educational reform. His conclusions contradict those reached by earlier researchers who used a more behavioral and less interpretive frame of
reference. For Shulman, the key constructs that guide the teaching process
are comprehension, reasoning, transformation and reflection, and his work,
"places emphasis upon the intellectual basis for teaching performance
rather than on behavior alone" (p. 20). (A similar perspective is apparent in
the work of Lampert 1985 and Munby 1982, among others.)

The preceding summarized studies were all carried out in content classrooms. There are relatively few parallel studies of planning and decision
making by language teachers, although this is beginning to change. One of
the earliest studies to investigate planning and monitoring by language
teachers is reported by Nunan (1988). The purpose of this research was to
explore the planning and decision-making behavior of teachers with varying degrees of experience. Twenty-eight teachers were categorized into
four different groups according to their amount of experience. Each teacher
was provided with an authentic tape and a set of activity sheets. Teachers
were asked to plan, teach and record a unit of work based on the materials.
Detailed information was collected on the aims of the unit, the modifications made to the materials, the length of time taken to teach the unit, and
the various grouping arrangements employed. Although a number of

differences were found between teachers with different levels of experience, these were relatively minor. Less experienced teachers varied their grouping arrangements more, from individual, to pair, to small group, to teacher fronted. In general, the more experienced teachers used more teacher-fronted tasks, indicating that they judged that innovative, authentic materials required more teacher intervention. In addition, as length of experience increased, so, too, did the length of the teaching unit. This trend would indicate that experienced teachers are able to exploit materials more effectively. There was no evidence in the data of any qualitative difference in the decision making of teachers with different levels of experience.

More recently, Johnson (1992, 1994) has explored the knowledge base of teachers. Johnson attempts to dig beneath the skin of what goes on in classrooms, attempting to obtain insights, not only into what teachers do, but why they do what they do. In her study of the emerging beliefs and instructional practices of preservice ESL teachers, she used narrative accounts from a number of teachers in preparation. She found four recurring images in these narrative accounts: images of formal language learning experiences, images of informal language learning experiences, images of themselves as teachers and images of the teacher preparation program. Her conclusions are telling. Although, on the surface, her findings reflect those from earlier studies in content classrooms, showing, for example, that belief and practice are resistant to change, Johnson is able to provide a deeper, more interpretive, and constructivist interpretation of the data:

In fact, the characterization of teachers' beliefs that emerged from this study is not one of "self-perpetuating, perservering even against contradictions caused by reason, time, schooling or experience" (Pajares, 1992, p. 324), but instead one of emerging beliefs based on conflicting images that require access to alternative images if preservice teachers' beliefs are to shift and mature beyond the current status quo, and ultimately, reconstruct a model of action that is appropriate for effective second language instruction. (Johnson 1994: 450)

In another investigation of preservice trainees, Johnson (1992) used a stimulated recall technique to obtain insights into teachers' actions and decisions. In this study, six preservice ESL teachers studied videotapes of their own teaching and made interpretive comments about the instructional decisions that they made. This study reinforces the emerging notion that teaching is cognitively demanding and that much of what goes on in the classroom can only be understood and interpreted if one goes beyond the surface behavior of teachers and students. Johnson found that for preservice teachers at least managing the learning process was a major factor in the decisions made in the classroom. As a result of the study, Johnson argues that second language teacher education programs need to go beyond the provision of methods and techniques and provide opportunities for teachers to "understand the dynamics of how they think and act as they learn to teach." (p. 507)

In a comparative study of experienced and inexperienced teachers' decisions, Nunan (1991) investigated the classroom decision-making processes of nine ESL teachers. The questions investigated in this study were as follows: What goes on when teachers make decisions? What do teachers focus on, when reflecting on their teaching? Are there differences in the ways experienced and inexperienced teachers make interactive decisions in the classroom? In the next task, some data from the study are presented. The task will give you an opportunity to relate issues dealt with in this section to authentic classroom data.

TASK

Aim To apply insights from the discussion in the preceding section to the analysis of interactive decisions in classroom interaction.

Procedure

1. What interactive decision does the teacher make in the following extract?
2. How does the teacher justify the decision in the follow-up discussion? Do you find this convincing? Do you agree with the teacher?

Data

T: What kind of . . . books, do you read? Yeah. What kind of books do you read? Or for her, for Alexandra, what kind of books does she read? So, what kind of books does Alexandra read? [History.] History books. History books. What about smokes? What's the question you can ask for smokes?

S: Are you smoke?

T: Are you smoke? Do you smoke, or does she smoke? Does she smoke? What question does the interviewer ask? The interviewer? What question does the interviewer ask? What's the question in here?

S: You smoke?

T: You smoke? You smoke? That's not a proper question, is it really? Proper question is do you smoke? So he says, "You smoke?" We know it's a question because . . . why? You smoke?

S: The tone.

T: The tone . . . the . . . the . . . what did we call it before? You smoke? What do we call this?

S: Intonation.

T: Intonation. You know by his intonation – it's a question.

T: Drinks. What's the question? Drinks. Do you drink? Yeah. What's the, what's the question he asks?

S: Drink?

T: Drink. Just one word. Drink? How do we know it's a question? Intonation. Drink? Usually, we'd say do you drink? Church? What's the question he asks?

Ss: Go to church? Go to church?

T: Go to church? What's the proper question – we ask? Do you go to church? Or, does Alexandra go to church? What about hours worked? We know that Alexandra doesn't work, she's a student. But what's the question we ask? Question?

S: We are you working?

T: Hours worked – what's the question, you'd ask?

S: Are you working?

In a post-lesson discussion, the teacher was asked why she had drawn the attention of the students to the issue of "proper questions." She replied that in fact it had been a spontaneous decision. When asked whether there was inconsistency between using authentic data, in which a native speaker must, by definition, be asking "proper questions," and insistence on complete question forms, the teacher replied that it had suddenly occurred to her that it would be useful to draw to the attention of the students the fact that they could recognize from the speaker's intonation that a question was being asked. She went on to say that, "I suppose it's recognizing one question form by the intonation, then being able to transfer it into the proper question 'Do you drink?' rather than 'Drink?' I mean, that would be good to spend a lot more time on at another point. But it seemed like it was good to bring up there. Just to transfer the information."

The problem here was that the teacher introduced an additional, unplanned objective to her lesson. Rather than being an aside, it grew into a major additional segment of the lesson that diverted both teacher and students from the original aim of the lesson. In terms of on-line monitoring and decision making, the incident demonstrated the importance of being aware of the potentially disruptive nature of unplanned modifications to a lesson, which may take it in unintended directions. A useful technique for dealing with these spontaneous additions to the pedagogical agenda is to record them in a notebook and then make them the focus of a review lesson later in the course. This technique gives time for reflecting on the implications of introducing additional material and enables important concepts to be expanded on and reinforced.

What conclusions about the management of the learning process can we draw from this investigation of experienced and inexperienced language teachers at work? In the first place, the findings from content classrooms relating to goals and objectives were largely borne out: there were few references to program goals and objectives, and the focus was on the exigencies of classroom management and organization. As with content teachers, the task was the basic unit of planning and instruction. In planning, teachers focused on tasks, and the lessons evolved through task cycles. In making on-line decisions in the classroom, perceptions of how well students were dealing with the tasks that prompted teacher action. Surprisingly, there was a relative lack of focus on language. In reflecting on and commenting on their classroom practice and managerial decisions, only 12 percent of inexperienced and 21 percent of experienced teachers' comments made any mention of language. Inexperienced teachers focused on classroom dynamics, discipline, and the general flow of classroom events significantly more than experienced teachers and seemed more concerned than experienced teachers about keeping things on an even keel. They also made significantly more negative evaluations of their own teaching performance than experienced teachers. Finally, in commenting on the management of the learning process, the most frequently expressed concerns by both experienced and inexperienced teachers were, first, the pacing and timing of their lessons, and, second, the quantity of teacher talk, and the quality of their explanations and instructions.

The more recent studies referred to in this section provide support for our vision of the self-directed teacher. If effective teaching requires high-level cognition, based on comprehension, reasoning, transformation and reflection, and if, as Shulman, among others, argues, teaching performance should have an intellectual basis rather than a merely behavioral one, then concepts of self-direction and autonomy should be at the center of both pre- and inservice teacher education programs.

Cross-cultural aspects of classroom management

Many of the classroom management problems experienced by teachers working in unfamiliar cultural concepts arise from a mismatch between the roles and expectations of the teacher and those of the learners. In some cases the mismatches and resulting management problems are a result of a clash of educational values and perceptions (for example, when teachers see themselves as facilitators, while students see them as dispensers of wisdom). In other instances cultural norms and values are at play, of which the teacher may simply be unaware. This problem is illustrated in a fascinating investigation of classroom decision making and management strategies in a cross-cultural context. Malcolm (1991) collected data from over one hundred classroom lessons in elementary aboriginal schools in Western Australia. He set out to investigate the management strategies as revealed through the discourse of the teachers, his ultimate aim being to identify good teaching practice in the context of aboriginal schools. In the next task, a critical classroom incident observed by Malcolm will be examined.

TASK

Aim To evaluate a critical decision-making incident in a cross-cultural context

Procedure

1. Study the following classroom incident observed by Malcolm. What basic mistake do you think that the teacher has made? Do you think that she should have abandoned her planned lesson in the way she does?
2. Have you ever witnessed or experienced a similar incident? If so, what happened? How was it dealt with?

Data

[I observed] a teacher in her first year of professional experience . . . trying her hardest to interest a large class of Aboriginal children, in their first year of schooling, in a story about a little white child whose pet kitten had broken its leg. While the teacher displayed a picture of a miserable looking girl looking at a kitten with a bandaged leg, the children fidgeted, jostled for places on the mat, went one after another to the table to get tissues on which to blow their noses, surreptitiously pushed, punched and poked at one another, or, if they were brave enough, came up to the teacher to whisper that they wanted to go to the toilet. The teacher at first sought to stimulate their interest in the picture by asking them questions about it, then she asked them about their pets, then read them the story. After that, she discussed the story with the children and sought to get children, one by one, to stand up and tell stories of their own about the girl and the kitten. All to no avail. It was at this point that the teacher abandoned her plan and, with the words we have quoted ("All right then, if you don't want to do that . . .") made the first of a number of changes of strategy which she would employ, under pressure from the children, before the lesson was over. (Malcolm 1991: 1)

Malcolm argues that there are three management tasks that need to be achieved in relation to classroom discourse. These tasks are the management of content, the management of student participation and the management of face. In relation to the management of content, Malcolm suggests that there are four areas of fundamental concern. First, the content must be relevant to classroom purposes. Second, there must be a basic level of shared knowledge. Third, teachers and students must share the same linguistic interpretation. Finally, they must share the same pragmatic interpretation. In managing participation, students must be able to see, hear, speak, and be heard. In the final area, the management of face, Malcolm suggests

that there are four "rights" that might be tested in the classroom and that can lead to loss of face. These rights are:
- The right to contribute
- The right not to contribute
- The right to acceptance of the form of one's contribution
- The right to acceptance of the content of one's contribution

In relation to the extract presented in the preceding task, the behavior problems occurred because the story itself was irrelevant and culturally alien to the students. In addition, it is not clear how the content relates to the pedagogical intentions of the classroom. It would have been preferable for the teacher to build the interaction around the stories and incidents that were relevant and real to the children themselves. (At the very least, the teacher should have determined whether or not the concept of family pet was culturally alien to these young learners.)

The following task is also based on data from Malcolm's research. According to Malcolm, each of these interactions are problematic when viewed from the perspective of the learner.

TASK

Aim To consider the rights of the learner within the context of classroom interaction.

Procedure

1. What is problematic about the following exchanges?
2. Place yourself in the role of the learner in each exchange. How would you feel or react if a teacher dealt with you in this way?

Data

1. T: Adele, what would you like to be when you grow up?
   A: A shop.
   T: A shop?
   A: Yeah.
   T: You mean you want to be a big building, a shop?
   A: I want to serve in a shop.
   T: You want to serve in a shop. Well, that's what you should say, isn't it?

2. T: [Showing a chart about seasons.] Who can read that? Hands up.
   E: [Bidding.] Oh
   T: Eileen.
   E: Sport?
   T: Spring, right.

3. T: Well, wait a minute. We've been talking about aboriginal food. . . . What white food, what white man's food do you like?
   S1: Ice cream.
   T: Which one . . . ice cream? Where d'you get your ice cream from?
   S2: In the shop.
   S3: Milk, milk, milk.
   T: Milk . . . you like milk, do you?

4. T: You tell me something you like about the pictures, Murray.
   M: I can see da ball.
   T: And what's the boy doing?
   M: No, a ball.

5. S: Two girls Miss C.
   T: Two girls? What're they doing?
   S: Same.
   T: Two girls the same. That's right.

6. T: Today I'm going to get you to write a story about . . .
   S1: Oh no. . . .
   S2: Circus.
   T: A day that you visited. . .
   S3: The circus.
   S4: But I've never been to the circus.
   T: A circus. But . . . if . . . if you haven't been to a circus, you can use your imagination to think what it would be like.

7. T: Anything else? Judith?
   [No reply.]
   T: You're not thinking.

All of these interactions are driven by the teacher's conception of appropriate classroom interaction. In almost all of these extracts, the teacher simply ignores the students' responses, partly because she has her own expectations of what should count as a "correct" answer. There is also evidence in the extracts of lack of cultural knowledge on the part of the teacher. In some instances, when students attempt to make relevant contributions, these contributions are overlooked.

Malcolm concludes his study by arguing that a "management strategies" approach to the study of classroom interaction is necessary if the active role of the student is to be recognized. In analyzing classroom discourse from a management perspective, it is necessary to go beyond the management of content and participation to a consideration of the management of face.

It is important that teacher recognize that the strategies which enable satisfactory management of classroom discourse to occur are essentially of two kinds:

teacher strategies and pupil strategies. Pupil strategies are often conducive to better communication and perhaps better learning in classrooms. It behooves teachers to take account of them. It is also important that teachers learn that strategies which go against the legitimate right of the learner to maintain face are likely to be counter-productive. Classrooms should be places where the self-esteem of teachers and pupils alike is respected and fostered. (Malcolm 1991: 16)

In summary, then, we can say that when working in an unfamiliar cultural context, it is important to determine the kinds of expectations that learners have of you as a teacher and of themselves as learners. When selecting content you should determine (perhaps by consulting a native-speaking colleague) whether the content is relevant to the learners. This matter is not always straightforward, because one of the functions of education is to introduce learners to new and unfamiliar concepts and content as well as teaching them new skills. However, this introduction should be done by taking them from the known to the new. Finally, you should determine typical patterns of interaction in the new culture you are working in. If, for example, it is culturally permissible for speakers to interrupt and to talk over one another, then you should consider allowing such behavior in your class. If you do not want such behavior patterns in your classroom, you should make this explicit, drawing a contrast between the interactional patterns the learners are accustomed to outside of your classroom and those you expect in your own classroom.

The "effective" teaching movement

Within the field of general education, there is a research tradition that seeks to identify teaching behaviors that are related to student learning. In other words, it seeks to establish a relationship between teaching and learning. This so-called effective teaching model is based on the premise that certain classroom teaching practices can be identified and related to successful learning outcomes. The methodology for identifying such behaviors is as follows:

1. Identify teachers whose students consistently obtain better than pre-dicted scores on standardized achievement tests.
2. Observe these teachers and compare their behaviors with those of inef-fective teachers.
3. Base teacher preparation programs on those behaviors that characterize effective teaching.

This particular tradition focuses on explicit classroom behaviors and tends to overlook the complex cognitive processes in which, as we saw in the section on classroom monitoring, teachers must engage in the complex environments within which they teach. To a certain extent, then the "effective, behavioral" teaching movement and the "cognitive process" movement represent opposing views of teaching. Although this opposition is evident within the research community, and although we subscribe to the reflective tradition, we believe that there is value in being familiar with the work that has been conducted within the "effective" teaching tradition. The important thing to keep in mind is that, to understand teaching, one must get at the cognitive proceses that lie behind the observable teaching processes.

According to Blum (1984:3–6), the following classroom practices are typical of effective teachers:

1. Instruction is guided by a preplanned curriculum.
2. There are high expectations for student learning.
3. Students are carefully oriented to lessons.
4. Instruction is clear and focused.
5. Learner progress is monitored closely.
6. When students do not understand, they are retaught.
7. Class time is used for learning.
8. There are smooth, efficient classroom routines.
9. Instructional groups formed in the classroom fit instructional needs.
10. Standards for classroom behavior are high.
11. Personal interactions between teachers and students are positive.
12. Incentives and rewards for students are used to promote excellence.

In this list, the behaviors that relate to time management are numbers 3, 4, 7, and 8. The rest relate to the management of the learning process in general. Although there are practices that we can say characterize effective teaching and learning, these are general principles to help guide us, not rules to be blindly applied to each and every class we teach. Additionally, we do not believe that one can simply put together a list of behaviors and assume that these will aggregate to good practice. (For a discussion on this, see Richards' discussion on the dilemma of teacher education in Richards and Nunan 1990.) Although we concur with Blum's list, we have one major concern with this line of research. Our concern relates to the fact the effectiveness is defined in terms of the ability of the students to achieve high grades on standardized tests. Such tests are not always the most reliable indicator of high-quality education.

One of the most consistent findings from research in content classrooms is that learner achievement is highly correlated with effective classroom management. In a major investigation involving over one hundred different elementary and secondary classrooms, Evertson (1985) studied the following aspects of classroom management: instructional management, room

arrangement, rules and procedures, student concerns, behavior and misbehavior, classroom climate, miscellaneous, and time on task. The following behaviors were consistent with enhanced student outcomes:

General area	*Specific behaviors*
Instructional management	– Describes objectives clearly
	– Uses a variety of materials
	– Has materials ready
	– Gives clear directions for assignments
	– Waits for attention
	– Gives clear directions for assignments
	– Waits for attention
	– Matches assignments to student needs and abilities
	– Paces lessons appropriately
	– Gives clear explanations
	– Monitors student understanding
	– Consistently enforces work standards
Room arrangement	– Suitable traffic
	– Good visibility
Rules and procedures	– Efficient routines
	– Appropriate general procedures
	– Suitable routines for assigning and checking work
Meeting student concerns	– High degree of student success
	– Low level of student aggressiveness
	– Attention spans considered
	– Activities related to students' interests
Managing student behavior	– Restrictions on student movement
	– Rewards appropriate performance
	– Signals correct behavior
	– Consistency in managing student behavior
	– Effective monitoring
Student misbehavior	– Stops inappropriate behavior quickly
	– Ignores inappropriate behavior

General area	*Specific behaviors*
Classroom climate	− Conveys value of the curriculum
	− Task-oriented focus
	− Relaxed, pleasant atmosphere
Miscellaneous	− Listening skills
	− Avoidance behavior during seatwork
	− Participation in class discussion
Percentage of students engaged	− Percent of students off task
	− Percent of students probably on task
	− Percent of students on task

This list of features all relate to observable behavior. Although behavior is important, we would also like to stress the importance of cognitive aspects of instruction and learning (which were dealt with in the section on classroom monitoring). The next task invites you to evaluate the behavioral aspects of classroom management and to relate these to your own teaching situation.

TASK

Aim To reflect on the outcomes of an investigation into the effectiveness of different managerial behaviors.

Data Outcomes of preceding summarized study.

Procedure

1. Which of the behaviors in the preceding list, in your experience, are most important in effective language teaching?
2. What similarities and differences can you find between this list and the one by Blum?
3. If you were to review an audio- or videotape of your own classroom, which of these features would you focus on? What would you expect to see?

Despite the diverse contexts and environments in which the studies reported in this section were carried out, the findings are consistent. Learning appears to be maximized when classroom tasks are clearly linked to student needs and broader curricular objectives that are conveyed to the students in ways that are meaningful to them. This link is something we have consistently argued for throughout this book and relates to all aspects of managing learning, not just the issues focused on in this chapter. In terms of classroom dynamics, all studies demonstrate that effective instruction is characterized by clear instructions, maximizing time on task (the time that students actually spend learning), and the establishment of smooth and efficient classroom routines.

Reflective teaching

In recent years the notion of reflective practice has been proposed as a counterpoint to effective instruction. Richards and Lockhart (1994: 202) contrast reflective teaching with a view of teaching as technology. The technological approach assumes that learning to teach is a matter of learning the theory and knowledge of applied linguistics and then applying this theory and knowledge to the classroom. In contrast, the concept of reflective teaching makes different assumptions about the nature of teacher development. It assumes that professional growth is a lifelong process, and that obtaining initial certification is only a first step in this process. Reflecting on one's teaching, and, in the process, developing knowledge and theories of teaching is an essential component in this lifelong process. The technological (and, up to a point, the effective) approach to instruction is deficient because it assumes that the ability to teach can be characterized by knowledge and skills that are somehow set. Reflective teaching, on the other hand, assumes that as our conceptions of language and learning evolve, what is considered appropriate in terms of teaching techniques and classroom management will also change. In other words, what is technically sound today may not be technically sound tomorrow.

Writing on the development of reflective TESOL teachers, Bartlett (1990) argues that becoming critically reflective:

means that we have to transcend the technicalities of teaching and think beyond the need to improve our instructional techniques. This effectively means we have to move away from the 'how to' questions, which have a limited utilitarian value, to the 'what' and 'why' questions, which regard instructional and managerial techniques, not as ends in themselves but as a part of broader educational purposes. . . . Asking "what" and "why" questions give us a certain power over our teaching. We could claim that the degree of autonomy and responsibility we have in our work as teachers is determined by the level of control that we can exercise over our actions. In reflecting on 'what' and 'why' questions we begin to exercise control and open up the possibility of transforming our everyday classroom life. (Bartlett 1990: 205)

Reflective teachers are ones who are capable of monitoring, critiquing and defending their actions in planning, implementing and evaluating language programs. Although there is a growing body of literature on reflective

Table 1   Knowledge and skills required for reflective language teaching

Curriculum area	Knowledge/skills
Planning	Sensitive to a range of learner needs (objective and subjective) and able to use these as a basis for selecting and organizing goals, objectives, content, and learning experiences of language programs
	Knowledge of the nature of language and language learning and ability to utilize this knowledge in selecting and organizing goals, objectives, content, and learning experiences of language programs
Implementation	Technical competence in instruction and classroom management
	Ability to analyze and critique their own classroom behavior and the behavior of their learners
Evaluation	Ability to assess learners in terms of a program's goals and objectives
	Ability to encourage learners to self-monitor and self-assess
	Ability to evaluate the effectiveness of teaching

learners (see, for example, Brindley 1984, Dickinson 1987, Nunan 1988), there has not been concomitant attention to the notion of reflective teachers (an exception being the work of Richards: see, for example, Richards & Lockhart 1994). Yet reflective, self-directed learners would seem to imply reflective, self-directed teachers: it would certainly be inconsistent for non-reflective teachers to encourage reflectivity in learners.

The aim of educating teachers to be reflective in the three senses outlined by van Maneen provides a focus for the development of goals for a teacher education program and is also supported by our views on the knowledge and skills required by language teachers. These views are set out in Table 1. We have chosen here to identify knowledge and skills in relation to the key curriculum areas of planning, implementation, and evaluation.

In the next task, you are invited to consider the issue of reflection in relation to your own teaching practice.

TASK

Aim To evaluate the concept of reflective teaching in relation to your own beliefs and practice.

Data The list of knowledge and skills requirements for reflective language teaching set out in Table 1.

Procedure

1. Can you add any items to the list?
2. To what extent do you see yourself as a reflective teacher? Give yourself a rating from 1 to 5 in relation to these knowledge and skills areas (1 = this does not describe me at all; 5 = this describes me perfectly).

In Table 1 we have tried to give some practical examples of the sorts of skills that might be expected of reflective practitioners in relation to curriculum planning, implementation and evaluation. Although the knowledge and skills set out in the table are suggestive rather than definitive, they are comprehensive enough to provide a point of departure for pre- and inservice education programs. We recognize that teachers in preparation will not necessarily have achieved these goals by the time they begin teaching. In fact, reflective teaching is predicated on lifelong professional renewal. However, we feel that novice teachers should have developed the essential attitude of reflectivity by the time they have begun teaching.

Dealing with behavior problems

As we saw in Chapter 1, some of the key themes underpinning educational change in the last ten to fifteen years have been the growth in learner-centered education, experiential learning, and collaborative learning. For a review of how these philosophical directions have found their way into the bloodstream of language education, see Nunan 1988, 1992b, Kohonen 1992, and Legutke and Thomas 1991. These new directions have changed the nature of the classroom, the roles implied for teachers and students, the managerial functions of the teacher, and the potential of the classroom as a place where genuine communication can take place. As a result, opportunities for low-structure teaching have greatly increased. On the negative side, they have also increased the potential for things to go wrong in the classroom, leading to problems of student discipline and behavior.

These issues of discipline and student behavior are the most frequently mentioned concerns of novice teachers. There is usually a tension between wanting to be respected and wanting to be liked. Over time, most teachers develop their own strategies and techniques for dealing with inappropriate behavior. A few seem to be able to manage behavior problems effectively from the beginning, while some never seem to develop effective strategies for dealing with unacceptable student behavior. As we shall see, behavior problems very often emerge as a result of confusion over rules, roles and expectations, as so the discussion in this section relates closely to the section on teacher and learner roles in the next chapter.

It is impossible to provide a set of rules and procedures that will work in all situations and settings. Some strategies that work with elementary students are highly inappropriate for secondary students and adults. Techniques that are effective in private schools may not work in inner city high school. Nonetheless, certain principles, we believe, are worthy of consideration, and we shall set these out in this section.

The first thing that needs to be said on the matter of student behavior is that prevention is better than cure. In other words, creating a classroom climate in which potential problems are preempted is better than trying to deal with problems once they have arisen. We cannot guarantee that problems will not occur, as they will, in part, result from the unpredictable interpersonal reactions triggered by different student (and teacher) personalities. However, there are some basic principles that we can follow. First, it is important to be clear in our own minds about our own role and that of the students. We need to decide before stepping into the classroom what we expect our students to be doing, and we need to formulate a set of strategies for dealing with situations in which our expectations are not met.

Research in content classrooms has shown that students have clear expectations of how teachers should behave, and behavior problems are likely to arise if these expectations are not met. In general, students expect teachers to provide leadership, to manage the classroom effectively and to provide instruction. The last imperative can be problematic of course, given our discussion on direct instruction in the preceding chapter. If learners believe that instruction is basically about bringing the good news, while the teacher believes that instruction involves acting as a facilitator so that students can manage their own learning, then there is likely to be conflict. It is therefore important, not only for the teacher to be clear on philosophy, roles, and responsibility, but to convey these to the students in a way that is meaningful to them. This can be difficult to do in classrooms with low-proficiency students when the teacher does not speak the students' first language. In homogeneous first language groups (that is, in those in which all students share the same first language), the rationale can usually be conveyed with the assistance of someone who speaks the teacher's and the students' first language.

Until relatively recently, it was assumed that classroom discipline problems were caused by a lack of firmness and reluctance to punish on the part of the teacher. However, as we saw in the section on effective teaching, it has been shown that the best classroom managers are those who prevent problems from occurring in the first place, rather those who deal with behavioral problems after the event by punishing students. Studies have shown that there was no appreciable differences in the ways in which effective and ineffective teachers dealt with behavioral problems. Rather, the difference lay in the fact that effective teachers created a classroom environment and adopted strategies which minimized opportunities for disruptive behavior. How did they do this? Strategies included:

1. Monitoring what was happening on a moment-by-moment basis
2. Setting up and monitoring multiple activities for different learning groups within the class
3. Being well prepared, and knowing precisely what they planned to do at each point in a lesson
4. Creating an environment in which students were able to work independently of direct teacher supervision on tasks that were at once challenging, yet within the capabilities of the students
5. Telling students what they expected, modeling the required behaviors, and giving them the chance to rehearse the behaviors if necessary
6. Teaching students effective time management strategies

(For a detailed review of this research, see Kounin 1970, Brophy & Good 1986, Doyle 1986, and Emmer, Evertson & Anderson 1980.)

In the language classroom, Harmer (1991: 250) suggests that disruptive behavior can be attributed to the teacher, the students, or the institution (although it is probably likely to be a combination of these). Student behavior can be affected by a desire to be noticed, by the proximity of another potentially disruptive student, or even by the time of day (most teachers dislike the first period after lunch or the period after gymnasium or sports). According to Harmer (1991), the teacher can do several things to minimize the chances of disruptive behavior:

− *Don't go to class unprepared*   Students automatically identify teachers who are not sure what to do in class.
− *Don't be inconsistent*   If the teacher allows students to come to class late without taking action one week students cannot be reproached for doing the same thing the week after.
− *Don't issue threats*   Teachers who threaten students with terrible punishments and then do not carry them out are doing both the class and themselves a disservice.
− *Don't raise your voice*   One of the great mistakes of many teachers is to try and establish control by raising their voices and shouting.
− *Don't give boring classes*   Perhaps the single greatest cause of indiscipline is boredom.
− *Don't be unfair*   Teachers cannot allow themselves to be unfair, either to the class as a whole or to individuals.
− *Don't have a negative attitude to learning*   A teacher who does not really care and who is insensitive to the students' reactions to what is happening in the classroom will lose the respect of the students − the first step to problems of disruptive behavior.
− *Don't break the code*   If part of the code is that the students should arrive on time, then the teacher must, too.

The following task contains a list of activities that Evertson et al. (1983) indicate are important for establishing an effective learning climate when beginning with a new class. In the task, you will be asked to evaluate each activity with reference to your present teaching context or a context in which you hope to teach.

TASK

Aim To develop a set of activities to facilitate the effective management of learning.

Procedure and data

1. Rate the following activities (adapted from Evertson et al. 1983) according to how much importance you would give them when taking a new class (5 = highly important, 1 = unimportant).

   a. Ensure that classroom space and materials are prepared.   1 2 3 4 5

   b. Decide what procedures are necessary for your classroom to function effectively, and develop a list of rules and procedures.   1 2 3 4 5

   c. Decide what you will do about appropriate and inappropriate behavior in your classroom, how you will communicate these to the students and how you will follow through.   1 2 3 4 5

   d. Teach students rules and procedures systematically.   1 2 3 4 5

   e. Develop activities for the first few days that will involve students and maintain a whole group focus.   1 2 3 4 5

   f. Plan strategies to deal with potential problems that could upset your classroom organization and management.   1 2 3 4 5

   g. Monitor student behavior closely.   1 2 3 4 5

   h. Handle inappropriate and disruptive behavior promptly and consistently.   1 2 3 4 5

   i. Provide learning activities at appropriate levels for all students in the class.   1 2 3 4 5

   j. Develop procedure that make students responsible for their work.   1 2 3 4 5

   k. Be clear when you present information and give directions to your students.   1 2 3 4 5

2. Review those items to which you gave a rating of 3 or less. Given your teaching situation or context, decide why you gave a relatively low rating to those particular items.

Even the best prepared teacher is going to encounter problems from time to time. Therefore it is worth spending some time in considering how these might be dealt with. In the first instance, it is worth thinking about the management of student behavior from the perspective of the institution in which you work. If you are lucky, there will be a clear school policy to provide guidance and coherence across the institution. In many places, however, the decisions will be left to the teacher. Wong et al. (1992) argue that an institutional approach will involve teachers and administrators formulating rules and procedures that apply to student behavior, deciding who is responsible for dealing with different sorts of problems as they arise, establishing lines of communication that teachers can use when they need help and advice, and determining how to match the curriculum to the needs of the students.

In some instances, behavioral problems occur because the students do not want to be in the classroom in the first place. In many EFL situations, English is a compulsory subject in the curriculum, but students cannot see why they have to be learning it. The same problem may arise in language institutes where students have been sent by their parents because the parents believe that a knowledge of English will give the students a comparative advantage in employment, that it will be useful for travel, that it will assist them when it comes to further education, and so on. In instances such as these, the key to minimizing problems is to find ways of making the class interesting, motivating, and worth attending for its own sake. We shall consider strategies for motivating students in the chapter on affective factors.

Wong et al. (1992) suggest that there are four basic strategies for coping with problems that arise during the course of instruction. These are the behavior modification perspective, the crime and punishment perspective, the effective teacher perspective, and the effective school perspective. (We have already dealt with the effective school perspective and therefore will not deal with it further here.)

The behavior modification perspective is based on the notion that behavior, whether good or bad, is likely to recur if it is reinforced in some way rather than being ignored. Using this approach, the teacher decides in advance which behaviors need to be either encouraged of discouraged. Behaviors to be encouraged are reinforced using various kinds of reward. These rewards can include tangibles such as high grades or intangibles such as teacher approval, which may be signaled through explicit praise, or even through a nod and a smile. For example, the teacher may decide that she wants a child who constantly leaves her place during seat work to remain seated. She can encourage this behavior by providing the child with individual attention every time she remains seated for two minutes. If the strategy proves effective, she can increase the length of time between reinforcing the behavior.

The adherent of behavior modification can employ five strategies:

— Desirable behavior should be reinforced so that it is more likely to recur.
— Immediate reinforcement is more effective than delayed reinforcement.
— Systematic reinforcement is more effective than inconsistent reinforcement.
— Reinforcement is more effective than punishment.
— Tasks in which students can succeed are more likely to lead to reinforcement than tasks that they cannot perform.

(Wong et al. 1992: 22)

The crime and punishment perspective, on the other hand, is predicated on the assumption that undesirable behavior can be minimized through negative sanctions of various sorts. The principles outlined by Wong et al. for this perspective include the following:

— Everyone should know what is punishable and what is not.
— The precise punishment for the offense should be known.
— The punishment of an offense should be agreed to be reasonable; within this, it should be as severe as possible.
— The offense should always invoke the punishment without favor and without remission for a first offense.
— The punishment should, in fact, be a punishment. What punishes one student may even be welcomed by another.
— The punishment should not be seen as a sort of expiation, after which the incident can be forgotten. It should be combined with a program to promote desired behavior.
— Schoolwork should never be used as punishment.
— Punishment should be administered as privately as possible, even though the fact of the punishment may be public knowledge.

We have already discussed the effective teacher movement in Chapter 3. Effective teachers are those whose students obtain better than predicted grades or who are identified through peer review as being excellent teachers. According to Wong et al. (1992), effective teachers share the following characteristics:

— They are masters of their material.
— They are well prepared and well organized.
— They are enthusiastic about the topic of the lesson.
— They are warm and approachable, but not familiar.

– They are alert and watchful.
– They are firm but reasonable; fair and consistent.
– They have a good sense of humor, but are sparing with jokes.
– They have clear and well-modulated speech.

TASK

Aim To summarize the management strategies presented in this section and to relate them to your own teaching situation.

Procedure

1. Review the content presented in this section and make a list of the strategies that you think are most appropriate to your own teaching situation or a situation with which you are familiar.
2. Which of these approaches seemed most in harmony (a) with your own teaching philosophy and style and (b) the teaching philosophy and style of the institution where you teach?

Summary and conclusions

A key element in the effective management of the learning process concerns the effective use of time, lesson pacing, on-line monitoring and decision making, and cultural factors in the classroom. In this chapter, we looked at these issues in relation to the dynamics of classroom interaction. We also looked at the concepts of effective and reflective teaching, for what they have to say about managing the learning process. In the final section the complex and sensitive issues associated with behavior problems were addressed.

PROJECT 1

Aim To examine the issue of lesson pacing and the decision-making processes associated with pacing.

Data A videotaped or live lesson.

Procedure Audiotape or videotape a lesson or observe a colleague's lesson, and note the pacing of the lesson. Were any tasks curtailed too soon? Did any go on too long? How were you able to tell?

PROJECT 2

Aim To develop skills in identifying and classifying different types of managerial decisions.

Data Your own data or the lesson transcript provided in the appendix to this book.

Procedure

1. Observe a lesson or videotape of a lesson (or use the lesson transcript provide in the appendix to this book), and classify the behaviors according to one of the schemes in the chapter.
2. To what extent did this exercise give you insights into the lesson that were not immediately apparent from the lesson itself?

PROJECT 3

Aim To evaluate Blum's effective teaching characteristics.

Data

1. Blum's list of effective teaching characteristics.
2. A videotaped or live lesson.

Procedure

1. Review Blum's list and identify those behaviors which are observable.
2. Observe a lesson or a videotape of a lesson, and note the extent to which these behaviors are apparent.
3. Make a note of the ways in which the lesson might have been modified to make it more effective.

PROJECT 4

Procedure As a preliminary task, carry out the following exercise, which has been adapted from Wong et al. 1992: 22–24).

1. Think back to your experiences as a student. Identify a teacher (Teacher X) who taught well, who aroused and maintained your interest in the subject, who encouraged to further your studies, or whose classes you particularly enjoyed. Now think of another teacher (Teacher Y) who was just the opposite, in whose lessons you learned very little and whose teaching you did not enjoy. For each teacher, write down two memorable events. These may be ordinary things,

but they have stayed in your mind and they help to express what it was like to be there. (Do not try to do this too quickly; you may need to give your memory some time to recall good examples.)

Teacher X

Event 1	Event 2

Teacher Y

Event 1	Event 2

2. With reference to these events, think of the teachers involved. Describe in your own words these teachers in terms of opposite dimensions (up to 10) in the following table. It is not likely that Teacher X and Y were exactly opposite in all dimensions. They might both be stern or caring or neither of these.

Example:

1 Caring	X	Cold	Y
2 Demanding in work	XY	Not demanding in work	
3 Hard working	X	Not hard working	Y

1		
2		
3		
4		

5	
6	
7	
8	
9	
10	

3. Now take five dimensions in which your teachers differ. In each case write down one teacher behavior, related to that dimension, that would promote good classroom management and one that would hinder good classroom management. (For example, if you made a mistake, a caring teacher might explain what went wrong, but a cold teacher might criticize you in front of the class.)

PROJECT 5

Aim To analyze and reflect on behavior problems and solutions found by teachers working in two different contexts

Procedure Study the following teacher statements and decide how you would deal with each. Which do you identify with most? What did each teacher learn from these exchanges about dealing with behavior problems?

Data

Statement 1 (By a teacher working in a one-to-one situation.) "Well, I was looked for by a psychiatrist. He seemed very eager to learn English. He wanted to participate in medical congresses, to be able to interrupt lectures, to give opinions, to ask questions and so on. So he wanted classes every day. But he worked like crazy, so I anticipated that he wouldn't be able to stand classes so regularly, so I suggested that he should only come three times a week, since he was actually a false beginner. I carried out a placement test, and he actually was a false beginner. We started using the material. He bought all the stuff. We started. After a month, he said he was bored, that he was a very interesting person, that his time was precious, that he felt ridiculous in class, and that he didn't want to continue with the work we were doing. He brought a text about Freud. What am I doing now? I'm adapting to what he wants. He is conducting the classes. He asked me to create a method only for him. So I bring texts, he reads, I focus on different aspects. For instance, I give him a lesson on adjectives. I ask him to read a text and underline the adjectives. He has a glossary, where he writes the words he doesn't want to forget. He writes sentences, and little by little I can introduce grammar. Now he's enjoying himself. One of the characteristics of a one-to-one teacher is flexibility. After each class, I usually get some feedback from him about how he liked it and how much he has learned."

Statement 2 (By a teacher working in a classroom situation.) "Well I had (and still have) this student. He's in his forties, and at first I just didn't like him very much. I thought he was analyzing me all the time — checking my explanations, this kind of attitude. Then, after some time, I decided to give him a lesson on how to describe people, using the questions 'What does he look like?' and 'What's he like?' There was a list of adjectives to describe physical appearance as well as to describe personality traits. There was a quiz entitled 'What sort of person are you?' He had to talk about himself. When he was answering, I thought to myself, 'This is my chance,' so I just said, 'Can I tell you something? In the beginning, I thought you were very defensive and fussy — almost unfriendly.' He replied that was the way he was, that it usually took a long time to get used to new people. He said that he analyzed, he got shy, he didn't know what to say, and that he didn't like to take risks that might result in making mistakes. He'd rather shut up and listen. As a result of this exchange, I was able to understand him better and also to tell him how I felt. Now things are going very smoothly."

5 Instructional groups

Introduction

In this chapter we look at the dynamics of interaction as learners move in and out of different learning configurations. Establishing effective learning groups and making decisions about how when and why to have students work in pairs, groups, or individually are central decisions that need to be made in order to manage the learning process effectively.

Because the dynamics of interaction and the problems that occur in different group configurations very often can be traced to the relationships that develop between teachers and learners, we begin the chapter by looking at teacher and learner roles. In the body of the chapter, we shall explore various modes of classroom organization, including small group and pair work, large classes, and self-directed learning.

Concept map of Chapter 5

In this chapter we deal with the following concepts and issues:

- *Teacher and learner roles*   dynamic nature of classroom roles, factors likely to affect roles, the teacher role continuum, learner roles and teaching methods, dealing with role conflicts
- *Small group and pair work*   dealing with learner resistance, factors to consider in implementing and evaluating pair and group work, assigning students to groups, optimum group size
- *Large classes*   location of students in classroom and effect on learning, problems and solutions, peer monitoring
- *One-to-one instruction*   advantages and disadvantages
- *Self-directed learning*   a rational for self-direction; developing self-direction in the classroom; experiential learning, intrinsic motivation, and self-directed learning; learning contracts
- *Mixed-level groups*   key factors differentiating learners, challenges and advantages of mixed-level groups, alternative ways of grouping learners

Teacher and learner roles

The roles which teachers and learners choose to adopt, or have forced upon them by institutional constraints, curricular exigencies, or classroom materials and tasks, will have a critical bearing on classroom atmosphere, patterns of interaction, and ultimately student learning. It is unlikely that the teacher and learners will always adopt the same role relationships whenever they step into the classroom. In the language classroom, as in life outside the classroom, teachers and learners will adopt a range or roles, although in any given classroom, the teacher or student may be characterized by a limited set of roles. As we shall see, these roles are not discrete. Rather they overlap, which can cause complications, confusion, and even conflict.

An additional factor to consider is that roles are dynamic, not static, and are subject to change according to the psychological factors brought by participants into the classroom and also the dynamics of group activity within the classroom. In a key text on roles in language learning, Wright (1987) identifies two groups of factors that are likely to affect roles. The first of these relates to interpersonal aspects, the second to task-related aspects.

1. Social and psychological factors. These include views about status and position, attitudes and values held by individuals and group and individuals' personalities. (Interpersonal aspects of role.)
2. Teachers' and learners' expectations about the nature of learning tasks and the way in which individuals and groups deal with learning tasks. (Task related aspects of role.)

(Wright 1987: 12)

The first set of factors derive from the personality and previous learning experiences of the teacher and students, and the expectations that they have about what is appropriate behavior for teachers and learners in the classroom. We indicated in the preceding section that behavior problems can occur if there is a mismatch between the perceptions held by teachers and learners about their respective roles. If learners expect that their role is to be the passive recipient of wisdom dispensed by the teacher, while the teacher expects the learners to be active participants in their own learning processes, then there is likely to be confusion, tension, and even conflict. If these are not resolved (or even acknowledged) through discussion and negotiation, the effectiveness of the classroom will almost certainly be affected and may even be destroyed.

The second set of factors identified by Wright relates to the role relationships inherent in classroom tasks. Underlying each and every classroom task, whether it be a role play, simulation, drill, cloze test, etc., is some sort of learning strategy (e.g., memorization, classifying, brainstorming, personalizing). Inherent in each strategy is a role for the learner. If the appropriate role is not identified and acted upon, the effectiveness of the task will be reduced.

The following classroom "snapshots" have been adapted from Good and Brophy (1987: 217–218). They are graded from most to least problematic in terms of participant roles and behavior. As we already pointed out, clarifying role expectations, and where necessary, negotiating these with the students, stating objectives clearly, linking tasks to learner needs, letting students know *why* they are being asked to take on certain roles can all serve to reduce the conflicts inherent in classrooms when learners and teachers either misunderstand or do not accept the different roles that they are required to play.

Snapshot 1   This class in continual chaos and uproar. The teacher spends much of the day trying to establish control but never fully succeeds. Directions and even threats are often ignored, and punishment does not seem to be effective for long.
Comment: Here the teacher is unsuccessfully attempting to adopt the role of controller, which is being resisted by the students. A possible response on the part of the teacher would be to try and exercise less control, positively reinforce appropriate behavior, and encourage students to take on more responsibility (for example, by playing a more collaborative role in the management of the classroom along the lines suggested in the preceding chapter.)

Snapshot 2   This class is also noisy, but the atmosphere is more positive. The teacher tries to make school fun for the students by introducing games and recreational activities, reading stories, and including lots of arts and crafts and enrichment activities. Still, there are problems. Many students pay little attention during lessons, and seatwork is often not completed or not done carefully. This problem occurs even though the teacher holds academic activities to a minimum and tries to make them as pleasant as possible.
Comment: Here the teacher has adopted the role of entertainer. Although this role is appropriate at certain times, at other times it is inappropriate. When to switch from one role to another will depend on the context and environment in which the learning takes place.

Snapshot 3   This class is quiet and well disciplined because the teacher has established many rules and makes sure that the rules are followed. Infractions are noted quickly and cut short with stern warnings, or with punishment when necessary. The teacher spends a lot of time doing this,

partly because he is so quick to notice any misbehavior. He appears to be a successful disciplinarian because the students usually obey him. However, the class atmosphere is uneasy. Trouble is always brewing just under the surface, and whenever the teacher leaves the room, the class "erupts."
Comment: This classroom is orderly because the teacher has taken on the role of disciplinarian. However, because the disciplinarian role often results in students who are other-directed, and who do not have not developed the role of self-directed adult, trouble of the kind indicated can occur when the controlling adult is not present.

Snapshot 4   This class seems to run by itself. The teacher spends most of her time teaching, not handling discipline problems. The students follow instructions and complete assignments on their own, without close supervision. Those involved in seatwork or enrichment activities interact with one another, so noise may be coming from several sources at the same time. However, these are the controlled and harmonious sounds of students productively involved in activities, not the disruptive noises of boisterous play or disputes. When noise does become disruptive, a simple reminder from the teacher is usually effective. Observers in this class sense a certain warmth in the atmosphere and go away impressed.
Comment: Here the students have embraced the role of inner-directed adult. The teacher's role has evidently been to develop a sense of independence and responsibility.

One of the problems that is brought about by the emergence of new models of language and learning and the development of innovative methodologies is that they generally entail new roles for teachers and learners. If these new role implications are not made explicit, then problems can arise, particularly if there is a mismatch between the expectations of the learners and the role implications of classroom tasks. This phenomenon occurred in many classrooms with the implementation of communicative language teaching.

The development of communicative language teaching has had a dramatic effect on the roles that learners are required to adopt. This is particularly true of oral interaction tasks. In small-group interaction tasks . . . learners are required to put language to a range of uses, to use language which has been imperfectly mastered, to negotiate meaning, in short, to draw on their own resources rather than simply repeating and absorbing language. This can sometimes cause problems if you are teaching learners who have rather set ideas on language and learning, particularly if these differ greatly from your own. In such cases you have a number of options. In the first instance you can insist that, as teacher, you know best and the learners must resign themselves to doing as you say. Alternatively, you can give in to the learners and structure activities around their preferences (assuming all learners think alike!). A more positive option would be to discuss the issue with the learners, explain why you want them to engage in communicative tasks, and attempt to come to a compromise. (Nunan 1989a: 86–87)

Teacher roles

Teaching is an exciting and uncertain profession because the personal chemistry between teacher-student and student-student means that no two classes will ever be exactly the same. Anyone who has taught for any length of time will have experienced the high of working with a class that "clicks," when the chemistry between the various personalities making up the class just seems to work. Unfortunately, the reverse can also occur. There are times when, through nobody's fault, the intangible and indefinable mix of factors fails, and every lesson is a struggle. In the following task, we look at the relationship between basic personality types and expectations we might have about student behavior.

TASK

Aim To reflect on the relationship between the notion between personality type and expectations of student behavior.

Procedure Wright (1987: 26) suggests that personality types such as the following can be found in most classrooms (although he is careful to point out that these are tendencies rather than absolute descriptions).

1. Which of these descriptions do you think is most like you? Which is least like you?
2. Can you think of any other personality types?
   a. *Authoritarian:* shows tendency for liking authority and exercising power
   b. *Affiliative:* shows tendency for preferring to form close relationships with others
   c. *Conformist:* shows tendency to for wanting to think as others do
   d. *Aggressive:* shows tendency towards aggressive behavior to achieve aims
   e. *Cooperative:* shows tendency to work closely with others in performing tasks
   f. *Achieving:* shows tendency toward wanting to achieve status, power, success.
3. What types of behaviors would you expect to see in teachers conforming to each of these types and students conforming to each of the types? Fill in the grid on the next page.

Role	Behavior	
	Teacher	*Student*
Authoritarian Affiliative Conformist Aggressive Cooperative Achieving		

In reality, we are all complex amalgams of a range of teacher roles. Any list such as the preceding one is bound to be a simplification of reality. It should also be kept in mind that the role and personality types are metaphorical. When we speak of Teacher A as a "ringmaster," for example, we do so to conjure up a particular image, to create a picture of someone who maintains tight control and who orchestrates a complex mix of activities. However, the metaphors can also be useful in helping us to identify and clarify our own self-concept and preferred teaching style, as well as that of our colleagues.

Harmer (1991) suggests that most classroom roles required of the teacher can be placed somewhere along a continuum, with "teacher as controller" and one extreme, and "teacher as facilitator" at the other. The controller role is appropriate at those times in the lesson when the teachers want the whole class to be attending to what they have to say, for example, when setting up a new activity, providing explanations or giving feedback. Other roles include the teacher as assessor (when the teacher corrects or provides feedback to the students), the teacher as organizer; the teacher as prompter (when the teacher needs to encourage students to participate or to provide information on procedural issues), the teacher as participant (Harmer points out that there is no reason why the teacher should not participate as an equal in communicative activities such as role plays and simulations), the teacher as resource (providing information and assistance as needed), the teacher as tutor (helping to clarify ideas, point out errors in rough drafts, etc.), and the teacher as investigator (in this role, teachers further their own professional competence through the observation and investigation of processes of teaching and learning in their own classroom).

Of all these roles, it is the teacher as organizer that is the most important and difficult from the perspective of classroom management:

The success of many activities depends on good organization and on the students knowing exactly what they are to do. A lot of time can be wasted if the teacher omits to give students vital information or issues conflicting and confusing instructions. The main aim of the teacher when organizing an activity is to tell the students what they are to talk about (or write or read about), give clear instructions about what exactly their task is, get the activity going, and then organize feedback when it is over. This sounds remarkably easy, but can be disastrous if teachers have not thought out exactly what they are going to say beforehand. (Harmer 1991: 239)

In the next task, we look at teacher roles and the high-structure to low-structure task continuum that we suggested at the beginning of the book could provide a rudimentary framework for teacher action.

TASK

Aim To consider the relationship between different teacher roles and high-structure/low-structure teaching contexts.

Procedure Put a number on the continuum to show where you believe the following roles would reside. (The first one has been done for you.)

Data

Teacher roles: (1) teacher as participant, (2) teacher as assessor, (3) teacher as prompter, (4) teacher as resource, (5) teacher as tutor.

Harmer goes on to document a list of "don'ts" for organizing activities, including the following:

– Don't assume that students have understood the instructions – always check that they have grasped what they are supposed to do.
– Never issue unclear instructions – plan carefully what you are going to say beforehand.
– Be careful about when students are to look at material.

(The vocabulary-in-context task in the section on teacher instructions provides a clear example of what happens if instructions are not given clearly. The students embark upon the task and then find themselves simultaneously trying to do the task as well as trying to determine what it is that they are supposed to do.)

In the next task, you are invited to consider the role relationships that are implied by different types of instructional activity. This task highlights the fact that everything that we do in the classroom (and, indeed, everything that we require our students to do) carries a clear message about the role of the teacher and learner.

TASK

Aim To identify the roles required of teachers in specific instructional tasks.

Procedure and data

1. Indicate what role the teacher has in each activity (a–k) by writing one of the numbers of the following roles in the empty space next to each activity.

Roles: (1) conductor of activities in the classroom, (2) foreign language informant, (3) coordinator of students and activities, (4) evaluator/observer of students' activities and performances, (5) animator of communicative tasks in the classroom.

a. [   ] Teacher knows the language, selects the new material to be learned, and presents it.
b. [   ] Teacher devises and provides the maximum amount of practice.
c. [   ] Teacher considers what, how much, when, and how to teach.
d. [   ] Teacher controls the amount of talking he or she does.
e. [   ] Teacher encourages the students to go on learning.
f. [   ] Teacher controls the quality of the students' output as well as the length of time they need to accomplish an activity.
g. [   ] Teacher provides ample opportunities for students to integrate new knowledge with established knowledge.
h. [   ] Teacher is well informed about the students' expectations and limitations.
i. [   ] Teacher prepares classes and provides students with appropriate strategies for understanding language.
j. [   ] Teacher does not depend on a textbook to develop the classes.
k. [   ] Teacher provides students with regular and frequent opportunities to use the language.

2. Can you devise some additional roles and situations?

When we did the preceding task, we came up with the following responses:

a. 3	c. 1	e. 5	g. 1	i. 2	k. 2
b. 3	d. 5	f. 4	h. 4	j. 5	

Learner roles

The different methods that have evolved over the years all imply different roles for learners (and teachers). The chart in the next task, created from material contained in Richards and Rodgers (1986), illustrates the range of roles required of learners in a number of methods that were fashionable when they wrote their book.

TASK

Aim To consider the relationship between teacher/learner roles and language teaching methods.

Procedure

1. Which of these methods are consistent with your preferred teaching style?
2. Which are consistent with your students' preferred learning roles?
3. Which are consistent with high-structure teaching and which with low-structure teaching?

Data The following learner role chart is derived from Richards and Rodgers (1986).

Method	*Learner role*
Oral/situational	Learner listens to teacher and repeats; no control over content or methods
Audiolingual	Learner has little control; reacts to teacher direction; passive, reactive role
Communicative	Learner has an active, negotiative role; should contribute as well as receive
Total physical response	Learner is a listener and performer; little influence over content and none over methodology
The silent way	Learners learn through systematic analysis; must become independent and autonomous
Community language learning	Learners are members of a social group or or community; move from dependence to autonomy as learning progresses
The natural approach	Learners play an active role and have relatively high degree of control over content language production
Suggestopedia	Learners are passive, have little control over content or method

This analysis shows that methods which differ widely on one level can be very similar at in terms of the roles they entail for teachers and learners. Parrott (1993: 63) points out that some models of learning and teaching see students as sponges who soak up knowledge from teacher and textbook. Other roles can include experimenter, researcher, negotiator, obeyer, explorer, struggler, path-follower, initiator. Although these labels are metaphorical, they do capture the spirit of many classroom task types. The fact that classroom tasks carry with them certain role implications is explored in the following task.

TASK

Aim To identify the roles implicit in different classroom tasks.

Procedure Study the following tasks and identify the learner roles that are implied in the tasks.

Data

1. Students in two groups listen to two different tapes in which several people are interviewed about their lifestyles. They summarize the information they hear and then work in pairs with a member of the other group to share information and complete a table.
   Role: _____
2. Students in pairs are given a situation in which there are several applicants for a job. They have to decide who is to get the job and justify their choice.
   Role: _____
3. Students read a short narrative and formulate the spelling rule for the simple past tense of the verbs.
   Role: _____
4. Students listen to a conversation and then practice it.
   Role: _____
5. Students obtain an English language newspaper out of class, select an article, and prepare a set of comprehension questions to accompany the article.
   Role: _____
6. Students record themselves carrying out discussion task and listen to the tape to identify their errors.
   Role: _____

Small group and pair work

One of the major changes to the dynamics of classroom interaction wrought by student-centered teaching has been an increasing emphasis on pair and group work. Pair and group work can greatly increase the amount of active speaking and listening undertaken by all students in the class. However, for inexperienced teachers, those working with unruly students, and those with large classes, setting up group activities can logistically be difficult. Such activities can consume precious class time, they can make the effective monitoring of student talk all but impossible, and they can lead to discipline problems. However, for the teacher who subscribes to an experiential view of learning; that is, for the teacher who believes that the most effective way to develop interactional skills in the target language is through guided opportunities to interact, pair and group work are indispensable.

Pair and group work can also be problematic in classrooms where there is a mismatch between the expectations of the teacher and those of the students. Consider the following case study from Nunan (1988: 167, 169; used by permission), in which problems arose because the teacher believed that students learned to speak by speaking and that pair and group work maximized opportunities to speak, while the learners believed that their role was to sit passively and absorb knowledge from the teacher.

By the end of the first week, Sally was experiencing a great deal of frustration. She felt lost, and, in her own words, like a beginning teacher. When asked what sort of assistance she would like, she replied that all she wanted was someone who would tell her what to do and how to cope with the complexities of the professional situation in which she found herself. She wanted to please her students and do what was best for each of them, rather than pitching her teaching to a middle level which would make the class too easy for some and too difficult for others. . . . At this early point in the course, students had been generally unable to articulate their feelings in any useful fashion, and the teacher was unsure whether she could begin by revising what she assumed they had covered. . . . When asked whether she felt that the idea of a negotiated curriculum was idealistic, she replied: "No, I agree with it. It's worked well with me before. I think of the curriculum as methodology as well as syllabus, and I've negotiated syllabus in the past rather than methodology." (Nunan 1988: 167)

The solution to Sally's problem can be found in her comment that methodology as well as syllabus ought to be negotiated. She realized that she had not negotiated the procedural aspects of learning with her students. When she did, the results were dramatic. By the end of the course, the attitude and motivation of the students had changed, they were much more interested in their work, more cohesive, and quite willing to engage in pair and group work. How had the change been brought about?

The change had been brought about by the teacher, in week four, deciding to conduct a fairly extensive survey of the students' attitudes towards the content, methodology, materials and class groupings. The students were asked to indicate what they found easy and what they found difficult, what they liked and what they disliked. . . .

The survey was followed by an intensive counseling session, in which Sally followed up on the major points arising out of the survey. All students had given a low rating to pair work. In fact, it was the only thing they hated enough to want to stop. This was a real problem for Sally, as a great many classroom activities were based on group and pair work, so she decided to pair work the focus of negotiation. She explained to them that she wanted to give them the maximum amount of practice, and if they had difficulty then this was part of communicating and learning to communicate, and that they had to work it out.

In reviewing reaction of the students to the consultative process, she stated that:

> At first they were a bit stunned and amused at the teacher wanting them to give their opinions on content and methodology. I explained that I'd been worried because of the disparate levels, and that some things would be difficult for some learners and that I was very interested to know. They were really pleased to be consulted. . . . Explaining and giving the rationale is crucial.

As a result of the consultation process, all learners were quite prepared to continue with the pair work. Clarifying the rationale also made 'an incredible difference to how they went about their pair work. Before, they were really sluggish and reluctant – just going through the motions. Now they really get into it.' (Nunan 1988: 169)

This case study illustrates in a rather dramatic way the changes that it is possible to bring about through a process of explanation and negotiation. It is simply not the case that, confronted with conflicting desires over such things as group and pair work, only two options exist – either adopt a "teacher knows best" attitude, or capitulate to the students. These are the extreme points on a continuum. Through negotiation and compromise, the teacher can usually find a point somewhere along the continuum that is mutually satisfactory to all parties concerned.

In implementing and evaluating pair and group work tasks in the classroom, there are several essential factors to consider. First, the teacher needs to think about the purpose of the task, particularly as it relates to the overall curriculum goals. Secondly, the teacher needs to decide how and why to group the learners and whether the composition of the groups is to remain static, or whether it will change. Group size is another pertinent factor. It is surprising how a task that is not particularly effective with groups of three can work well with a slightly larger group, and vice versa. When collecting data for this book, we found it interesting to observe a class in which the teacher found it impossible to motivate students to speak when they were in groups of seven or eight. Once the group size was reduced to five, however, the students became animated and carried out the task with no further prompting.

Generally speaking, odd-sized groups work better than even-sized groups. We also find for most communicative tasks that it is desirable to limit the number of students in a group to five or less. As students will be working independently for at least part of the time, an additional factor to consider is how feedback will be provided. The feedback can be related to the content of the task, the linguistic performance of the students or both content and linguistic performance.

Some teachers worry that students working in pairs or small groups will make errors that may go uncorrected, or, even worse, that students will learn each others' errors. Our own belief is that at certain times during a lesson it does not matter whether or not the students make errors. From the limited amount of available evidence, it would also seem that learners do not, in general, appear to learn each others' errors. If you are bothered by students' errors, you can circulate during group work, and make a note of the more frequently occurring errors. These errors can be dealt with during a subsequent review session.

Another problem is that of noise. Group work, by its nature, is designed to generate noise, and in many classrooms this can be disruptive to other classes in adjoining rooms. We have worked in schools where the principal would appear at the window within minutes of a group activity being started. As he was not a language specialist, he had great difficulty in equating noise with learning. Luckily, he was prepared to tolerate what he considered to be our deviant views on the subject.

A major issue in the management of group work is deciding on a policy for assigning students to groups. In some contexts and situations, it may be natural to allow students to self-select, in which case they will tend to work in friendship groups. However, there are also other possibilities and considerations:

Some teachers use what is called a sociogram where, for example, students are asked to write down the name of the student they would most like to have with them if they were stranded on a desert island. This technique certainly tells the teacher who the popular and unpopular students are, but will not help to form groups of equal sizes since popularity is not shared round the class in such a neat way. At the beginning of a course a sociogram may not be appropriate anyway since students will often not know each other. . . . A lot of teachers form groups where strong and weak students are mixed together. This is often a good thing for the weak students (although there is a danger that they will be over-powered by the stronger members of the group and will thus not participate) and probably does not hinder the stronger students from getting the maximum benefit from the activity. Sometimes, however, it is probably a good idea to make groups of strong students and groups of weaker students. (Harmer 1991: 246)

Honeyfield (1991) considers two important aspects of managing group work. The first of these relates to the optimum size of the group. The second is concerned with grouping criteria other than size. He reviews several recent investigations of group work in the language classroom and draws the following conclusions (some of these are self-evident, others are less so):

1. There is no conclusive evidence from research which can tell us how big small groups should be in the language classroom, or what other criteria we should follow in allocating students to groups.
2. It seems likely that the smaller groups are, the more "talking time" there is for each participant.

3. Some theories of second language learning seem compatible with the idea that quantity of talk (which can be thought of as "input" or "output") is important for learning. This argument could be used to favor smaller groups, especially pairs.

4. On the other hand, having say four learners in a group may make group tasks more complex (e.g., because of more opinions being expressed), and therefore more interesting. In any case, varying the size of groups from time to time could in itself help make lessons less monotonous.

5. There is some evidence from general education and social science research that groups beyond six members in size change their character. Some of the changes may not be helpful for learning.

6. The ideas set out in (2)–(5) above suggest the size of small groups in the language classroom should normally range between two and six members.

7. It seems likely that many types of group tasks can be adapted for groups of varying sizes. Some "real world" tasks that may be needed in ESP courses are exceptions to this, with group size depending on participation patterns in real life.

8. Language teaching methodologists (at least those working in the "communicative" tradition) currently favor mixed proficiency level grouping, but suggest that this can generally be arrived at by allocating students to groups on a random basis.

9. There is a limited amount of research evidence that lends some support to mixed proficiency level groupings.

10. Some reasons can be given to support the allocation of students to groups on the basis of other differences (e.g., mother tongue, ethnic origin), but this too can probably be achieved by random grouping.

(Honeyfield 1991: 16)

Once group activities have been set up, it is crucial to monitor and evaluate group dynamics and individual member contributions. Things to note as you monitor groups at work include those who contribute and those who do not, those who facilitate and those who inhibit the group, whether the atmosphere is positive, negative, or neutral, whether members are actively involved in the group task, or whether they are simply going through the motions. (One of the projects at the end of this chapter is designed to help you as the facilitator to observe your groups and notice how they behave.)

The preceding discussion sets out just some of the factors that need to be taken into consideration in setting up successful group work activities. Once the teacher steps back and observes group work tasks in action, it is surprising how many insights can be generated and how much more successful group tasks can become. In the next section of the chapter we turn from small groups to large classes and explore some of the problems and practical solutions to issues associated with instructing large groups of second language learners.

Large classes

For teachers who have spent most of their professional careers working with comparatively small classes, it comes as something of a shock to visit classrooms containing over one hundred students. For most of us, classrooms of more than fifty are considered large. It is only comparatively recently that teachers and university-based researchers have begun to explore the particular problems created by large classes. This work has been led by a group of students, teachers, and researchers based at the University of Lancaster in the United Kingdom (see, for example, Colman 1989a, 1989b; Nolasco & Arthur 1988.)

One piece of research that has emerged from the group is that of Shamin (forthcoming). She points out that large classes are a fact of life for EFL teachers working in developing countries such as Pakistan, India, Sri Lanka, Indonesia and Nigeria. In some of these places it is possible to come across classes comprising upward of 200 students. Shamin's research, which was carried out in Pakistan, focused on the effect of physical location on motivation and achievement in large classes. Given the teacher-fronted nature of instruction and the difficulty teachers have in moving about the classrooms by virtue of the overcrowding, students who sit or who are seated at the front of the class have a greater academic advantage than those seated further back because they can actually take part in the lesson. As a consequence, Shamin reports that there was a great deal of competition for the front seats, and students adopted a range of strategies to get the front seats. One student reported that, "If you come regularly you can come early and grab the front seats," while another stated, "I grabbed my seat in the front row the very first day before other boys had come."

The effect of location on the management of the learning process is captured in the following quote:

A few students at the back also commented on the difference in teachers' wait time between questions which were directed at the students in the front or the back of the class. According to them, this reflected a difference in teachers' expectations from students at different locations in the classroom. However, it was not possible to record the incidence of this phenomenon in any systematic way.

It was also observed that the majority of large class teachers created, within their large class, a smaller class of students in the front only. They seemed happy to teach this 'smaller' class of students in the front and ignored the students at the back as long as these students tacitly agreed not to disturb the class and at least copied down the answers from the blackboard. An extreme example of this phenomenon was observed in the class of one teacher who enjoyed the reputation of being a 'good' teacher in her school. She had 65 students in her class. However, in actual effect, she was really teaching a class of 8 students – the class monitors who sat in the first row. They answered all the questions and served as barometers for pacing the classroom activities. One day when she had given them dictation, it was very obvious that she only considered the students in the front as worthy of her attention. (Shamin forthcoming)

Shamin concludes from her research that physical location is perceived by students as critical to their chances of partaking in the educational "goods and services" on offer in large classrooms. Physical location creates two psychological zones. The front is where all the pedagogical action seems to take place. Here students can hear the teacher, can read what is written on the board, and get to take part in teacher-student interaction. Monitoring and supervision results in higher motivation. The students at the front therefore tend to be considered academically more able. Those at the back often cannot see or hear. They do not pay attention, their motivation is lower, and they tend not to pay attention to the content of the lesson. They are considered academically less able and create their own psychological and cultural space, which has it own rules and norms of interaction. Needless to say, these differ from the norms and rule in force at the front of the classroom. The teachers perceive that those at the back are lazy; the students' own perception is that they are doomed.

Shamin concludes her study by pointing to a dilemma in teaching in Pakistan. On one hand, the most sensible way of dealing with the two-zone problem, would be to devolve responsibility in the classroom by using different instructional and classroom management techniques such as pair and group work. However, it seems that in Pakistan, students learn most effectively when under the direct control of the teacher, where control is external and imposed rather than internal and voluntary.

TASK

Aim To brainstorm and prioritize ideas for dealing with the dilemma created by class size and a teacher-centered philosophy.

Procedure Make a list of ideas for dealing with this dilemma. Prioritize these and, if possible, discuss them with another teacher.

It would be worth experimenting with the notion of learner training in classrooms such as those described by Shamin, although the learners may, at the outset be unwilling to take part in devolved activities such as pair and group work, which are designed to enhance their own self-direction and motivation. At the outset, these innovative techniques may not result in effective learning. However, it may be possible to measure progress over the medium to longer term. We know from research in more privileged contexts that it takes considerable time and effort to engender change in the attitudes, habits, and learning approaches of students.

Duppenthaler (1991) points out that one of the first and most daunting tasks confronting the teacher of large classes is to learn the students' names. The problem is usually compounded by the fact that the teacher will probably be teaching several large classes concurrently. He suggests that one way of learning names is to create a student picture roll card file. This file consists of a passport-size photograph of each student that is pasted or taped onto a small, stiff card, which also contains the student's name. The back of the card can be used to keep a mini-record of the student. The record might be diagnostic information about learning difficulties or might contain biographical data on such things as hobbies, interests, learning preferences, and so forth. Duppenthaler says that, when possible, the teacher should take the photographs to ensure uniformity.

Duppenthaler also describes a classroom task designed for large classes called "passages for peer monitoring." This task is designed to enable students to practice a variety of skills while at the same time minimizing the chance of error. The task required a series of handouts, each containing a number of short passages followed by questions and answers. The handout is used in the following way:

You will need a handout with a set of instructions. . . . Divide the students into pairs, pass out the handouts (only 1 handout to each pair of students), have the students read the instructions, and quickly check to make sure that all the students know what they are supposed to do. Student A then reads passage 1 to student B who is not allowed to look at the handout. Student A then asks B the comprehension questions and checks B's answers using the models provided. Student A can read the passage as often as B wants and can help B with the answers if B either has trouble or asks for clarification or help. After A has finished with passage 1, A gives the handout to B, the students change roles, with B acting as teacher for the next passage and A as student. Students continue to alternate roles until all the passages have been read and questions answered. (Duppenthaler 1991: 65–66)

One-to-one instruction

Teaching on a one-to-one basis requires quite different skills from teaching classes and groups of students. When we talk about one-to-one teaching, we are generally thinking of the situation in which a teacher has a private student to work with. However, it can also occur within the context of a larger class, when the teacher chooses to work with a single student. Increasingly, one-to-one teaching is also being carried out in self-access and individualized language centers where teachers are available as resource persons to assist students who may or may not be concomitantly enrolled in a regular class (Murphey 1991; Wiberg 1987).

Teachers and students will have their own preferences when it comes to modes of learning. The following interviews indicate some of the attitudes held by teachers and students regarding one-to-one learning. They partly reflect individual learning style preferences, are partly concerned with achieving a closer match between the objectives of the teacher and those of the learner, and also reflect issues of simple convenience.

Interview with teacher

I: What do you think about one-to-one teaching?

T: Well, I think it can be more interesting, sometimes, than teaching a "normal" class.

I: In what ways?

T: It depends on the kind of student you have. If you meet an interesting person, the subjects you'll be talking about, no matter whatever they are, will be interesting to talk about. If the student is intelligent, or has traveled a lot, or shares the same interests, he or she will make the classes richer.

I: It's easier than having to cater for different interests all at the same time.

T: Yes.

I: Can you see any disadvantages in one-to-one teaching?

T: Yes. What if the student is boring? You have to put up with him for an hour or so.

I: And then what do you do?

T: I try to be as professional as possible – be nice, polite, do my job. It's difficult when you don't like the other person!

I: Can you think of any other disadvantages?

T: Yes, when they cancel classes, for example. You prepare the lesson, they phone and call it off. But you still have to charge them, and I feel embarrassed – so all these "practical" issues are bad. But I think that despite all this one-to-one classes are more rewarding because you can observe the improvement of the student better.

I: What do you see as the important characteristics of the private teacher? Do you think that they should have special training?

T: I think so. But also, I think that it has to do with empathy. It's something you won't find in books. It's something that either goes or . . .

I: It's as if you're making a new friend – you never know what it's going to be like.

T: Yes, but I think training is always necessary.

I: How do you plan your classes? Do you plan them in advance?

T: Usually, yes. But, for instance, one of my students is taking a very hard course now, and she's been working hard, as well. She gets here very tired, so I try to adapt the lesson to her mood. For example, I try to give her lighter classes with songs and that sort of thing.

Interview with Student A

I: Do you see any disadvantages in private lessons?

S: It's when you don't like the teacher, but you keep going, because they live near your house or they offer you a special price or a specific schedule, then you go on, but you don't have interest. I think it's better to try to find a new teacher for you – someone who will meet your goals and objectives.

I: For you, what is a good teacher?

S: Well, it's someone who understands my problems. We talk about them, or when I'm tired do lighter activities. We can discuss our problems, we can exchange ideas, we can discuss interesting texts, we can listen to some music, we can do a lot of things we can't do in school. There you have to follow rules, and when you get to a certain level, it's hard to follow a class with some boring things and so you have to find another kind of teaching or class.

I: Don't you like to have classmates?

S: Sometimes, only to discuss some topics, but not to study grammar rules, because you waste a lot of time while you wait for others to have their doubts solved. I prefer when the teacher can tackle my difficulties more objectively. And if you want to do something like study for a test – for TOEFL, for instance, you can have specific preparation.

I: We have been talking about the role of the teacher. What do you think the role of the student is?

S: To be punctual, try to study, to be interested in everything, be nice, be kind, not only as a student but as a friend. Then you can have a good relationship, and then the classes get better. We can do a lot of different things, like we can exchange ideas. For me this is the important thing. The possibility of exchanging ideas and seeing what you have to do to become a good speaker.

I: Have you had any bad experiences before?

S: No. The only problem was that the teacher had a British accent, and I prefer the American one. I have lived in L.A., you know. I just love the way Americans talk, the expressions they use. I've had bad experiences with large groups, because sometimes the subject was boring, and the teacher had no flexibility – she had a syllabus to follow.

I: Couldn't you the students ask the teacher to change the syllabus or the textbook?

S: We tried, but she had to follow the lesson plan she was given by the school. I think that sometimes there are boring texts, but the teacher could explore them in a more interesting way. It's a question of preparing the classes better. Teachers are not very well paid, and they don't dedicate much of their time to preparation. So it's an easy option to just open the book and follow it. Sometimes you don't even have to give that exact text, you can give something else, which will include the same topics to be analyzed. Another problem is when the students are messy, and then the teachers get tired, they decide to keep going anyway. This is a vicious circle, and if they keep going like that things get even worse. They have to try to reverse the situation. Also, teachers should not let their private problems interfere with the lessons. That's why I'd rather have private lessons – in large groups you don't have a chance to ask and solve your doubts.

Interview with Student B

I: Why do you look for private lessons?

S: First of all, I worry about being misplaced. Once I had an interview and I was completely misplaced. Also I think that in one-to-one classes you have all the time for yourself; you don't have to share with other slower, weaker students. Listening to too much wrong English, you start copying and teachers lack time to correct everybody appropriately. I also think that the student should always choose the teacher they want to have lessons with.

I: What are the characteristics of a good teacher in your opinion?

S: Realizing the needs of the students, for instance things they have difficulty with, things they don't know. A good teacher keeps the students' interest in the classes, exchange ideas, get things off the chest. We always end up doing a little psychoanalysis. I don't mind having other classmates as long as they have the same interests and are at the same level. I think that language schools should be teaching schools, not commercial companies. They should worry about the student as an individual, not as a source of making money. That's the main reason I look for private lessons – to be treated as someone special, not as if I were part of the herd.

(Authors' data)

There are obvious advantages in being able to match content and procedure to the needs, interests and proficiency level of a single student. However, in many ways it is more demanding and tiring. There are fewer opportunities to vary the pacing and timing of the lesson, and dealing with an unresponsive student can be painful.

There are several practical problems lying in wait for the teacher wishing to teach on an individual basis. Problem number one is where to get the customers. In foreign language contexts, many native speakers, or trained non-native speakers become involved in one-to-one instruction without planning to do so: a student from the regular class approaches, wanting additional instruction, a colleague, who does one-to-one teaching passes an unwanted student on to us, our aerobics instructor wants English lessons, our landlady's brother-in-law wants to improve his English in advance of a business trip to the United States and so on. The second problem is where to conduct the lessons, at your place, your student's place, or neutral territory. A third problem, and one that can cause a great deal of embarrassment relates to how much teachers should charge for their services. These fees will be standardized in some contexts, and the teacher can generally obtain guidance from colleagues in other contexts. However, situations will often arise in which the teacher will be confronted with a moral dilemma over how much to charge.

There is also the issue of what to do when either the teacher or student is forced to cancel or to skip a class. If teachers are forced to cancel an appointment, they arrange an alternative time to meet (and therefore do not suffer financially). However, when students cancel or fail to meet appointments, teachers generally do not receive the money. One solution to this dilemma is to charge students in advance for a predetermined number of lessons (which, after all, is the policy of language teaching institutions). Then, if the student misses a class, the teacher is not penalized financially.

Additional problems are concerned more directly with pedagogy. How planned and structured should the lessons be? Should we use commercial materials, or try and structure the contact sessions around the needs and interests of the student. Should we assess progress in any formal way?

In many, if not most, institutional contexts involving large classes, the input is provided by the teacher or a textbook nominated by the institution. In such contexts, the learners themselves, their needs and wants, may be forgotten, and teaching may (and usually is) based on a stereotypical view of learner needs. In contrast, in one-to-one teaching, the teacher has an opportunity to find out who students are, and is able to determine their linguistic, communicative, and affective needs. Content and methodology are determined through a process of consultation and negotiation between teacher and student. Although this method requires skills not always demanded of the classroom teacher, freedom from the imperatives of institutional lesson plans and the exigencies of the whole class allows the teacher to tailor-make instruction for each particular learner. The disadvantages of not having opportunities for peer correction, pairwork, and small group discussion are compensated for by the ability to work at the learner's own pace, opportunities to record and transcribe dialogues for student self-correction, and, above all, authentic teacher-student communication.

Despite the obvious differences between one-to-one and whole group teaching, issues of teacher talk, planning, time management, resources, affective issues, and monitoring and evaluation remain important. However, this is rarely pointed out in teacher education programs. "There is a temptation to think no group dynamics is involved in one-to-one teaching, and that there is only a single relationship involved in the classroom activities" (Wiberg 1987: 10). The many different roles that teachers are required to play in the language classroom are also paralleled in one-to-one teaching. Particularly with adults, the teacher has to be colleague, friend and psychologist as well as language expert. A major difference between in-class and one-to-one teaching is that with the latter the student has much more control over the content and process of learning – in a sense, it is the student who directs the teacher. It is therefore important for both teacher and student to be aware of the role requirements of different learning moments.

TASK

Aim To consider problems and possible solutions in one-to-one teaching.

Procedure

1. Take a few moments to make a list of the problems or challenges that you have encountered (or anticipate encountering) in one-to-one teaching.
2. The following observations or reflections on one-to-one instruction have been adapted from Murphey (1991). They contain a variety of practical suggestions for dealing with some of the issues already discussed. Read them, and check off those that contain possible solutions to the problems you listed.

Data

1. Your students are your best publicity. Let them know you are looking for other students, and the connections multiply.
2. If possible, make English the only language of communication from the very beginning, and it becomes the accepted standard.
3. Agreeing (or suggesting) to meet with no obligation to discuss possible lessons gives more control to the student. Clients may be more apt to consider teachers who don't give them a hard sell. It's a start of unequal encounters.
4. The flexibility of the teacher is of great importance in regard to meeting place and time.
5. Often the clients still need something to make them feel your meetings are somewhat like school. Even if they are progressing a lot, the enjoyment and naturalness may make them doubt the efficacy of the method because they learned in school that studying is supposed to be more difficult.
6. The pain of error correction can be avoided by taking notes and only interrupting if the communication breaks down (i.e., you don't understand).
7. When the teacher generates an intense and genuine interest in the client and the client's interests, feeling sincerely that the client has

as much to teach as to learn, the creation of an equal encounter situation is easier.

8. A teacher may plan extensively and have a stock of topics to discuss and materials to exploit, but does not need to feel tied to them.
9. The teacher needs to figure out to what extent the student wants lessons resembling school or simply social contact.
10. Adjusting to your student's enthusiasm and interests may necessitate a readjustment of your own priorities at a given moment in your life or at least an acceptance of their interests without derogatory judgment.
11. Although the traditionally professed goal for language teachers is student progress, for certain students at certain levels, maintenance and "keeping the batteries charged" may be their primary reason for taking lessons. Social contact may be primary for others.
12. Students should be encouraged to select materials themselves, although this role is traditionally the teacher's.
13. Students dropping the one-to-one meetings after a while should not necessarily be taken as a sign that something was wrong with a teacher or her way of teaching. The good thing about most one-to-one is that it is ecologically self-regulating; if, for either of the parties, meetings become unwanted, for whatever reason, they can be discontinued — a very healthy option not available in public schools.

One-to-one teaching is rarely dealt with in teacher education programs. However, most teachers working in EFL settings end up doing one-to-one at one time or another. In this section we have seen that one-to-one teaching has several advantages. The most obvious is that in a one-to-one situation, it is easier to respond to the needs and interests of the learner. From the learner's perspective, this mode of learning offers flexibility, the opportunity for personal attention, and the possibility of being able to choose the teacher the student wants. Based on data from teachers we interviewed, the major disadvantage was the financial implication of students canceling class at the last minute. Another disadvantage for both student and teacher could be lack of empathy between teacher and student. Students nominated as disadvantages the occasional lack of preparation on the part of the teacher, the cost compared with regular class, and the lack of contact with other students.

Self-directed learning

At first sight, there may seem something paradoxical about discussing self-directed learning in a book on the management of the learning process. However, our view is that all instruction should ultimately point learners toward self-directed learning because, in the final analysis, it is the learners who have to do the learning. An additional compelling consideration is the fact that if the learners are seriously interested in becoming proficient in the language, then they are going to have to do most of the learning on their own. The most extensive and prolonged period of classroom instruction can only provide a limited introduction to the chosen language. The self-directed learner is one who is able to make informed choices about what to learn and how to learn. The ability to make informed choices takes knowledge and skill, and for most people the best way to obtain such knowledge and skill is through instruction. However, those who are enthusiastic about self-directed learning should proceed with caution.

Only a few people are spontaneously self-directed. Many turn to self-instruction as a solution to an otherwise intractable problem – for example, an inability to get to classes because of family or job responsibilities, or because their language learning objectives would not be met in the course available. It is not desirable to thrust self-instruction and self-directed learning on to learners who are resistant to it, and it is very important that those of us who are enthusiastic about self-instruction do not confuse the idea, or our enthusiasm to introduce it, with the learner's ability or willingness to undertake it. I believe that the way forward is to introduce into the learning program elements which train learners towards greater autonomy and aim towards a gradual development towards full autonomy. (Dickinson 1987: 1–2)

Dickinson, who has been a leading figure in the application of ideas on self-direction to language learning, goes on to point out that many different terms and concepts describe situations and contexts in which the learner is in control, or in partial control, of the learning process. He makes the point that self-direction differs from other concepts because it refers to attitudes rather than to techniques or modes of instruction. He also makes the point that the self-directed learner may choose classroom instruction. The interlocking terms and the glosses provided by Dickinson (p. 11) are as follows:

- *Self-instruction.* This is a neutral term referring generally to situations in which learners are working without the direct control of the teacher.
- *Self-direction.* This term describes a particular attitude to the learning task, where the learner accepts responsibility for all the decisions concerned with his learning but does not necessarily undertake the implementation of those decisions.
- *Autonomy.* This term describes the situation in which the learner is totally responsible for all of the decisions concerned with his learning and the implementation of those decisions. In full autonomy there is no involvement of a "teacher" or an institution. And the learner is also independent of specially prepared materials.
- *Semi-autonomy.* This conveniently labels the stage at which learners are preparing for autonomy.

- *Self-access materials*. These are materials appropriate to and available for self-instruction.
- *Self-access learning*. This is self-instruction using these materials. The term is neutral as to how self-directed or other-directed the learners are.
- *Individualized instruction*. Once again this term is neutral as to who takes the responsibility for the learning. Chaix and O'Neil (1978) define it as: "a learning process which (as regards goals content methodology and pacing) is adapted to a particular individual, taking the individual's characteristics into consideration."

One of the major challenges to the effective management of learning in classroom contexts is the fact that learners are different and learn in different ways. They have different attitudes, expectations and preferences. They want to learn different things, and they want to go about learning in different ways. In a sense, each learner is an island, and each learner interprets a particular classroom even in a slightly different way. In other words, each learner constructs an individual vision of reality in an individual way.

This tension between the individual and the group has given rise to a number of interesting theories and models of the learning process. One of these is experiential learning, which attempts to incorporate the learner's personal experiences into the substance of the classroom. For the experiential teacher, each learner's personal experience gives "life, texture, and subjective personal meaning to abstract concepts and . . . at the same time providing a concrete, publicly shared reference point for testing the implications and validity of ideas created during the learning process" (Kolb 1984: 21). Critical to experiential learning is the creation of opportunities for the learner to reflect on the learning experience. Such reflection provides a link between immediate experiences and higher-level conceptualization.

Kohonen points out that there is a close relationship between the concepts of experiential learning, intrinsic motivation and self-directed learning because:

Learners are encouraged to see themselves as increasingly competent and self-determined and to assume more and more responsibility for their own learning. Intrinsic motivation:

1. satisfies needs such as belonging, acceptance, satisfaction from work, self-actualization, power, and self-control;
2. manifests itself primarily in the form of feelings, e.g., feelings of success and competence;
3. is connected with work, involving feelings of relevance of work, satisfaction derived from work, feelings of progress and achievement, and feelings of growth as a person.

(Kohonen 1992: 18)

One practical way of giving individual learners the space for self-directed growth is to develop individual learning contracts. In a self-instructional context, such contracts provide a supportive framework, a sense of direction and a means of evaluation. Within the social and pedagogical constraints of the classroom, a learning contract can be extremely motivating for the student.

What does a learning contract look like? There is no limit to the possibilities. Figure 1, which has been adapted from Dickinson (1987: 100), will provide some idea of what a contract might look like.

If you are thinking about using contracts with learners, it is important to decide how much of the contract is going to be drawn up by the learner independently and how much will be completed collaboratively with you. The following key questions can help in the development of a contract:

1. What are the learning objectives?
2. What activities will help to reach these objectives?
3. What resources will be needed?
4. What evidence will satisfy the learner or an outside observer that the objectives have been achieved?
5. What is an appropriate time frame for achieving the objectives?

The form in Figure 2 (on page 160) can be modified, adapted, and used to provide a framework for the student and teacher to negotiate the content of a self-directed learning package. This pro forma can also be used in cases in which students are being guided toward self-direction through a program devised by the teacher. It is essential to give the students an outline of the course. This will help the teacher establish clearly what will be taught. It also acts as an aid to assist the teacher to foresee potential problems as well as to anticipate what extra materials will be needed, for example, handouts to be reproduced, pictures to be collected, videos to be prepared, songs to be recorded, and so on.

Mixed-level groups

In recent years teachers working in many different contexts have begun to experiment with alternative ways of grouping students for instruction. Rather than taking chronological age or current proficiency, several alternative grouping criteria have been suggested including learning style and strategy preferences and communicative goals. Some teachers argue that they would rather have a group of learners who had the same end in view (for example, to obtain employment in an English speaking country) and who were heterogeneous in terms of proficiency than a group in which students were all at the same proficiency level, but which contained stu-

Language Skills Contract			
NAME _Djibril_	GROUP _Advanced_	DATE _1 October_	
Skill area for improvement – learning objectives	Proposed activities – what you are going to do	Proposed resources – what you are going to use	Ways of demonstrating achievement – how you are going to test yourself
1. *Reading speed* Improve reading speed from 100 w.p.m. to 120 w.p.m. without reducing comprehension.	Timed reading of prepared passages.	Reading speed builders. Box IV; Level – blue.	Use test items in the card for comprehension and get >80%. Reach >120 w.p.m. on five consecutive cards.
2. *Seminar discussion skills* Break into a discussion. Disagree politely with another speaker. State an alternative viewpoint.	Take part in oral skills options. Try to arrange additional discussions with friends. Practice during tutorials and seminars in other subjects.	Supplied by tutor. Try to get a native speaker to take part. Watch TV news and discuss current issues; use newspapers. Supplied by tutor.	Judge reaction of other participants: Do they look startled/irritated when I join in? Do I convey my viewpoint? Do I manage to persuade people? Try to get a native speaker to monitor your performance.
3. *Essay writing* Improve my planning of essays. Write essays.	Plan essays on many topics Write one essay per week on one of the topics above.	Wallace Study Skills in English. For self-help group from friends (tutor will help with this).	Use the guide in the book. Self-assessment schedule. Ask tutor. Assessment by self-help group. Tutor to check some essays.

Figure 1 Language skills contract (Adapted from Dickinson 1987; used by permission)

dents with very different learning goals. In fact, in many contexts, particularly in smaller language schools, simple economics dictate that the class will be heterogeneous along a number of dimensions, including proficiency, goals and learning preferences. This heterogeneity highlights the fact that, although proficiency is the learner variable that springs most readily to mind when we think of mixed-level teaching, it is by no means

1. Period of instruction
   From: _____   To: _____

2. Scheduled meeting time(s)
   _____

3. Course objectives
   a. _____
   b. _____
   c. _____

4. Textbook(s) to be used
   _____

5. Extra materials and suggestions for additional reading (extra-class activities)
   a. _____
   b. _____
   c. _____

6. Requirements and grading criteria (if applicable)

7. Syllabus items to be covered
   Week 1: _____
   Week 2: _____
   Week 3: _____
   etc.

8. Extension and enrichment resources
   a. _____
   b. _____
   c. _____

Figure 2   Form for negotiating a self-directed learning package

the only criteria. Also to be borne in mind is the fact that learners have different degrees of aptitude for language learning. Therefore, learners who are homogeneous in terms of proficiency at the beginning of a course are likely to be at different levels of proficiency after several weeks or months of instruction.

In thinking about multilevel instruction, it is useful to consider the key factors which differentiate learners, the reasons for such differences, the problems and challenges to the management of learning brought about by such differences, and, on the positive side, the advantages of multilevel classrooms. Key considerations in each of these areas are set out in the following table with material extracted from Bell (1991: 2–18) and have been summarized and commented upon by us in the following list.

1. Factors

Educational experience At its simplest, variance in educational background means that some students have more experience in the classroom than others. They have acquired and developed learning strategies that they can bring to the task of learning a new language in a classroom setting.

Country/culture of origin The culture of the student's educational background also plays a role in student progress. In some areas of the world the student role is seen as essentially a passive one. To question the teacher in any way would be an insult to the teacher's authority. A student's role is to absorb whatever the teacher presents, not to critically evaluate it.

Individual factors Students are individuals, and the teacher should be very wary of racial stereotypes. Younger students generally find learning less difficult than older students do and are more flexible in adapting to new methods of learning.

Situational factors The amount of time and effort students can devote to the task [of learning another language] will vary enormously, as will the amount of support available. Many ESL students go home from the class to a milieu where the only place they hear English is on television. Another personal variable is length of time in the country.

2. Reasons

Administrative benefits Although a few large educational institutions have deliberately opted for heterogeneous groupings within their classes, for the most part multilevel classes are found in locations where only one or two classes must satisfy all comers.

Convenience for the learner Many students, too, find small multilevel classes attractive. Even in large cities, where ESL centers offer classes at all levels, there will be students who prefer to attend a mixed-level class in their immediate neighborhood.

Companionship and support Many students prefer mixed-level classes, generally because they have friends or relatives who are also interested in English and they want to be assured of being in the same class.

3. Problems

Methodology Teachers generally identify their biggest problem with multilevel classes as being one of techniques. "What can I give them to do that won't bore the advanced students and won't be too difficult for the beginners?" is a fairly common question.

Curriculum   In a class with fairly homogeneous levels of English ability, the first steps in developing a curriculum would be the performance of a needs analysis, in which we discover what we want our students to learn English for. We identify their weak areas and assess what skills they already have. This assessment is not so simple with a multilevel class.

Group conflict   Another challenge for the teacher is to avoid the students' perceiving the mixed ability levels as a problem. Lower-level students may feel intimidated by the competition and may not make the same effort that they would in a more homogeneous classroom. The more advanced students may feel that they are being held back and may become impatient with the beginners.

Assessment and evaluation   Many institutions offering a single multilevel class feel that placement evaluation is irrelevant as there is only one class in which the students can be placed. This attitude fails to take into account that such evaluation information is highly useful in developing curriculum and is critical in measuring the students' progress.

Preparation   There is no doubt that a multilevel class makes heavy preparation demands on the teacher. Teachers of these classes cannot just pick up an assigned text and work through it.

Teacher attitude   Sometimes we feel that it is our responsibility to make the students learn. The truth is that it is the students' responsibility to learn.

4. Advantages

Flexibility   One of the most common advantages is that the teacher is unlikely to be forced into teaching a set syllabus. Very few multilevel teachers have to worry about covering a certain amount of material to give their students fair chance at an examination.

Diversity   The very variety of age, race, and background leads to interesting differences in viewpoint and experience, so that natural interactions are possible between students.

Interaction   Beginners have the opportunity to call on a wide range of potential helpers rather than relying solely on the teacher. The advanced students get the satisfaction of demonstrating their prowess and the opportunity to check their control of language items by attempting to teach them themselves.

It is clear that multilevel groups pose particular challenges for the management of learning in the classroom. In the first place, it may be impossible to find a set text that will suit the range of learner types to be found in the classroom. In addition, most of the techniques already discussed, such as pair and group work, which will find a place in the multilevel classroom, will need to be modified. According to Bell (1991), the problems that are inherent in the multilevel classroom are compounded by the fact that classes are often irregular, as is the attendance of the learners. These factors can hinder learning as well as militate against the development of a cohesive group identity, an identity that greatly facilitates the management of learning. Bell suggests that the judicious choice of group tasks can help build group cohesion.

Any task that must be done cooperatively helps to start the seeds of group feeling. This need not be a complex linguistic exercise. One of the best icebreakers I know is to get the students to rearrange the furniture, a cooperative task that will involve students from all levels of ability. There are linguistic icebreakers you can use, but sometimes the best task is one that students value as a real-life activity, not just a language game in which they become self-conscious of their linguistic abilities. Asking students of widely varied ability to fetch a box of books from the staff room is often a more useful task in the long run. (Bell 1991: 70)

Bell's analysis raises some interesting issues. In relation to educational background, we need to consider in what ways strategies are qualitatively different and therefore beneficial to the learning situation. Our own view is that students who have developed an awareness of learning strategies can make invaluable contributions to the classroom. If we accept that there may be variance in educational backgrounds, we can assume that the roles of the learner and the teacher in different cultures may provide a rich resource of for open-ended discussions and learner strategy training.

As far as methodology is concerned, there are tasks that can exploit mixed levels of ability. They include peer teaching, observing others' presentations, exchanging written work, writing tasks and exercises for others, and working on large group projects. These tasks all allow students to work at their own levels of ability and enable the creative teacher to exploit the relative strengths of different learners in the class.

Although needs analysis may be more complicated in mixed-level classes than in homogeneous ones, it is certainly not impossible. Needs analysis procedures of the type set out in Chapter 1 can be given to any group of students to identify strengths, weaknesses and learning purposes. Hicks (personal communication) points out that students can create their own questionnaire that would be suitable for the group. The needs of the group then become the knowledge and property of the group and a target to be achieved by both the individuals and the whole group. Ongoing needs analysis that is carried out collaboratively with students can also be useful in overcoming some of the group conflicts mentioned by Bell. In fact, it may be that teachers see mixed-level classes as being more problematic than do the students. Many students come from less competitive cultures than our own and often expect to help each other out in class. If this does not happen, it is the job of the teacher to help them how to do it.

In terms of assessment and evaluation, it is rare that placement test evaluation coincides with the subsequent methodology of the course. It is particularly rare if the emphasis of the multilevel class is to be on group involvement, effort and achievement. In such a class, it may be more beneficial to allow the evaluation process to develop organically as a combined process between teachers and learners. This development leaves room for greater negotiation in terms of syllabus and methodology and eliminates the dangers of prejudgment. Student progress throughout a course can be evaluated through a variety of means that fall outside the narrow confines of initial student assessment.

Although it may be true that multilevel classes make heavier preparation demands on teachers than homogeneous groups, it needs to be pointed out that teachers often spend a lot of time preparing materials, tasks, exercises, and games that students could create, at their own pace, and in their own way, in class. As we shall see in the next chapter, course books and supplementary materials are essential vehicles for learning, given adequate and appropriate learner training, but the drivers and navigators can be the students themselves. The multilevel classroom requires open-ended tasks that learners can handle in their own style, individually, in pairs or in groups. Many tasks and exercises are too closed to all allow for a range of responses that are equally valid. Multilevel classes can encourage learners, despite their varied cultural backgrounds and educational experiences, to make their own decisions about learning strategies at the same time as encouraging peer involvement, assessment, and evaluation.

As we have already seen, literally dozens of different variables and dimensions can be employed in characterizing learners, although some will be more significant than others. Age can be important in certain contexts and with particular learner groups. For example, we have worked in some cultural contexts in which younger and older adults are placed in separate groups, because it is considered unproductive and demotivating for older and younger learners to communicate with each other. In most educational contexts, teachers are simply not in a position to have control over how learners are subdivided for instruction. However, we have worked in a number of contexts in which teachers have been given this opportunity. The data in Table 1 were taken from a language center for adult immigrants in which the teachers had the opportunity of grouping the learners for instruction. We extracted the following 21 sets of data at random from 120 learners, all of whom were to be grouped into six classes.

This type of data is obtained through various needs analysis procedures of the type described and exemplified in Chapter 1. These data were selected through precourse interviews and questionnaires. In the following task, you are invited to decide how you would group these learners for instruction. This is an interesting exercise, because in the course of decid-

Table 1 Student data

ID	Age	Time in country	L1	Years of education	Occupation	Proficiency	Aptitude	Goal
1	26	1.6	Vietnamese	5	Dressmaker	1–	Average	Mix with parents of children's friends
2	35	2.0	Chinese	8	Small business	0+	Slow	Get a better job
3	62	12.0	Russian	6	Home duties	0+	Slow	Mix with native speakers
4	31	1.1	Spanish	5	Bricklayer	0	Average	Get a job
5	59	12.0	Arabic	4	Plasterer	1	Average	Talk to grandchildren, doctor
6	55	3.0	Chinese	3	Cook	0	Slow	Read English
7	33	1.0	Chinese	6	Factory	0+	Average	Communicate at work
8	26	1.2	Polish	12	Secretary	0+	Fast	Retrain, get better job
9	28	2.0	Spanish	6	Dressmaker	0+	Average	Talk to employer, clients
10	20	1.6	Arabic	12	Student	0+	Fast	Undertake tertiary study
11	46	2.0	Hungarian	11	Secretary	1–	Average	Get a better job
12	19	1.0	Vietnamese	10	Student	1	Fast	Undertake tertiary study
13	39	8.0	Croatian	6	Mechanic	0+	Average	Social, job retraining
14	37	5.0	Korean	8	Police officer	0+	Average	Social, child's school
15	27	1.0	Czech	12	Nurse	0+	Very fast	Retrain as nurse
16	54	3.0	Khmr	–	Home duties	0+	Slow	Make friends
17	61	7.0	Spanish	5	Home duties	0+	Slow	More confidence in speaking
18	25	1.0	Vietnamese	10	Welder	1–	Average	Retrain for better job
19	32	1.0	Turkish	14	Accountant	2	Fast	Further study, better job
20	58	18.0	Russian	12	Librarian	0+	Average	Talk to neighbors
21	44	9.0	Croatian	6	Cleaner	0+	Average	Talk to employer, workmates, children

Key to proficiency ratings
0 = Zero proficiency   1 = Minimum survival proficiency
0+ = Initial proficiency   1+ = Survival proficiency
1– = Elementary proficiency   2 = Minimum social proficiency

ing which factors to take into consideration, you will need to make explicit to yourself those factors that you think are central to the language learning process.

TASK

Aim To determine those factors to which you would give most weight in grouping learners for instruction

Procedure Consider the learner data presented in Table 1. Which factors would you take into consideration in subdividing these students for instruction?

As we have already indicated, numerous criteria can be employed when grouping learners for instruction. There are costs and benefits whatever criteria are selected. For example, if the learners in Table 1 were grouped according to their level of education, they would be heterogeneous in terms of proficiency, aptitude and learning goals. If they were grouped according to their goals, they would be mixed in terms of their proficiency, aptitude, levels of education, and so on. In such cases, when teachers have a choice, the criteria they select will reflect their beliefs about the nature of language and language learning. In the language center from which these data were extracted, the teachers chose to assign students to class according to two criteria: learning goals and proficiency. Notice how this procedure results in groups that are mixed in terms of their aptitude, first language background, age, occupation, and time in the target country (Table 2 on page 168).

It is worth noting that there was one student who was impossible to assign to a group. This student was given an individual course of study in the individualized learning center.

TASK

Aim To identify the criteria used to group the learners in Table 2.

Data The grouped set of learners set out in Table 2 (on page 168).

Procedure

1. Which criteria are considered by this center as being the significant ones for instruction?
2. What challenges to the management of learning will be posed by the employment of different grouping criteria?

The center in which these learners were studying employed proficiency level and educational and employment needs as the basic criteria for grouping the learners. This grouping posed significant educational challenges, and the resulting groups were heterogeneous in terms of aptitude, age and ethnicity. One of the most significant factors reported by the teachers working with these students was the mixed age levels. They said that having older and younger learners from Asian backgrounds in the same classroom posed challenges when it came to things such as group work, because there were certain things that the younger learners simply could not do or say in front of their elders.

In some situations, it may also be possible for students to group themselves. This grouping could be done after an initial contact session in which the students meet each other and share some information about each other. Responsibility for establishing grouping criteria would form a suitable basis for the development of collective responsibility for learning. Some years ago one of us experimented with this notion of learners taking responsibility for grouping themselves and found that it worked very well.

Summary and conclusions

In this chapter we dealt with a wide range of issues concerned with constituting and managing learning groups. We examined different grouping criteria and looked at practical problems and solutions in relation to group and pair work, as well as the issue of large classes. Also considered in the chapter, is one-to-one teaching. In considering teacher-student role relationships, we raised some questions that will be revisited when we look at affective aspects of language teaching. Some degree of overlap between chapters is inevitable in a book of this kind. We do not see it as a problem. In fact we believe that there are definite advantages in revisiting key issues and problems from several different perspectives.

Table 2 Assignment of students

ID	Age	Time in country	L1	Years of education	Occupation	Proficiency	Aptitude	Goal
Group 1: General communicative/social orientation – beginner								
1	26	1.6	Vietnamese	5	Dressmaker	1–	Average	Mix with parents of children's friends
3	62	12.0	Russian	6	Home duties	0+	Slow	Mix with native speakers
7	33	1.0	Chinese	6	Factory	0+	Average	Communicate at work
14	37	5.0	Korean	8	Policeman	0+	Average	Social, child's school
16	54	3.0	Khmr	–	Home duties	0+	Slow	Make friends
17	61	7.0	Spanish	5	Home duties	0+	Slow	More confident in speaking
20	58	18.0	Russian	12	Librarian	0+	Average	Talk to neighbors
21	44	9.0	Croatian	6	Cleaner	0+	Average	Talk to employer, workmates, children
Group 2: General communicative/social orientation – intermediate								
5	59	12.0	Arabic	4	Plasterer	1	Average	Talk to grandchildren, doctor
Group 3: Employment focus – beginner								
2	35	2.0	Chinese	8	Small business	0+	Slow	Get a better job
4	31	1.1	Spanish	5	Bricklayer	0	Average	Get a job
8	26	1.2	Polish	12	Secretary	0+	Fast	Retrain, get better job
9	28	2.0	Spanish	6	Dressmaker	0+	Average	Talk to employer, clients
13	39	8.0	Croatian	6	Mechanic	0+	Average	Social, job retraining

Group 4: Employment focus – intermediate

11	46	2.0	Hungarian	11	Secretary	1–	Average	Get a better job
18	25	1.0	Vietnamese	10	Welder	1–	Average	Retrain for better job

Group 5: Literacy skills – beginner

6	55	3.0	Chinese	3	Cook	0	Slow	Read English

Group 6: Further study

10	20	1.6	Arabic	12	Student	0+	Fast	Undertake tertiary study
12	19	1.0	Vietnamese	10	Student	1	Fast	Undertake tertiary study
15	27	1.0	Czech	12	Nurse	0+	Very fast	Retrain as nurse

Individualized learning center

19	32	1.0	Turkish	14	Accountant	2	Fast	Further study, better job

PROJECT 1

Aim To explore the relationship between roles and tasks.

Procedure

1. Divide the students into groups of six to eight. Appoint one observer for each group. Tell the class that these observers will sit a little apart from the group and act as group secretaries, making notes on what is said in the discussion.
2. Then call the secretaries up to the front as a group and give each a copy of the first questionnaire and ask them to fill it in by placing a check mark in the appropriate column each time a member of the group does one of the things mentioned on the questionnaire. There is no need to specify which member of the group did these things.
3. Ask the students to return to their groups and give each group its first discussion task. The secretary should play no part in the discussion but should fill in the questionnaire while the students talk.
4. When the students have finished the discussion, give each member of the group a copy of the questionnaire and ask the members to try to remember exactly how they contributed to the discussion and to place a check mark in the appropriate column to record how many times they performed each action. Ask them to reflect (privately) on their roles in the group and decide if they need to change roles in any way.
5. Ask the observers to show their completed questionnaires to the group.
6. Give out the second questionnaire to each group and ask them to discuss the questions on it.

Data

1. Two discussion tasks suitable for the level of your group (either from a textbook or a speaking skills resource book).
2. A copy for each student of the following questionnaires.

Questionnaire 1

Roles in groups Put check marks (✓) in the end column to show how many times each action was performed.

Action	Number of times
Organized the other members of the group	_____
Contributed an idea	_____
Encouraged others to say something	_____
Tried to get everyone to come to an agreement	_____
Summarized what other people had said	_____
Evaluated other people's ideas	_____

Action	*Number of times*
Asked people to explain what they meant	_____
Made everyone laugh	_____
Tried to smooth out problems	_____
Was rude about other people's ideas	_____
Distracted the group by talking about something else	_____
Interrupted other people to state my own ideas	_____
Did something else while everyone was talking	_____
Didn't listen to other people's ideas	_____
Didn't talk in English	_____
For observers only: Number of people who didn't speak at all	_____

Questionnaire 2

Evaluate your group performance.

1. Where are most of the check marks? If they are all in the top half of the questionnaire, then you can congratulate yourselves: you are a generally helpful and cooperative group! Well done! If there are some check marks in the bottom half, then you need to think carefully about how you can cooperate better as a group and be more considerate of the feelings of each member of the group. If all your check marks are in the bottom half, well . . . ! Perhaps you had better ask yourself if you really want to learn English.
2. Are there any gaps? For example, have you got enough encouragers in your group? Have you got a peacemaker – someone who tries to smooth over problems and difficulties? Do enough people contribute ideas? Try to see where your deficiencies are as a group.
3. Are there too many people doing the same thing? For example, are there too many organizers? A group really only needs one! And if there are too many contributors and not enough summarizers, then your discussions will have plenty of ideas but no direction! Try to see what your excesses are as a group.
4. Make three lists:
   a. Things we should stop doing
   b. Things we should do more of
   c. Things we should do less of

Decide individually what you can do to help the group work more smoothly and to make group discussions more successful and enjoyable for yourselves.

Now try the second discussion!

(Adapted from Hadfield 1992; by permission of Oxford University Press)

PROJECT 2

Aim To evaluate factors associated with effective pair/group work tasks.

Procedure

1. Review the evaluative checklist that follows, and modify it if necessary.
2. Observe another teacher implementing a group task and then interview the teacher using the checklist as a guide.
3. Evaluate a group work task in your own classroom using the checklist as a guide.

Data

Pair/Group Work

1. (a) What was the purpose of the pair/group work?
       To increase student talking time and input   [ ]
       To relieve pressure from the individual   [ ]
       To give the teacher opportunity to check on individuals [ ]
       To cater for disparate levels   [ ]
       To allow more advanced students to help others   [ ]
       To provide variety and a change of pace and focus   [ ]
       To minimize teacher domination   [ ]
       Stimulation/motivation   [ ]
       Follow up   [ ]
       To build up rapport   [ ]
       Other   [ ]
   (b) Do you see any other purpose for which you could use pair/group work in the future?

       _____

       _____

2. (a) What was your basis (criteria) for grouping students?
       Random selection   [ ]
       Common interest   [ ]
       Level of English   [ ]
       Friendship   [ ]
       Other   [ ]
   (b) Who decided on the criteria?
       You   [ ]
       The students   [ ]
       Why? _____
   (c) Was the criteria suitable for the task?
       How do you know?

       _____

       _____

(d) Would you make any changes next time?

_____

3. (a) How many groups were there?

_____

(b) What was the size of each group?

_____

(c) Could different organization of these factors have been more effective?

_____

4. (a) Did the pairs/groups remain the same or did they change?

_____

(b) Can you see any advantages in changing the pairs/groups around, e.g., preventing the same pairs always forming?

_____

_____

(c) Can you suggest ways of doing this, for example?
   i. Have students walk around the room and on cue from you stop and find the nearest person.
   ii. Have individuals from each group keep circulating to other groups.
   Your suggestions:

_____

_____

_____

5. (a) When did the pair/group work take place?
   Introductory stage   [ ]
   Practice stage   [ ]
   Extension stage   [ ]
   Other   [ ]
   (b) Is there any other stage in the lesson when pair/group work could have been used effectively?

_____

_____

6. (a) Did you have to clarify your instructions? Why?

_____

_____

7. (a) What form did the feedback take?
   Written on the board   [ ]
   Individual reporting to class   [ ]
   Individual reporting to other groups   [ ]
   Reporting to other individuals   [ ]
   Written reports   [ ]
   Other   [ ]

(b) Was there a purpose in the feedback so it was meaningful and not boring, e.g., passing on necessary information to another pair/group to compile a story?

_____

(c) Did the feedback prove that your instructions and guidance were clear and were understood? How?

_____

(Source: Pak 1986; used by permissoin)

PROJECT 3

Aim To explore and evaluate the logistics of setting up group tasks and managing group activities. [This task has been adapted from Wajnryb (1992: 109–110).]

Data A language lesson of your choosing.

Procedure

Before the lesson
1. Arrange to observe a lesson that will contain a range of interactive patterns.
2. Familiarize yourself with the chart that follows so that you can use it effectively for taking notes on the various phases of the lesson.

During the lesson Monitor the teacher's way of getting students in, through, and out of activities. Try to record details of, (a) a moving-in phase, (b) a monitoring phase, and (c) a moving-out phase.

a. *Moving into an activity*   Observe the teacher and comment on the following features:
   i. Organizing the groups and seating
   ii. Giving instructions including modeling and checking
   iii. Appointing and briefing group leaders
b. *Monitoring pair/group work*   Observe the teacher and comment on the following features:
   i. How the teacher monitors
   ii. In what circumstances the teacher speaks to a group
   iii. The teacher's voice, position, proxemics (the distance between people who are conversing)

c. *Moving out of an activity* Observe the teacher and comment on the following features:
   i. Winding pairs/groups down
   ii. Signaling for everyone's attention
   iii. Reorienting group to new phase of lesson
   iv. Organizing and monitoring the report-back phase

Phase	Subskill	Observation	Comment
a. Moving into an activity	i. Organizing groups, seating, etc. ii. Instructions iii. Appointing, briefing leaders	*T selects group members*	*T seems to be deliberately creating groups*
b. Monitoring pair/group work	i. Monitoring ii. Verbal contact iii. Teacher's voice, position, etc.		
c. Moving out of an activity	i. Winding down ii. Signaling iii. Reorienting iv. Reporting back		

After the lesson
1. Discuss your notes with the teacher. Together, compile a list, in roughly chronological order of the various subskills involved in both moving into and out of an activity. Consider the purposes of each.
2. Consider the skill of teacher intervention during group work. Do you consider the following statements (based on Brown 1989: 9) to be totally true or false or partially true or false? Add any relevant comments or qualifications as necessary.
   a. A teacher monitoring a group is there to listen, help and monitor, but not to teach.
   b. Any teacher comment must be preceded by the teacher listening closely to the group to find out how they are getting on.

   c. Any interaction must be initiated by the group or its members but
      not by the teacher.
   d. The teacher must give equal time to the groups.
   e. The teacher must give equal time to individuals within the groups.
   f. The teacher must sit or crouch down to be at the same height as
      the students.
   g. Proxemics, eye contact, and tone of voice in group work are
      necessarily different from those in full-class activity.
3. There are different ways of grouping students. Recall the one used in
   the class you observed and consider it from the point of view of the
   group member. Consider the ease with which members of the pair or
   group were able to communicate; relax, be comfortable; concentrate
   on the activity; see the board; see/hear the teacher; work silently; be
   included as an equal member.
4. One way of organizing report-back is to call on each of the group
   leaders to present their reports. Are there other ways? What are the
   advantages and disadvantages of each of these? Is there a
   correlation between task type and report-back style?

PROJECT 4

Aim To develop skills in observing group behavior and facilitating
interaction.

Data An audio/video recording of a small group task.

Procedure

Pre-observation
1. Review the following questions and select five to six that are
   interesting or important to you.
2. Record a small group task, and evaluate the task according to these
   questions.
3. As an alternative to (2), invite a colleague to attend your class to
   observe one of the groups and to evaluate you and the students
   according to the questions you have selected.

a. *Participation*
   – Who are the high/low contributors and are they aware of it?
   – Who are the silent people in the group? Why do you think that they
     are not speaking? Is it because they are shy, because they
     disagree with the other students, because they do not know, etc.?
   – Who talks and doesn't talk to whom? Is there any reason why this
     should be so?
   – Is there a rigid contribution hierarchy?
   – Is there a gender bias?
   – Do the men speak and act first? Do they seem to interrupt without
     realizing it?
   – Do the women wait for the men to finish?

b. *Group roles*
   − Apart from you, as the leader, who takes what roles and are these roles beneficial or inhibiting (e.g., clowns, despite their disciplinary laxities, may help the group to relax and laugh)?
   − Is there a rebel? A bully? A timekeeper? A critic? A scapegoat?
c. *Decision making*
   − Is it autocratic or democratic?
   − Do some people impose autocratic decisions on others?
   − Is there any proposing, consulting or supporting?
   − Is there any negotiating, bargaining or compromising?
   − Are some people's proposals always accepted or others' always ignored?
   − Do some people abstain from decision making?
   − What is the effect of all these behaviors on the group?
   − Are there any reasons why they continue to occur?
   − How can you encourage the unresponsive students to participate?
d. *Group atmosphere*
   − What is the atmosphere, climate or morale of the group? Is it friendly and congenial, or tense and sluggish?
   − How is the atmosphere maintained?
   − Do the group members attack or withdraw rather than relate constructively?
   − Are they dependent on one or two members to achieve a task or support one another?
   − Do people pair off or develop cliques or subgroups that destroy the unity of the group?
   − Is there any sense of collective unity or fun?
   − Do people harmonize and pull together or are they uncoordinated and lacking in coordination?
e. *Group norms and ground rules*
   − Does only one person talk at once? Is this person actively listened to?
   − Is it acceptable for some members to break group norms and rules but not others?
   − Is it permissible to express or talk about feelings in relation to the group or what it is doing?
   − Is conflict between members avoided? How?
   − Are decisions only made by the leader?
   − Is too much initiative resented?

Post-observation
1. What did you learn about (a) your students' behavior (b) your own behavior?
2. Was there a disparity between your own perceptions and those of your colleague?
3. What would you do differently next time?

PROJECT 5

Aim To develop skills in planning and implementing a learning contract.

Procedure

1. Work with a group of learners and help them to design a learning contract. How proficient is the learner? Should the contract be in the student's first language? (Alternatively, design a contract for yourself in relation to a language you are learning, you once studied or are proposing to study).
2. Review the following evaluation questions (from Dickinson 1987: 156), modifying or adding to them if necessary.

Learning objectives
— Are the objectives clear and understandable?
— Do they describe what the learner is setting out to *learn* (rather than what he plans to *do*)?
— Is each objective stated in such a way that the learner can know when it has been achieved?
— Are they limited and so achievable within a week or two (i.e., the time span of the contract)?
— Are there sufficient/too many objectives for the time available?

Proposed activities (what the learner is going to do)
— Are the proposed activities relevant to the achievement of the objective?
— Are the activities feasible, given the time and resources available?
— Are there other activities that could be used?

Proposed resources (what the learner is going to use)
— Are the resources relevant for undertaking the proposed activities?
— Are there other resources, particularly human resources, that could be helpful?
— Has the learner considered using relevant authentic documents for practicing the activities?
— Are the resources easily available at times the learner wants them?
— Is it desirable and possible to organize a group of learners to work on this/ these objectives?

Ways of demonstrating the achievement of the objectives
— Is the self-assessment technique proposed clearly relevant to the objective and the activities used?
— Are there tests available in the materials being used?
— Are there relevant tests available elsewhere?
— Are the criteria proposed clear, relevant, and able to be applied?
— Is the self-assessment technique convincing to other members of the group?
— Is there a way of using a peer (or group of peers) to help with the assessment?

3. Get students in groups to evaluate their contracts using the evaluation questions.

6 Managing resources

Introduction

This chapter examines the professional resources which exist to help (or which are intended to help) the teacher and the student exploit classroom learning opportunities more effectively. Although the focus in the first part of the chapter is on commercial textbooks, we also look at other types of support, including audio visual materials. From one perspective, anything that exists within the classroom can be a resource for learning, not just technical hardware and software such as books, tapes and video, but also the human resources that exist in the shape of the teacher and students. In this chapter we have chosen not to focus on human resources as aids to the management of learning because these are exhaustively dealt with in other chapters.

Concept map of Chapter 6

In this chapter the following ground is covered:

— *Using commercial teaching materials*   course series versus supplementary materials, criticisms and benefits of commercial materials, matching textbooks to learner needs, task sequencing in commercial texts
— *Making the most of the teacher's book*   the teacher's text: an underutilized resource, the strengths of a good teacher's book
— *Exploiting resources that lack a teacher's guide*   techniques for introducing and exploiting different types of task
— *Electronic support*   video: an underutilized resource in language education, using video with learners at different levels of proficiency, linking the syllabus and video resources
— *Using computers in the classroom*   computers in high-structure and low-structure contexts, the electronic blackboard, computers and small group work, advantages of computers in managing learning, concordancing packages

- *Visuals and realia*   exploiting the resources around us, as a springboard
  for learner-created materials

Using commercial teaching texts

There are many different types of commercial textbooks available on the
market today. These can be divided into comprehensive course series,
which are intended to provide the basic syllabus and core of materials on
which a course is based, and supplementary source books, which are intended to support programs that are based on basal series or programs
created by the teacher. Multilevel courses contain numerous components.
They typically include a student's book, teacher's manual, cassette tape,
and student's workbook. Most series these days also contain a video, as
well as a testing program. Supplementary textbooks generally consist of
one or two levels. These usually contain a student's book, teacher's manual,
and cassette. Both types of resource can be used in many different ways.
The extent to which teachers draw upon and depend on commercially
produced materials will depend on the teachers' training, the context and
environment in which they are working, the institutional philosophy of the
school in which they teach, and the needs and interests of the students. We
believe that both basal texts and supplementary course materials provide
invaluable support to teachers, that they can facilitate the introduction of
new ideas and can act as teacher training tools, and that they can save the
teacher a great deal of time.

However, this does not mean that commercial materials have escaped
criticism. There are some who take a negative line on the place of textbooks
in the classroom, arguing that commercially produced texts are incapable,
by virtue of the very processes through which they are produced, of providing for the needs of learners, that they are extremely blunt instruments
which, because they have been created without input from learners themselves, make invalid assumptions about what learners want to learn and
how they want to learn it. Those who subscribe to this view believe that
resources should be tailor-made by the teacher for each new group of
learners and that classroom input should flow from initial and ongoing
assessments of learner needs. In its most extreme form, this negative view
of textbooks also has it that commercial materials are to be avoided because
they present sanitized stereotypes, they stifle the creativity of teacher and
students, and they ignore, and thereby devalue, the culture of the students.

It must be admitted that there is some truth in these criticisms. Econo-
mies of scale dictate that most commercial materials have to be produced
and marketed in a wide range of cultural contexts. This means that they
cannot focus heavily on one particular culture at the expense of others. In
addition, the list of taboo topics becomes alarmingly long as the market for

a particular work becomes more diverse. Most editors working for commercial publishing houses become extremely nervous if their authors present draft materials containing references to crime, homelessness, single-parent families, or homosexuality (in fact, we even heard of one group of publishers that refused to allow the word "sex" to appear at all in any of the materials they published). There are, however, indications, that these attitudes are beginning to change.

Despite the criticisms, valid and otherwise, commercial materials can be an invaluable aid to the classroom teacher providing structure and support for the inexperienced teacher, and a bank of useful and usable ideas for the more experienced teacher. Although self-directed teachers will be independent and resourceful, they should also be able to derive a great deal of professional support from textbooks that are appropriate to the contexts in which they work. Such texts can facilitate or obviate the need for teachers to construct their own curriculum, to think of bright new ideas for introducing the present perfect, for collecting and reproducing listening and reading texts, and for sequencing and integrating the various tasks and activities within a lesson. In addition to the resources they provide, good textbooks are invaluable teacher-training and development tools in their own right. In short, they can relieve the overburdened, as well as the underprepared, teacher of a great deal of stress, time, and additional work. As Richards (1993) points out, many language schools around the world are staffed by native speakers of English who have little or no formal training, and for these people, the textbook and teacher's manual are primary teacher training as well as teaching resources. Harmer (1991: 257) also points out that:

Good textbooks often contain lively and interesting materials; they provide a sensible progression of language items, clearly showing what has to be learnt and in some cases summarizing what has been studied so that students can revise grammatical and functional points that they have been concentrating on. Textbooks can be systematic about the amount of vocabulary presented to the student and allow students to study on their own outside the class. Good textbooks also relieve the teacher from the pressure of having to think of original material for every class. Indeed there is a greater variety of published material for teaching and learning English than ever before.

For reasons already indicated, no textbook is going to be a perfect match for your students. However, it is clear that some will be more appropriate than others. Achieving a reasonable match between the needs of your learners and the provisions of the textbook is obviously a key consideration in selecting print materials. Unfortunately, it is not always the most, or even the only consideration. In many institutions, teachers have little or no say in the materials which are selected. This task is very often carried out by program administrators or directors of studies with little or no consultation with the classroom teacher. Economic considerations often take precedence over learner needs.

Assuming that you are in the fortunate position of being able to select a textbook for your students, several key variables need to be juggled in making your selection. These include the proficiency level targeted by the text; the experiential content, themes, and so on and the methodology, including learning strategies, implicit in the materials.

How do teachers use commercially produced textbooks, and what do they see as the major functions of the textbook? There is comparatively little data on this question, although a study reported in Richards (1993) makes interesting reading. In the study, carried out by Richards, Tung, and Ng (1992), 249 ESL teachers in Hong Kong reported that:

> their primary teaching resources were textbooks, supplementary materials, and audio tapes. The primary functions of the textbook were to provide practice activities (64%), to provide a structured language program for teachers to follow (56%), and to provide information about the language (50%). Most teachers reported that they do not rely on a single textbook (83%), many using a separate textbook for listening (86%), reading practice (66%), and writing (56%). Only 28% of the teachers reported that they made a significant use of exercises and materials which they prepare themselves. (Richards 1993: 2)

Richards is critical of an over-dependence on the use of commercially produced materials. He singles out for specific criticism a lack of focus on student needs, a lack of local content, and a "reification" of textbooks. The tendency to invest in textbooks with qualities of excellence, authority, and validity:

> may be more prevalent among ESL teachers for whom English is not their native language (or who do not speak English very well) than among those for whom English is a mother tongue. Or it may be a factor of experience. In EFL situations, relatively inexperienced ESL teachers whose mother tongue is not English may tend to follow the textbook very closely, or to be very uncritical of their textbooks, and to be relatively reluctant to discard sections of the book and replace them with other materials. . . . Other teachers (often native speakers with some teaching experience) are more sceptical about their textbooks. They criticize the content and design of exercises, and are more likely to dip into their textbook rather than go through it lesson by lesson. (op cit.: 7)

Most serious, in Richards' view, is the potential of the textbook to de-skill the teacher, because all of the key decisions about what to teach, when to teach, and how to teach (and also often how to assess) are based on the textbook and teacher's manual, not on the professional judgment of the teacher. The role of the teacher is reduced to that of a technician, to study the resources that have been provided, and to follow the procedures laid out there in much the same way as a neophyte cook might follow the recipes in a cookbook. Higher level management of learning, interactive decision making, and reflective teaching are largely absent from the textbook driven classroom. This problem is serious if, as we saw in Chapter 3, interactive decision making is a significant feature of good teaching.

The solution would appear to be not to abandon the use of commercially produced resources, but to ensure that they are used to support rather than dominate the teaching learning process. Textbooks should be seen as source books for creative teaching, not as technical manuals to be slavishly followed in a step-by-step fashion. According to Richards, the most effective way of promoting a source book rather than course book approach is by training teachers to evaluate and adapt textbooks. This approach can be partly achieved through the sorts of evaluative tasks we appended as projects to this chapter.

TASK

Aim To demystify and thus reduce the dependence of the teacher on textbooks.

Data A textbook or course materials of your choice.

Procedure

1. Select a textbook you are currently using or have recently used.
2. Analyze one of the units to identify the content. You may like to focus on the following:
   - Language content (e.g., grammar, pronunciation)
   - Language skills (e.g., listening, reading)
   - Test-taking skills (e.g., answering multiple-choice questions)
   - Real world tasks (e.g., filling out a job application)
   Try to estimate how much of the unit is devoted to the various elements you have identified.
3. Reanalyze the unit, this time focusing on the nature of the instructional tasks. Some of the things to examine include:
   - The type and quantity of form-focused activities
   - The opportunities provided for genuine communication
   - The balance between receptive and productive tasks
   - The learning strategies implicit in the tasks
   - The balance between teacher-focused and learner-focused tasks
   - The mix of whole class, small group, pair and individual tasks
4. Working with a number of other teachers, draw on the results of steps 1 and 2, to brainstorm and identify criteria to use in evaluating a textbook, unit or learning task.
            (Steps 2 and 4 are adapted from Richards 1993: 10–12.)

Choosing a textbook is not an easy task. In case of language schools, the book chosen has to cater for the needs, objectives, and philosophy of the school. Language schools that are sponsored by larger institutions, such as the British Council or the American Consulate are required to adopt the text determined by the organization. The overriding principle in many countries is whether to adopt an American or British model.

Once that is established, the academic directors or pedagogical coordinators have to identify a course book that will offer their students a complete course, from elementary to advanced levels, and that will develop all their basic skills: speaking, reading, listening and writing. A textbook can provide time-saving short cuts, saving teachers from having to waste time in creating different activities and topics for each group and class. Also, a textbook provides a pedagogical rationale that is consistent with the philosophy of the school.

In one-to-one teaching, it is more difficult for the teacher to be the sole arbiter, since the student has greater control over what to learn and how to learn it. Again, having a textbook can facilitate things for the teacher. Occasionally it may be possible to find a single text that will meet the student's needs. More usually, however, it is necessary to bring together material from several sources to meet the student's objectives. Textbooks can provide useful input for the teachers on specific matters, if they have to read about issues their students are interested in. Matching material to students' needs can result in a rewarding pedagogical experience for teacher and student.

One main disadvantage of having to follow a textbook in a language institute is the lesson plan. Having a lesson plan to follow narrows possibilities of catering for the students' needs or opening a space to deviate from the book and show the students other texts, video, or even discussing topics that unexpectedly arise during class. Usually the schools devise a lesson plan that allows teachers to insert any kind of extra material they might find interesting or useful. If this type of lesson plan does not exist in your institution, it is a good idea to get together with the coordinator and negotiate for greater flexibility.

It is true that having a textbook to follow can encourage complacency in some teachers, and simply following the textbook might be a very practical solution to the pressures caused by lack of time. However, if such a practice is widespread within an institution, it is unlikely to keep the students in the school in the long run. Additionally, such an approach is antithetical to the self-directed teaching approach that we have developed in this book.

TASK

Aim To collaborate with colleagues to develop and extend skills in integrating lesson plans and materials.

Procedure

1. Get together with another teacher or fellow student to devise a lesson plan based on some commercially produced material.
2. If possible, compare the plan with another pair of colleagues or students.

Data

1. Input on lesson planning provided earlier in the book
2. Commercial materials relevant to the students you currently teach or anticipate teaching

Having a textbook to follow as well as an organized lesson plan does not guarantee that the same kind of teaching will take place in all classes using the textbook, although it should ensure a greater degree of consistency across classes than if different teachers go their own way. Having a good textbook means having lively and interesting material, thus freeing the teacher to focus on other tasks such as monitoring the progress of their students, developing revision materials and activities, and so forth.

As already mentioned, the textbook can have a constraining effect on teachers and their views on what they are supposed to do. By their very nature, textbooks are generally rather rigidly sequenced. A typical pattern is for units to be initiated with the presentation and practice of new vocabulary, followed by activities designed to integrate known vocabulary with the newly learned items. Reading and listening also tend to have a predetermined place in the lessons. The self-directed teacher is the one who can experiment with this set order, selecting the parts that will cater to the students' needs and discarding other more inappropriate parts. The self-directed teacher will also find ways of varying the sequence of the activities, thereby avoiding the boredom which students sometimes express with the set format of the textbook, without, at the same time upsetting the balance between language input, practice and communicative output (what Harmer calls "the balanced activities approach"). It is through this balance that students are exposed to a variety of learning experiences that will help them to acquire and learn a foreign language.

In one-to-one classes, it is very important that the teacher be aware of the student's needs. It is also important to bear in mind the fact that the student who seeks private tuition wants to be treated differently from those who opt for classes in a language school. The student's age, gender, social background, interests, occupation, and background knowledge base are important factors to be considered when planning the classes. Sometimes (in most cases, we daresay) the use of more than one textbook is necessary, and again, the self-directed teacher will be able to balance the needs of the student with the diet offered by the textbook.

Making the most of the teacher's manual

Many teachers and teacher trainers assert that teacher's manuals are a waste of time and that they never consult them. Although many manuals are overwritten, it would be unfortunate if they were ignored on these grounds alone. Writing teacher's manuals is hard work. In fact, many writers would argue that they are more difficult to write than the students' books. There must be some reason that a great deal of effort and energy goes into their production, and it is worth identifying what it is without dismissing the teacher's manual out of hand. The fact that teachers' manuals and guides tend to be underutilized is unfortunate, as the teacher's book can be a very useful tool, containing the author's philosophy and approach, as well as essential information on ways of optimizing the students' book. It also gives teachers' insights on what the authors had in mind when they wrote the books. In fact, the best manuals are not only useful guides to the materials they accompany, they can also act as a teacher-training course, providing information on points of grammar, general guidance on language teaching methodology, and tips on classroom management.

Far from constraining the self-directed teacher, a good teacher's book is the one that tells the teachers not only how to deal with the material but also provides information on the theoretical orientation of the course as a whole. It should also indicate alternative sources for teachers to improve their knowledge. A good teacher's book will help teachers function more effectively in the classroom, without constraining them unnecessarily.

The following statements were made by a group of teachers we engaged in a discussion on the use of teacher's books. The discussion was prompted by the perception that teachers tend not to use the teacher's guide that accompanies the basal series. We asked a group of teachers to comment on the strengths and weaknesses of the teacher's books they used and have extracted those comments that focus on the strengths.

- "It helps/guides me when I'm preparing my classes, it helps me keep in mind the balance between activities, and allows me to 'play' with the material presented, not having to follow it as a 'bible.'
- "For me, a good TB is that one which allows the teachers to identify all the methodological principles underlying the course, helps them make decisions about the course design, what skills are needed for each task, what emphasis should be given to each one, if on oral, writing, etc."
- "A good teacher's book also 'teaches' the teacher to show the student how to evaluate their own development in their learning process."
- "A good teacher's book is that one which is 'open' enough to provide opportunities for the teachers to make decisions based on their student's

needs, not having to follow it slavishly, otherwise the flow of learning is interrupted."
— "It is very important that the teacher's book show the aims the teacher should have for the students as far as the activities, skills and language are concerned."
— "The teacher's book must help the teachers plan their classes according to context, establishing what the situation is, class organization, indicating if the tasks are to be done individually or in groups, teaching aids, indicating if the teacher needs extra material such as pictures, tape recorder, etc., what the language focus is and how to present the language items, helping the teacher anticipate what language will be used by the students, and also anticipated problems, providing alternatives for problematic tasks and generally giving ideas on how to vary ways in which some tasks can be done."

From these comments, it seems that a good teacher's manual:

— Sets out the rationale for the course, and the methodological principles underpinning it
— Indicates how the course book can be used in a variety of flexible ways
— Provides guidance on introducing learning strategies and learning-how-to-learn
— Shows how the course can meet a range of student needs
— Indicates alternative ways of doing tasks
— Gives advice on modes of classroom organization

TASK

Aim To evaluate a teacher's book against the strengths set out in the preceding lists.

Data One or two teacher's manuals for course books you are currently using or might potentially use.

Procedure Examine the teacher's manual(s), evaluate one or more teacher's books, and decide how successfully they meet the needs as identified by the teachers who contributed the comments in the preceding list.

Some (usually more experienced) teachers hold the view that teacher's guides are a waste of time. Others, usually less experienced and lacking in confidence, tend to over-rely on the teacher's manual. For most teachers, however, the teacher's manual can provide a useful set of signposts, enabling them to maximize the student's text, without being enslaved by either teacher's manual or students' text.

Exploiting resources that lack a teacher's guide

Some materials and other resources do not provide explicit guidance for the teacher. Also on occasions you will not have access to teacher's manuals. In this section we therefore set out some general principles to follow when introducing different types of pedagogical material. Some of these points have been adapted from Nunan, Lockwood, and Hood (1993).

Introducing a unit of work

Begin each unit by explaining the objective of the unit. This can be done either by referring students to the unit summary provided on the contents page of the book or by looking at the language review that is generally attached to the end of the unit. Statements about objectives best include information about the topic and the kinds of tasks and texts with which students will become more competent. You may also choose to explain specific grammatical features that students will learn to use. A discussion of objectives at the beginning of each unit gives students a clearer sense of purpose and direction. It also provides a point of reference for reflecting on and assessing their learning as the course proceeds.

At all points in the course, every opportunity should be taken to relate the content of the unit to the student's own background knowledge and interests, to their particular goals and aspirations and, when appropriate, to the experiences they have encountered in using English outside the classroom.

Warm up

Most units of work have some sort of starter task or tasks, the purpose of which is to introduce the topic, to motivate the students, and to provide them with enough grammar, vocabulary and content to help them deal with the challenging language and learning experiences to come.

Listening

General English course books covering the four skills invariably have one or more listening tasks. These generally appear fairly early in the unit and are often intended to introduce key grammar and vocabulary in context as well as to provide models for later speaking practice. Listening texts are increasingly based on authentic input, which learners who have only had experience with non-authentic data will find challenging and possibly a little off-putting. It is crucial to convey to such students the fact that it is not necessary for them to understand every word for the listening to be effective. Decisions that need to be made in relation to listening include the following:

Is it necessary to provide a context for the listening?

Should students' books be open or closed?

Should one or two items from the listening exercise be modeled for the whole class so that students know what to do?

Should the task be done individually, in pairs or in groups?

Does the task require the listening to be played more than once? If so, does your cassette recorder have a numerical counter so that you can rewind the tape and find the beginning of the listening efficiently?

How will students check their answers? Is it possible for checking to be done independently or collaboratively?

Reading

Reading texts, like listening texts, may be authentic or adapted from authentic sources. The type of text and the purpose for reading will determine the kinds of reading strategies required in the task. These strategies will vary from skimming the text for the gist to reading carefully for detailed comprehension. In some cases students will be required to read the text more than once. In preparation for reading, it is usually a good idea to discuss as a whole class students' experience and knowledge relevant to the subject matter of the text. This discussion enables a sharing or pooling of knowledge, introduces some relevant concepts and language and sets up expectations about the information contained in the text. You may also need to cover key vocabulary and/or difficult structures before students begin the reading task. Reading tasks generally begin with a specific prediction or orientation activity. This activity may be done as a whole class, in groups, pairs or individually depending on the level of support needed. You may need to draw special attention to the kind of strategy students should employ in their first reading of the text. You will also need to decide whether or not to allow students to use dictionaries, and, if they are to be permitted, when they should be used.

Writing

In most general course materials, which are generally designed to develop oral language skills, writing is used to provide variety. The first thing to do is to determine the purpose for the writing task. Check to see whether a model is provided, and if it is not, then you may need to create your own. Ensure that students understand the purpose of the model text, where they would find such a text, who wrote it to whom, what it is about. You should then explain the context for the writing task that the students will undertake (that is, purpose, reader, situation, and subject matter). You may also need to introduce or revise important language features and key vocabulary.

If you feel that the writing task will be too challenging for the students, you can construct a text on the board or overhead projector as a whole class activity with the students contributing the language. This will enable you to identify and explain language features that are problematic and to model the editing process for students. Having modeled the writing process, give students the time to prepare for and to draft their texts. Group or pair work is a useful way to help students prepare for writing as they can share ideas and rehearse some expressions they intend to use. Encourage them to edit and revise, paying particular attention to language features highlighted earlier. Students can swap texts and give each other feedback. Reading their own text aloud will also help students to pick up parts that need revision. Writing dictionaries may be used in the self-correction of spelling. With more advanced students, who are capable of producing extended texts, a major problem is how to provide corrections and other forms of feedback. This process can be extremely time consuming, and it is worth thinking of ways in which students can collaborate in correcting their own work. Alternatively, you can read the drafts, identify the more commonly occurring errors and deal with these with the whole class.

Speaking

These tasks provide learners with an opportunity of activating the language they have been learning. When planning speaking tasks, you will need to decide whether these are high structure (for example, drills and controlled practice) or low structure (for example, role plays, simulations, and information gaps). Questions to consider in relation to speaking include the following:

Is it necessary to review the language to be exploited in the task?
Will the students work in pairs or small groups?
Will the task be too challenging for some of the students in the group, and if so, is it feasible to model the task for the rest of the class, using two or more of the better students?
How will you monitor students as they complete the task? What will you do if it is too challenging for the students and if it breaks down?
How will you provide feedback? (One idea that works well with certain communicative tasks is to video- or audiotape native-speaking friends or colleagues doing the task. When students have completed the task, play the native-speaker version, and have students compare this with their own performance.)

Information gap and role play tasks

Information gap tasks can be difficult to manage, particularly in larger classes. Here is one suggested procedure:

1. Explain the context of the task.
2. If there are two roles, divide the class into two groups. If there are three or four roles, then divide the class into three or four.
3. If the task requires the use of role cards, indicate which group is to look at which role play cards. (In the case of information gaps, these cards are generally to be found at the back of the book.)
4. Each group studies and discusses the role card they have been asked to work with. Circulate between the groups, ensuring that they are clear on what the role card requires them to do.
5. Recombine the students into pairs or small groups, depending on the requirements of the task, so that each pair or small group consists of one representative from the larger groups. If there are odd numbers of students in the class, one or two students can share a role or act as observers.
6. Get students to complete the task. Circulate, giving assistance as required, and make a note of any difficulties or problems with grammar or vocabulary for later follow up work.
7. If the task is too difficult for a majority of students, some of the better students can model the task to the rest of the class.
8. It is a good idea to video- or audiorecord some of the better groups from time to time. These recordings can be used for revision or follow-up lessons.
9. Check answers, and discuss the task with the class.

Pronunciation

Pronunciation is an important and difficult skill for any foreign language learner. Unfortunately, many textbooks introduce discrete pronunciation features such as minimal pair exercises out of context. Additional pronunciation practice, focusing on fluency, rhythm and intonation in context, can be provided by working with the short practice dialogues contained in most course books.

Grammar

These days the emphasis tends to be on the "communicative" teaching of grammar through inductive discovery of rules and principles and the provision of opportunities for group discussion. Questions to consider in relation to the teaching of grammar include:

Should the item be taught deductively (giving the rule and then getting students to produce examples of the target structure) or inductively (giving examples of the target structure and getting students to generate the rule)?

Which approach is favored by the author of the textbook? Does the approach suit the students? If not, can it be modified in any way?

Are the examples and models clear? Should additional examples be provided?

Should the exercises be done individually, in pairs or in small groups?

Does the book contain an answer key? If not, how will you provide correction and feedback?

Are you sure of the rule(s) yourself?

Out-of-class task

Some textbooks provide out-of-class tasks so that students can activate their language outside of the classroom. Despite a reluctance on the part of many students to practice outside of the classroom, it is an excellent way of encouraging the growth of learner independence. In foreign language classrooms, students may carry out certain tasks in their native languages and then report back using the target language. It is a good idea to go over each task in class with the students, making clear what is required, and reviewing the language needed in each case. When appropriate, get two or three students to model the tasks in front of the class. If you want students to report back (reporting back is generally a good idea to maximize the effectiveness of the task), tell students when and how.

Language review

In some textbooks, there is a section encouraging students to review and reflect on the material covered in the unit. If checklists are involved, they can be completed individually out of class. Students can compare their responses in pairs or groups, before being debriefed by you in a whole class session.

Electronic support

The ubiquitous videos seem to have been with us for a long time now, and even in developing countries, they can be widely found in people's homes. Despite this, we would argue that the video has been one of the most underutilized resources in language education. In fact, it is only in the last three or four years that publishers have accepted that international ELT courses should have a video element to accompany the standard offerings of students' course book, students' workbook, audiotape, and teacher's manual. At first sight, this seems rather odd. Consider the benefits of the video. It can bring an immediacy and directness to the relative artificiality of the classroom. It can allow the non-native teacher to bring samples of genuine interaction to the classroom and enable the student to eavesdrop on that communication, studying it repeatedly, and absorbing aspects of communication that are difficult to access in any other way, such as proxemics, non-verbal communication, ways of holding the hands, the head, and the body, and so on.

In fact, video can fulfill different functions for learners at different levels of proficiency. For beginning learners it can provide examples of authentic language use in limited contexts of use. In this way, it can validate the language they are learning and demonstrate its use in the world beyond the classroom. With higher-level students, it can provide variety, interest, and stimulation and thereby help to maintain motivation. It can also be used for extensive listening and listening for gist. With advanced students, video can fulfill the same functions as for native speakers, to provide information and entertainment. At this level, it can be used as a stimulus for discussion and debate.

Why is it, then, that we are only now on the verge of seeing video's widespread use within the classroom? We believe that there are several reasons, most of which have to do with classroom management. Until relatively recently, video players, as expensive items of equipment, were kept under lock and key, rather than provided as standard equipment in the classroom. Teachers wanting to show a video would have to go through the cumbersome business of obtaining a machine, getting it to the classroom, setting up the program, and then going through all of these procedures in reverse at the conclusion of the lesson. Being extremely busy people, many teachers decided that it was simply too much trouble. In addition, few teachers have received explicit training in how to integrate video into their lessons. Without appropriate training or the opportunity to experiment with the medium, teachers tended not to use it effectively. We have observed lessons in which teachers, having gone to the bother of liberating the machine from its place of security, felt constrained to overuse it, showing lengthy stretches of programs of dubious relevance. The result is confusion and boredom on the part of the students and disillusionment on the part of the teacher. At a practical level, video and television are not used in many classrooms because the classes are too large, and most students would simply not be able to make out what was happening on screen. Attitudinal factors have also militated against the use of video. Many teachers (and learners) see it as a form of entertainment and therefore a distraction from the serious business of learning.

It must be added that hardware and software manufacturers have not helped the cause in some regards. The lack of standardization of operating systems can be a major problem. In fact it caused us considerable inconvenience and expense in collecting much of the classroom data for this book.

As most of the book was written while one of us was in Australia and the other in Brazil (countries with incompatible operating systems), we were forced to go through the expensive business of having videotaped material dubbed from one system to the other.

Until recently, there was little appropriate software for use. Much of the material developed specifically for ELT was not particularly exciting or interesting, and there seemed to be confusion as to the role of video. Should it be basically the same as the material on an audiocassette with talking heads added? Should it attempt to introduce a note of drama into the classroom? Or should it act a vehicle for adding a touch of naturalism? In selecting material for use in the classroom, a number of options present themselves. These include teacher- and student-made material, videos made specifically for the language classroom, material taken from television programs (these might include advertisements, news and weather, drama, comedy and documentaries), videos made for content area classrooms, and movies, which can be hired from video outlets.

Assuming teachers have a range of materials at their disposal, the major problem from the perspective of the management of learning is how to integrate the video into their language programs. Allan (1985) has a number of useful techniques and suggestions in her book on teaching English with video. She begins by evaluating the strengths of video as a classroom resource and suggests that there are four principal benefits. First, it presents realistic slices of life, which give a more comprehensive picture of communication than can be provided by sound and still pictures. Second, it has the potential to get students talking. In addition, it provides visual support, which makes it an excellent medium for extended listening to the target language. Finally, it offers variety and entertainment (although, as we already noted, in some contexts, these will not necessary be seen as an advantage). According to Allan, the ways in which video is integrated into the syllabus will depend on the kind of video installation the teacher has, the maximum flexibility being offered by a classroom with a permanently installed video with playback facilities and a good choice of materials.

In terms of syllabus integration, there is not always an obvious link between the bank of available materials and the syllabus. The most obvious link is through the specific language structures and functions you are teaching. Assuming you have managed to locate a video sequence that fits the language items in the syllabus, a number of possibilities present themselves:

- it could be used to present language – either for the introduction of new areas of language or to supplement what has been taught by other means and methods;
- it could be used to check whether students are already familiar with the language and can use it confidently, to help the teacher diagnose problems;

– it could be used to stimulate learners to produce the language themselves through roleplay or discussion.

(Allan 1985: 50)

Other ways in which video can be linked to the syllabus are through the topics you are dealing with or through activities: "Your syllabus may include slots for the development of certain skills such as listening to lectures or writing reports. You could think of using video material occasionally as an input to these activities" (Allan 1985). In integrating video into the lesson, the medium can be used for eliciting the target language, for presenting examples of new material, or for reinforcing, in a naturalistic context, language that has already been introduced.

Using computers in the classroom

Although computers in language learning are still a comparative rarity, this picture is rapidly changing. More and more courses, particularly those in universities and colleges are augmenting conventional forms of instruction with the use of computers. The growing interest in computers has been accelerated with the falling cost and increasing power of hardware and the increasing availability of interesting, high-quality software. In terms of our high-structure to low-structure continuum, there are instructional programs that span the range. High-structure programs give little control to the student. They are often based on principles of programmed learning that are designed to lead the student step-by-step through a learning routine. Traditionally, of course, this carefully sequenced design was the hallmark of the computerized learning package.

However, there are also many programs that offer a great deal of power and responsibility to the learner. We have found that some of the more exciting programs are those that were not specifically designed to teach language. These programs include simulations, design programs, and word processing packages. Such packages can stimulate a great deal of interactive discussion if students are given the opportunity of working on the programs in pairs or small groups rather than individually.

Almost twenty years ago, an evaluation was carried out in Britain of a number of different computer-aided instructional projects. The evaluation showed that even in those comparatively early days a number of educational paradigms could be tapped by computer-aided instruction. Although these paradigms included the "Instructional" (what we earlier called "direct instruction") of the drill and practice type, they also included paradigms consistent with low-structure learning, including discovery learning, experiential learning, hypothesis testing, and what is called "emancipatory" learning. (In this final type, students engage in learning for its own sake, rather than being instrumental to other types of learning.)

In one of the most useful early books on computers in the classroom, Higgins and Johns (1984) suggest a wide range of uses of computers in the classroom, including its employment for small group work and as an electronic "blackboard" as well as for individual study.

As the name suggests, when used as an electronic blackboard, the computer takes the place of the conventional blackboard (or white board). The advantage of the computer is in the speed and flexibility with which language can be produced and transformed. The obvious disadvantage is in the size of the screen (although devices projecting the image from the computer onto an overhead projector screen are now available, which can overcome the problem of screen size).

High-structure uses of the computer include conventional drill-and-practice exercises of various sorts. The advantage of the computer in drill work is that it never gets tired, distracted or bored, as many teachers do with rote work. However, as already indicated, restricting the computer to high-structure instruction, in which the students have little initiative and control, is unfortunate. Some of the most successful lessons we have observed are those in which the computer is used for interactive group work involving problem solving and simulations. Computer-mediated simulations can be extremely absorbing. In fact, we have observed classes in which students literally have to be chased out of the room during breaks (a reversal of the usual situation).

There are many different types of simulation, for example, developing an economy by producing different kinds of products, buying and selling players to create the perfect football team. What they share is a decision-making framework and a set of data. Students manipulate the data, feed their manipulations into the computer, and then deal with the challenge posed by the computer. In many of these situations, the students (and also the teacher) are collaborating in a competitive effort against the computer (Higgins and Johns 1983: 63). "The common feature of all simulations is that the computer is representing some of the consequences of decisions or actions on its screen, so that the user can follow a process through to uncertain outcome."

Simulations and other relatively low-structure computer-mediated tasks raise management issues similar to those of low-structure small group tasks. Their success depends on adequate preparation, briefing students clearly on what is expected of them, establishing different roles within the small groups, if this is appropriate (at the very least you need to designate, or have the students choose, someone to operate the keyboard or mouse). If you anticipate that students will work at different rates, or if you are teaching a mixed-level class, you may need supplementary material for those students who finish before the others. Alternatively, you can get the students collaboratively to plan a report on the simulation and its outcome.

Following the simulation, it is generally desirable to debrief the class on the activity. Higgins and Johns see this phase, in which the teacher gets participants to say what they did and what they might have done, as particularly important:

The teacher's most important function occurs at the de-briefing or post-mortem phase, when the participants review what they did and what they might have done. The computer can be used to recall a 'history' of the simulation, or to calculate the effects of other decisions, for example in commercial simulations, in which the participants have had to decide on the scale of investment or the price of a commodity. (Higgins & Johns 1984: 67)

Many teachers appear to be frightened of computers, although we have anecdotal evidence that this is beginning to change as computers become more and more integrated into many aspects of everyday life. Apart from a general fear of technology, some teachers have expressed a general concern that introducing computers into their classroom will involve a loss of control. As we have seen already in this section, the amount of control that teachers give up or retain will depend on the type of program they are using. This control in turn will (or should) depend on the objectives of the course and the needs of the learners.

In managing language learning, computers have four main advantages. They can allow the user to:

1. carry out tasks which are impossible in other media (such as automatically providing feedback on certain kinds of exercise);
2. carry out tasks much more conveniently than in other media (such as editing a piece of writing by deleting, moving or inserting text).

The main effect that these features have on methodology is that students can:

3. work through some exercises on their own and have them marked automatically by the computer (multiple-choice and total-deletion programs provide examples of this);
4. carry out exploratory work which is not assessed by the computer, but which allows them to see the results of their decisions (word-processing, spreadsheet and simulation programs provide examples of this).

(Hardisty & Windeatt 1989: 8)

Hardisty and Windeatt go on to suggest that all of the interactional patterns typically seen in non-computer classrooms are also possible with computers. In managing the learning process through computer-mediated instruction, one needs to ask:

What have the students been doing?
What has the teacher been doing?
What has the computer been doing?

Hardisty and Windeatt illustrate the range of learning modes, student configurations and interactional patterns by showing what students, teacher and computer were doing in a single lesson.

Students
writing / editing / commenting / reading each others' work / asking for help / learning terminology / talking to each other / operating computers / listening to an implementing instructions / laughing (a lot)/

Teacher
guiding / explaining / editing / keeping control / reassuring and encouraging / doing other class work / giving instructions / observing / correcting /

Computer
memorizing / storing / providing a stimulus / moving and transferring information / saving time / anonymous editing / printing/
(Hardisty & Windeatt 1989: 90)

One of the problems in writing about the application of computers to learning is that the field is changing so rapidly, one's words may well be out of date before they are published. Recently in Japan, we observed a lesson using the latest computer technology. Several students were working on a state-of-the-art computer with CD ROM drive, high-resolution color monitor, and so on. They were involved in making a radio program and newspaper. In the lesson we observed, they were rehearsing and recording the radio call sign (each student had created their own call sign, following a model that had been taped from a commercial radio program). The computer gave a visual graph or "voice profile" of the original as well as a profile of their own output. By constant rehearsal, and guided by the visual feedback from the computer, the students were able to approximate the fluency and intonation contour of the original. They worked intensively on both fluency and accuracy of pronunciation because there was a reason for doing so. They would not have achieved the same success without the assistance of the computer.

Another potentially exciting development is the use of concordancing in language learning. Concordancing has only become feasible in language classrooms with the increasing power and sophistication of microcomputers. Concordancing software enables us to identify patterns that exist in authentic language that are not easily identifiable from a casual inspection of the printed text. Students can therefore study the contexts in which particular words occur. The following concordancing extract shows some of the contexts in which the word "fun" appeared in the newspaper *The Independent.*

. . . hackers who access systems for	fun	and would be intended to act
. . . on the soundtrack. This was often	fun	and sometimes funny
. . . daughter out of a window. Rather more	fun	and doubtless just as fruitful

... me to the giantists. It's a bit of	fun,	and if it appeals to the young
Leo McKern has some	fun	answering frequent calls of nature
... arden fashion. Anthony Dowell is most	fun	as the glitteringly seedy bridegroom
Marcos loyalists now poke	fun	at the Aquino administration's
... presumably is where the	fun	begins
... without, perhaps a great deal of	fun,	but one with considerable insight

(Scott & Murison-Bowie 1993: 8)

TASK

Aim To consider the use of concordancing in language learning.

Procedure How do you think that such a program might be used in language learning?

There are many different ways of using concordancing programs in language learning. For an excellent introduction to these, see Tribble and Jones (1990) and Scott and Murison-Bowie (1993). Such programs enable learners, either working collaboratively in the ways suggested in this section, or independently, to explore differences between words that are often treated synonymously. Learners can also explore the core meaning of a word such as "jump" or "interest" as well as the particular uses to which the words are put in special purpose contexts. ("Jump" for example, will display very different collocation patterns in an economics text compared with a sporting report.)

In this section we looked briefly at some of the ways in which computer-aided instruction can assist and enhance the quality of learning. We also tried to suggest that teachers have nothing to fear from the advent of new technology. Although there are some aspects of computer-aided instruction that will make different demands on the teacher, managing the learning process in computer-mediated classrooms will present similar problems and respond to similar solutions as those in regular classrooms. The important thing is to see the computer as a tool to facilitate the learning process, not a monster that is going to highjack your classroom.

Visuals and realia

Many of the comments already made in this chapter are also relevant to the use of visuals and realia in the classroom. One of the problems of teaching in foreign language classrooms is that such resources are hard to come by. However, a carefully assembled collection of resources (culled from trips abroad by you or your friends, or obtained locally) can act, not only as a survival kit and supplement to the commercial resources you use, but also as the genesis for the development of your own teaching materials.

Some of the resources we have collected include the following. (This list could be extended almost infinitely, so the following is suggestive only.)

Print/visual
— Slides of environmental print, such as public signs and notices
— Postcards and letters
— Official notices and letters (e.g., from banks, building societies)
— Notes from school
— Bulletin board notices
— Job applications
— Extracts from newspapers, including articles, advertisements, classifieds, crosswords, horoscopes, features, editorials, and foreign exchange information
— Calendars, diaries, and planners
— Airline disembarkation, immigration and customs forms
— Written instructions on how to assemble toys, pieces of furniture, etc.
— Photographs
— Picture sequences
— Imaginative material including poems and extracts from plays, short stories, and novels

Audio
— Casual conversations among native speaking or bilingual friends
— Radio and TV news and weather broadcasts
— Public announcements (e.g., from departmental stores)
— Messages recorded from answering machines
— Telephone conversations
— Transactions in shops and public institutions such as libraries
— Sporting commentaries
— Formal lectures
— Songs and music extracts from radio
— Talk-back radio and radio "advice" segments

These pieces of realia can be used as the raw materials or input data for a task, or they can be used as they are to provide cultural background, to assist in explaining new vocabulary and as a stimulus for students (for example, pictures and picture sequences are excellent for encouraging the production of oral and written narratives). Visuals help to supplement the input provided by commercial and teacher-produced material, they can help to stimulate motivation and interest, and they can help to show learners how language is used in genuine contexts of use. In short, they can help to bring the language classroom to life.

We have also found that with intermediate- and advanced-level students, realia can be used for learner-created materials. Students working in small groups can create tasks based on various forms of input and then exchange these with another group. In this way, creativity and independence are encouraged.

Summary and conclusions

In this chapter we dealt with the use of resources in the classroom. We argued that, far from constraining the self-directed teacher, resources, including course books and teacher's manuals, can provide a great deal of freedom and flexibility. This is not to say that all commercially produced materials are equally noteworthy, and we tried, in this chapter, to provide evaluative questions and criteria whereby teachers might make their own determinations as to the worth of materials of various sorts.

We should like to conclude by pointing out that the deployment of the sorts of resources discussed in the body of the chapter is critical to the effective management of the classroom. In fact, without skills in using educational software, facilitating the learning process will be a difficult task indeed. We realize that, in many teaching contexts and situations around the world, high-quality materials, videorecorders, computers, and even audiocassette recorders are well beyond the reach of the classroom teacher. We have a great deal of sympathy with the plight of such teachers. However, we would like to think that even consumers of home-grown materials can benefit from the critical ideas and evaluative schemes which we have set out in this chapter.

PROJECT 1

Aim To link textbook selection to learner needs.

Procedure With reference to a group of learners you are currently teaching or who you are familiar with, complete the following textbook selection procedure (from Harmer 1991).

Data

Description of students
1. Age _____
2. Sex _____
3. Social/cultural background

_____

4. Occupations

_____

5. Motivation/attitude

_____

6. Educational background

_____

7. Knowledge (a) English level

_____

(b) Of the world

_____

8. Interests and beliefs

_____

Based on the above, what conclusions can you draw about the kind of material that would be suitable for your students?

_____
_____

Description of student needs
1. What contexts and situations (if any) will your students probably use English in at some future date?
   (a) _____
   (b) _____
   (c) _____
2. Give an order of priority for the different language skills (including subskills) that your students will need when using English.
   (a) _____
   (b) _____
   (c) _____
   (d) _____
   (e) _____
3. Now say what percentage of class time should be spent on these various skills.
   (a) _____   (d) _____
   (b) _____   (e) _____
   (c) _____
4. Based on the above say (a) what level the students need to reach and (b) what kind of language they need to be able to use or understand (e.g., formal/informal, spoken/written, scientific/business, etc.).

Conclusions: Type of materials appropriate for students
Based on the description of students and their needs, say what type of materials you think would be most appropriate for these students.

_____
_____
_____

(Harmer, J. 1991. *The Practice of English Language Teaching*, pp. 277–278. London: Longman. Used by permission.)

This project will provide you with a description of the ideal materials for your students. Having come up with a description of the ideal materials, you will now have to try and achieve a match between the ideal and the reality. Although Project 1 focused on the learners, Project 2 begins with the materials themselves. It provides a comprehensive range of evaluative questions that will enable you to determine the extent to which any given set of materials will suit your students.

PROJECT 2

Aim To help you identify your own priorities and develop your own criteria for selecting commercial materials.

Procedure   Create a checklist from the following list of questions for evaluating the materials you are currently using or are contemplating using.

Data

Phase one: Initial questions
I.   What do the materials aim to do and what do they contain?
   1. When they finish their course, what should your learners know of and about the target language?
   2. What should they be able to do in and with the language?
   3. What knowledge about language and what guidance for using language appropriately for different purposes in various situations are offered in the materials?
   4. What do the materials offer which your learners will need to know?
   5. What do the materials offer which the learners will need to be able to do?
   6. What is missing from the materials?
II. What do the materials make your learners do while they are learning?
   7. How do you think you best learn a language? What is most useful for learners to do to help them learn?
   8. What procedure or sequence of work does the learner have to follow in order to be successful at the task?
   9. Which types of task seem to be most conducive to learning?
   10. Which helpful ways of learning seem to be missing from the tasks provided in the materials?
III. How do the materials expect you to teach your learners in the classroom?
   11. What can I do as a teacher which can best help my learners to learn a new language?
   12. What are you expected to do to help your learners work successfully through the materials?

13. Do materials give you enough freedom to adopt those roles which for you are most helpful to learners discovering a new language?
14. Are you asked to take on roles you do not regard as appropriate?
15. Do the materials limit what you want to do as a teacher in using them with your learners?

IV. Are materials the only resource in classroom language learning?
16. What contributions can a classroom and its participants make to learning and teaching languages?
17. Which of your contributions to classroom work are referred to and extended in the materials: your contribution as a teacher; your learners' contributions (as individuals or as a group); or the contributions of other classroom resources?
18. During classroom work, which of those contributions are additional to those referred to and extended in the materials?

Phase two: Your learners and the materials
I. Are the materials appropriate to your learners' needs and interests?
19. How and to what extent do the materials fit your learners' long-term goals in learning the language and/or following your course?
20. How far do the materials directly call on what your learners already know *of* and *about* the language, and extend what they can already do *with* and *in* the language?
21. How far do the materials meet the immediate language learning needs of your learners as they perceive them?
22. Which subject matter (topics, themes, ideas) in the materials is likely to be interesting and relevant to your learners?
23. In what ways do the materials involve your learners' values, attitudes and feelings?
24. Which skills do the materials highlight and what kinds of opportunities are provided to develop them?
25. How much time and space, proportionately, is devoted to each skill?
26. How is your learner expected to make use of his or her skills?
27. How are the learners required to communicate when working with the materials?
28. How much time and space, proportionately, is devoted to your learners expressing meaning?
29. How and how far can your materials meet the desire of individual learners to focus at certain moments on the development of a particular skill or ability use?

II. Are the materials appropriate to your learners' own approaches to language learning?
30. On what basis is the content of the material sequenced?

31. On what basis are the different parts of the material divided into "units" or "lessons," and into different sub-parts of units/lessons?
32. On what basis do the materials offer continuity? How are relationships made between "earlier" and "later" parts?
33. To what extent and in what ways can your learners impose their own sequencing, dividing up and continuity on the materials as they work with them?
III. Are the materials appropriate to the classroom teaching/learning process?

(Breen & Candlin 1987)

PROJECT 3

Aim To design and evaluate a lesson based on a piece of videotaped interaction.

Procedure

1. Study the videoscript and list the language features that the extract could be used to teach.
2. Design a four to five stage teaching sequence, and set it out as a lesson plan.
3. Study the following lesson plan, adapted from Allan, and identify the purpose for which the video is used (e.g., whether it is used for reinforcement, presenting new material, as a source of information etc.).
4. In your view, what are the (a) most effective and (b) least effective aspects of the lessons?
5. What similarities and differences are there between this plan and the one you developed?
6. What features of the plan would you incorporate into your own?
7. What management problems or challenges would you anticipate in the lessons? How might these be preempted?

Data

Videoscript
(Time)
0.00   [A woman carrying a tray with food on it, approaches a man sitting at a table in a crowded canteen.]
0.04   Woman: Hello. May I join you.
         Man: Mm. Please do.
         [The woman puts her tray on the table. She goes to the next table to get a chair.]
0.09   Woman: Do you mind if I take this chair?
         2nd woman: Somebody's sitting there actually.
         Woman: Oh.
         [She goes to another table.]

0.15   Woman: Could I take this chair?
       2nd man: Please.
       The woman takes the chair and then sits down.
0.22   Man: So, how are you?
       Woman: Fine, and you?
       Man: Yes, very well.
0.26   End of sequence

Lesson plan – Teaching suggestions

Stage one: Defining the context – What is happening?

1. Play the first section (0.00 to 0.04) with sound only, up to the part
   when the woman begins to speak. T ask Ss to listen to the sound and
   then guess where they are.
   – Where are they?
2. Play the first section (0.00 to 0.04) with picture and sound. Did Ss
   guess correctly?
3. T asks Ss to predict what is going to happen next. If necessary, T
   asks prompt questions.
   – Is she going to sit down?
   – Where?
   – Where will she put the tray?

Stage two: Predicting the language – What are they saying?

1. View without sound until where the woman puts her tray on the table
   (0.00 to 0.07). T asks Ss:
   – What did she say?
   – What did the man say?
   – Does she know him?
   T asks Ss in pairs to guess the dialogue and make notes of their
   guesses.
2. View without sound until the woman puts her hands on the chair at
   the other table (0.07 to 0.10).
   – What did she say?
3. T asks Ss to guess what is going to happen.
   – What is the second woman going to say?
   – Ss offer suggestions.
4. View next section without sound until where the woman moves to the
   next table (0.10 to 0.14). T asks Ss:
   – Were you correct?
   – What did the second woman say?
5. View final section without sound. T asks Ss:
   – What did she say to the second man?
   – What did he say to her?
6. Role play whole sequence without sound. T asks Ss in groups of four
   to perform their predictions of the whole dialogue.

Stage three: Summarizing the language

1. T summarizes on the board possible ways of asking and giving permission. For example:
   - Can I . . . ?
   - Could I . . . ?
   - May I . . . ?
   - Is it all right if I . . . ?
2. Ss practice these structures by asking each other if they can borrow a book, a pen, a chair, etc.

Stage four: View, listen, and compare

1. Replay the whole sequence with sound. T asks Ss to look and listen in order to compare what they hear, with their own guesses. Who guessed correctly?
2. Replay the whole sequence again, pausing to ask comprehension questions, for example: "Why can't she take the first chair?" If necessary replay with sound only for intensive listening to parts of the dialogue.
3. To aid comprehension T give Ss a gapped videoscript. In pairs, Ss listen to the sound only and try to fill gaps.

Stage five: Acting out the scene

1. Ss act out the sequence in groups of four. T monitors the groups and corrects the language and pronunciation if necessary. T chooses one or two groups to provide a model to the other Ss.
2. After acting out the sequence T asks Ss to act out similar but not identical situations, for example:
   - You are in a train. Ask if you can sit in an empty seat.
   - You are in a canteen. You need some salt. Ask somebody at the next table.
   - You want to use somebody's telephone.

7 Affective issues in the language classroom

The ideal of using the present simply to get ready for the future contradicts itself. It omits, and even shuts out, the very conditions by which a person can be prepared for the future. We always live at the time we live and not at some other time, and only by extracting at each present time the full meaning of each present experience are we prepared for doing the same thing in the future. This is the only preparation which in the long run amounts to anything.

(Dewey 1963: 49)

Introduction

Within the field of education, there seems to be almost universal agreement that affective factors are critical to effective learning. The folk wisdom of the staff room has it that "unmotivated students just won't learn," that "you can lead a horse to water, but you can't make it drink," and "it's only Ali's attitude that prevents him from achieving his full potential." Unfortunately, affective factors are notoriously difficult to pin down. Because they are difficult to define, they are extremely difficult to measure, and it is almost impossible to specify the contribution they make to the learning process. Despite all this, they refuse to go away, and so it is necessary for us to deal with them, doing the best we can with the blunt instruments at our disposal.

Although the principal focus of attention in this chapter is on motivation and attitude, we also deal with aptitude, even thought it is not, strictly speaking, an affective factor. We have chosen to deal with it in this chapter partly as a matter of expediency, but also because we believe that aptitude will impinge directly on motivation and attitude.

Concert map of Chapter 7

In this chapter the following ground is covered:

– *Motivation* motivation and achievement, instrumental and integrative motivation, enhancing motivation by tailoring instruction to learner needs, preconditions for effective motivation

- *Attitude* relationship between attitude and motivation, cultural attitudes and language development, dealing with negative attitudes, attitudes from the learners' perspectives
- *Anxiety* anxiety and learner performance, causes of anxiety, anxiety
and the mother tongue

Motivation

All standard books on educational psychology have chapters on motivation
and its effect on the learning process. Most studies report a high correlation
between motivation and achievement, and this correlation is taken as evidence that a highly motivated student will do well in school. Of course the
relationship may be in the opposite direction from that which is commonly
assumed. In other words, it may be superior achievement that enhances
motivation rather than high motivation leading to superior performance.
Given its obvious importance, the ability to motivate students to learn is a
key skill in every teacher's repertoire. Although we do not disagree with
teachers' efforts to motivate students, we do believe that ultimately students should become self-motivated. We base this assertion on the article of
faith central to learner-centered instruction that ultimately it is the student,
not the teacher, who must do the learning.

Although virtually everyone associated with education agrees that motivation is important, it is difficult to find a clear definition of the concept.
Motives are inner psychological drives that impel people to action. Or, to
put it another way, psychologists have invented the concept of motivation
to account for certain observable behaviors. These behaviors are more
readily observed and therefore more easily accounted for when they relate
to physical needs such as hunger and shelter than when they relate to
abstract concepts such as the motivation to learn. Why does an individual
decide to learn? Is the motivation to begin learning similar to or different
from the motivation to continue (or to discontinue) learning? What part
does motivation play in situations in which it is someone other than the
student who decides what will be learned, and how? Even more crucially,
what part does motivation play when it is someone else who decides that
the course of instruction shall take place at all, as is often the case in foreign
language instruction when the parent or even the government decides that
instruction will take place?

In foreign language teaching, motivation as a critical variable was placed
on the agenda by Gardner and Lambert (1972). (See also Gardner 1985.)
Gardner and Lambert argue that there are two basic types of motivation,
instrumental and integrative motivation. Instrumental motivation drives the
learner to acquire another language for money, career, or power. Integrative
motivation, on the other hand, arises out of a desire to identify with the

culture or community that speaks the language. Gardner and Lambert argue that integratively motivated learners will do better than instrumentally motivated learners. In his seminal book on the role of attitudes and motivation on the language learning process, Gardner (1985: 10) suggests that motivation:

refers to the combination of effort plus desire to achieve the goal of learning the language plus favourable attitudes toward learning the language. That is, motivation to learn a second language is seen as referring to the extent to which the individual works or strives to learn the language because of a desire to do so and the satisfaction experienced in this activity. Effort alone does not signify motivation. The motivated individual expends effort towards the goal, but the individual expending effort is not necessarily motivated. Many attributes of the individual such as compulsiveness, desire to please a teacher or parent, a high need to achieve might produce effort, as would social pressures, such as a demanding teacher, impending examinations, or the promise of a new bicycle.

One of the challenges for researchers in the field of language education is the fact that important concepts such as motivation, anxiety, and, indeed, language proficiency are invisible mental qualities that can only be investigated indirectly. Motivation is generally investigated through questionnaires and rating scales of various kinds which require learners to reveal their attitudes toward the language, the culture, and the learning process. Examples of such scales can be found in one of the projects at the end of this chapter. Researchers collect responses from learners using such scales and then infer the existence of psychological qualities such as motivation.

The integrative/instrumental distinction was first drawn by Gardner and Lambert in a study published in 1959. The researchers used a scale in which learners were presented with four reasons for studying French and asked to rank order these in terms of their personal significance for the learner. If learners gave the highest ranking to "meeting and conversing with more and varied people or as a means of better understanding French Canadian people and their way of life" (Gardner 1985: 11), they were classed as integrative. They were classed as instrumentally oriented if they gave a higher rating to getting a better job, or education.

The basic claim here is that intrinsically motivated people do things for their own sake, rather than for an external reward. Extrinsically motivated individuals, on the other hand, engage in activities, either for the rewards that such engagement is likely to bring, or because they face the prospect of being punished if they don't do the task. A number of researchers have presented data to support the notion that intrinsic motivation is superior to extrinsic motivation. Would learning not be maximized, then, in a learning environment in which both extrinsic rewards and intrinsic motivation are present? Apparently it would not. The distinction between instrumental and integrative motivation has recently been called into question. Brown (1992: 139), for example, reports that:

Perhaps because of its simplicity, the integrative/instrumental dichotomy has tempted many to believe that it captures "everything you always wanted to know" about motivation. Motivation to learn a foreign language is, of course, much too complex to be explained through one dichotomy, as criticisms of Gardner's work has shown (see especially Au 1988 and Crookes & Schmidt 1990). It is especially problematic to do so as second languages are increasingly being learned outside of what once were closely allied cultural contexts. English as an International Language (EIL), for example, may be learned and used extensively without reference to a particular native culture. Rather, learners become highly proficient in the language in order to carry out specific purposes and/or to communicate almost exclusively with other nonnative speakers of English.

Brown (1992) provides data suggesting that the introduction of extrinsic rewards into an intrinsically motivating situation can actually decrease the intrinsic motivation. He goes on to point out that the only extrinsic reward that enhances intrinsic motivation is the provision of positive feedback: "sincerely delivered positive feedback in a classroom, seen by students as a validation of their own personal autonomy, critical thinking ability, and self-fulfillment, can increase or maintain intrinsic motivation" (p. 143).

One important way of enhancing motivation is to develop courses that are relevant to the needs and interests of the students. This can be done through the procedures that were presented and discussed in Chapter 1. Ongoing needs analysis, which actively involves the learners, can also enhance motivation. Involving learners in the decision-making process about what to learn and how to learn and encouraging them to take responsibility for their own learning can be a major way of enhancing motivation. In many situations, this simply does not happen. Teachers ignore the needs and interests of the students and simply follow the textbook. In situations in which there is no immediate need to use the language outside of the classroom, classroom tasks and activities need to be made interesting for their own sake. Students at all ages and levels of proficiency bring many experiences and a great deal of world knowledge into the classroom, and where possible these should be related to the content of the lesson.

TASK

Aim To explore the relationships between students motivation and teacher action/belief.

Procedure

1. Read the following scenarios and decide what the major motivation of the students of each teacher is likely to be.

2. Think of your own students, or recall when you were a student. Which of these approaches would you or they be more likely to respond to? (Or would this depend on the context in which you were studying? If so, what contextual variables would be the important ones?)
3. Imagine that you are the director of studies in a school where these teachers work. Which would you rather supervise? Rank them from most to least desirable.

Data

Teacher A: "This week we are going to be revising the things we studied in Units six through nine. This work is really important because it forms the basis of the end of week test, and, as you know, this will comprise thirty percent of your final grade and could even play a major part in whether or not you graduate."

Teacher B: "This week we are going to be revising the things we studied in Units six through nine. This work is really important because it will help you to be a more effective user of the language in social situations, and you may find this useful at some point in the future when you are communicating with native speakers."

Teacher C: "This week we are going to be revising the things we studied in Units six through nine. The skills you develop will be particularly useful when you begin your student exchanges next semester. In fact, they will make the social situations you will find yourself in a little easier to deal with."

Teacher D: "This week we are going to be revising the things we studied in Units six through nine. You should enjoy these revision lessons, because I've thought up some games that involve using the language. We'll divide the class into five groups, and the group that wins the most games can skip homework on the weekend."

Each of these teachers makes a rather different sales pitch to the students. Teacher A appeals to the students' self-interests in terms of upcoming examinations. In a sense the subject matter being taught is irrelevant. This appeal might just as well have been made by a teacher of science or mathematics. Why would the teacher make such an appeal? It may well be that the teacher believes that students are basically interested in examination results. With good reason, the view that "if it isn't tested it won't be taken seriously" is widely held in many educational circles.

Teachers B and C attempt to motivate students by pointing out the future value of the content they are studying. Teacher B appeals to the investment theory of motivation, that is, "make an effort to learn now, even though it might seem rather pointless, because you might find the stuff useful at some indeterminate time in the future." Teacher C is more concrete, reminding students that they will indeed be given the opportunity of using the language when they go on a student exchange to the target country in the following semester.

Teacher D adopts a different motivational strategy. She seems to subscribe to the view that if learning is fun then motivation will be enhanced. There also seems to be an implicit acknowledgment that the subject is not really worth studying for its own sake. She therefore tries to make the class time worthwhile in its own right. She also tries to appeal to the competitive ethic of the students. As an additional form of insurance, in case these strategies should fail, she caps off her motivational speech with a bribe.

All of these approaches are, in themselves, probably inadequate. As Good and Brophy (1987: 306) point out:

the topic of classroom motivation did not receive much systematic scholarly attention until recently, so that teachers were forced to rely on unsystematic "bag-of-tricks" approaches or on advice stemming from questionable theorizing. Much of the latter advice flowed from one of two contradictory yet frequently expressed views that are both incorrect (at least in their extreme form). The first view is that learning should be fun and that when classroom motivation problems appear it is because the teacher somehow has converted an inherently enjoyable activity into drudgery. We believe that students should find academic activities meaningful and worthwhile, but we would not expect students to typically find such activities "fun" in the same sense that recreational games and pastimes are fun. The other extreme view is that school activities are necessarily boring, unrewarding, and even aversive, so that one must rely on extrinsic rewards and punishments in order to force students to engage in these unpleasant tasks.

According to Good and Brophy, these views – that learning is either fun or drudgery – are based on folk wisdom rather than research. They go on to point out that recent theory and research reject both views. These days, it is generally accepted that a more balanced and sophisticated approach is needed in which a wide range of motivational strategies is pressed into service.

TASK

Aim To identify the different motivational strategies implicit in teacher statements.

Procedure Identify the motivational strategies behind the following teacher statements.

Data

Statement	Strategy
a. "You know your parents are paying a lot of money for this course."	_____

b. "Don't forget, you'll need this
   language when we go to Miami
   next month."   _____
c. "The first one to finish can leave
   early this afternoon."   _____
d. "Don't forget that the end of
   semester exam is on Friday."   _____
e. "You'll soon come to appreciate the
   fact that being fluent in another
   language brings its own rewards."   _____
f. "Last year, promotions all went to
   those students who did best in the
   Report Writing course."   _____
g. "If you can finish the translation
   quickly, I got a great computer
   simulation game for you to try."   _____

Each of these statements focuses on a rather different aspect of motivation. The first statement is an attempt to appeal to the rather negative factor of the student's sense of guilt. The success of such factors is highly problematic and will depend on external issues over which teachers have little control, such as the relationships that children have with their parents. For an adolescent who has parental conflicts, such statements may actually decrease rather than increase motivation. All of the other statements, apart from statement "e" attempt to appeal to the extrinsic motivation of the students ("if you apply yourself, you will receive some reward or avoid some punishment beyond that of improving your proficiency.") Statement "e" is an attempt to appeal to the intrinsic motivation of the student. Although we agree that learning something for its own sake is a good thing, we do not believe that simple assertions such as these are likely to make the slightest difference to the motivation of the student.

According to Good and Brophy (1987: 310–11), it is pointless even discussing the issue of how to motivate students without prior discussion of four essential preconditions without which no motivational strategies will succeed. These are the need for a supportive environment, matching the difficulty level of the material to the ability of the student, developing objectives which are meaningful to the students and sensitivity and moderation in the use of strategies for motivating students. Table 1 sets out these preconditions. As you read them, you might consider the extent to which your own teaching environment, or an environment with which you are familiar, is consistent with these preconditions.

Thus far, we have focused on strategies which teachers can employ to motivate students. This focus is reasonable in a book addressed to teachers.

Table 1   Preconditions for effective motivation

Factor	Characteristics
1. Supportive environment	— Orderly classroom — Teacher with highly developed management skills — Students non-anxious and comfortable with taking risks
2. Appropriate level of difficulty	— Tasks are challenging but not impossible — Students know what they have to do — Criteria for success are clear
3. Meaningful learning objectives	— Activities are meaningful and worthwhile — Relationship between objective and activities is clear — Students can relate content to own experience — New tasks build on and extend existing skills — There is a learning-how-to-learn dimension to instruction
4. Moderation and variation in strategy use	— Motivational strategy is matched to instructional need — Particular strategies are not overused — Teacher uses a range of strategies

However, it is also worth looking at motivation from the point of view of the students. Collecting data from students through observation, question-naires, diaries, and informal interviews can be highly rewarding. As soon as learners begin talking about the learning process, they will inevitably begin making references to affective factors such a motivation and anxiety. In the next section, we present some data from learners themselves that illustrate the importance of affective factors in the learning situation.

Attitude

The attitude of learners toward the target language, the learning situation, and the roles that they are expected to play within that learning situation will have an important effect on the learning process. It will therefore have implications for the management of learning. If the learner has a negative attitude toward the language, the culture, the classroom, or the teacher, learning can be impaired or even rendered ineffective. Attitude is closely related to motivation. In fact it could be argued that learners' motivation will be largely determined by their attitude toward the target culture, language, and learning environment.

There are comparatively few investigations of attitude in the language teaching literature. One large-scale study reported by Lawrence and Andrich (1987) investigated the relationship between attitude and language development among non-English-speaking background immigrants in Australia. Using a questionnaire, the researchers obtained data from over 600 immigrants from the following language backgrounds: Vietnamese, Turkish, Chinese, Spanish, Arabic, and Polish. One of the end of chapter projects utilizes the Lawrence and Andrich attitude scale, and we refer you to the scale if you are interested in learner attitude. Lawrence and Andrich discovered that although the learners they surveyed were generally positive in their attitude toward the target culture and language, there were some negative factors, and that these did indeed have an effect on the learning situation.

The extent to which teachers are required to deal with negative attitudes toward the target culture and/or the target language will very much depend upon the context and environment in which the teaching takes place. In foreign language contexts, there may be fewer negative attitudes toward the target culture than in second language contexts. (In the latter, some students may feel alienated.) However, in foreign language contexts it may also be more difficult to engender positive attitudes toward the target culture. Another problem for teachers working in foreign language contexts is to decide *which* cultural context to present to the student. Although countries such as Mexico and Brazil will, understandably, relate to North American contexts, and countries such as Hong Kong and Singapore will tend to think in terms of British culture, the issue is becoming increasingly blurred (and in one sense increasingly irrelevant) with the growth of English as an international language.

Attitudes toward the target language will also be colored by the environment in which the learning takes place. Foreign language teachers working in high schools often complain about the difficulty of motivating their students because the students have no immediate need to use the language. Negative attitudes develop because the students see the subject as irrelevant. In a recent workshop in which this issue came up, we brainstormed pros and cons of foreign language instruction in the context in which the teachers taking part in the workshop were working. We took a step back and looked at the educational context and environment in which the foreign language instruction was taking place. We then looked at the language program in light of the educational goals of the school. Having done that, the teachers were able to argue that no other subject on the curriculum was better placed than language to realize the goals of the school. The goals included intellectual and cognitive development, social and interpersonal development, and intercultural appreciation, tolerance and understanding. The teachers then looked at ways in which their programs could be modified to bring them into closer alignment with the school goals in ways in which the relationship between educational goals and language programs were transparent to the learners. These issues are contextualized in the following task.

TASK

Aim To identify the philosophy and goals of the educational institution you work for, or one you are familiar with, and to consider the relationship between institutional goals and factors internal to the learner.

Procedure

1. Working with several colleagues, examine the educational philosophy and goals of the institution you are currently working in. To what extent is there a match between these goals and your language programs? If there are mismatches, what can be done to bring these into alignment? To what extent is your language program tailored to the intellectual, social, and intercultural needs of the learner?
2. Brainstorm strategies for conveying the goals and content of the language program to learners in ways that are meaningful to them.

In the preceding section, we suggested that there was value in collecting data from learners themselves about their language learning. These data can be obtained relatively informally through interviews or learner journals and diaries and will provide a wealth of detail on the attitude of the learner toward the learning process. The following extract is from a diary kept by a native speaker of English who was learning another language (Thai). As you read the extract, you might like to consider the attitudinal factors that are revealed:

I'm seriously considering dropping out of class. Today we practiced the structure: "pick up the pen/book/ruler" and pass it to. . . . When it was my turn, I tried to give the exercise a bit of meaning by actually picking up a book and passing to Alan, my classmate. As I did so, the teacher, [name deleted], rapped me quite hard on the back of the hand with her ruler, and told me not to do it. I was aghast, and I think the other students were as well. I'm not sure how useful the classes are anyway. The other day I asked Khun Matana about a language point I needed and she refused to tell me, saying that we'd deal with that particular item in week six. I don't mind compromises, and I'm happy to accept that she's the boss, but if I'm paying a considerable amount of money for the lesson, then I do expect to have at least some of my needs met. The constant drilling, incomprehensible grammar explanations, and lack of real, meaningful conversation are turning me off. The other problem is that most of us work all day, so we're all exhausted by the time class begins. I figure that I'm just about at the stage when I can start learning independently. The advantage of attending class is that it stimulates me to make an effort. I'm afraid that I'll find other things to do if I give up classes. (Authors' data)

The impact of learner attitude on the learning process is borne out in the work of Block (see, for example, Block 1994, forthcoming). This impact is vividly illustrated in the following extracts from learner diaries, which have been translated into English. Some of the things that seemed to affect Block's learners particularly are listed with the illustrative extracts:

Fatigue
Today I really felt passive. Also, I didn't feel up to learning a lot of English. I even talked about it with several classmates and everyone said the same thing. It's because we had an exam yesterday which we had to study a lot for. (Block 1994: 477)

Perceived purposelessness
. . . first of all there were words that we already know. And we never get to see words that we don't know, which means that the only thing we do is review the words we already know. (Block forthcoming)

. . . so far we have been using the book too much because all of its exercises are usually too mechanical. If you understand a little grammar, if you do them ten times, in the end you know the mechanism, the trick. But doing them just to be doing them, it's actually so mechanical that in the end you don't even see the sentence. (op cit.)

Failure to identify or accept the roles implicit in a particular task (in this case to accept responsibility for their own learning)
. . . going outside of class in groups, it's a little difficult to control us. So we can talk about anything, like we were talking about life in Sitges and life in Barcelona . . . and we were speaking in Spanish. (op cit.)

Disparity between instruction and assessment
Actually these exams are proving to be really stupid because what we do in class has nothing to do with what we do in the exams. (op cit.)

Boredom
After that, we did something in groups, an exercise we did last week. Today of course we had to remember because we hadn't dealt with it for a week, which was boring and the people didn't do it. . . . A task has a time limit regarding its relevance. (op cit.)

Failure of teacher to specify objectives
We never knew what the outcome was going to be. So we did exercises and exercises without ever knowing that we would end up doing this. Maybe if we'd been told from the beginning, it would have been more interesting. (op cit.)

In one way or another, all of the factors identified by these students have to do with the issues raised in this book, and we have made numerous suggestions about practical ways of dealing with them. In the opening chapter, for instance, we stressed the importance of conducting an initial needs analysis to identify the attitude of the learners toward language content and learning processes. We suggested that the initial analysis should be supported by ongoing needs analysis and monitoring. We also stressed the importance of developing appropriate goals and objectives and conveying these to the students in ways that were meaningful to them. The result of failing to deal with the issues through the sorts of strategies set out in this book will be a deterioration in classroom atmosphere. This deterioration will compound the problems that already exist, increase the negativity of the students and lead to a further deterioration in classroom climate.

Anxiety

Anxiety is another contentious aspect of the affective state of the language learner (Horvitz & Young 1989). Some argue that mild anxiety facilitates the learning process (although, to our knowledge, no one has yet been able to offer a satisfactory operational definition of "mild," nor of procedures for ensuring that such "mild" anxiety as might be provoked does not become acute anxiety). Most people seem to believe that anxiety is detrimental to effective learning and that the first task for the language teacher is to reduce anxiety in the learner. (An excellent way of turning learners rigid with anxiety is to tell them you are going to make them "relax.")

The complexity of issues associated with affective factors in the learning process, and the oversimplistic assumptions we sometimes hold is highlighted by the available research in this area. In 1975 Chastain carried out an investigation into the relationship between anxiety and foreign language proficiency. Chastain administered tests purporting to measure anxiety to a group of college students in the United States. He then correlated the results of the tests with the students' foreign language grades. Chastain found that in some cases high anxiety was associated with poor language performance, while in others it was associated with superior performance. It is suggested that there are two types of anxiety, facilitating anxiety, which assists performance on such things as language tests, and debilitating anxiety, which impedes it. (For a discussion, see Scovel 1978.)

One of the most widely cited studies of anxiety in language learning is Bailey (1983). Bailey kept a diary of her experiences of learning a foreign language and used the journal as a database for her research. She found that at times her anxiety appeared to help her in her efforts to master the language, but that at other times, the anxiety got in the way. She noticed as well, in her own diaries and the diaries of other language learners, that there was a systematic relationship between anxiety and competitiveness.

It is not only fear of failure that can lead to anxiety. In many cultural contexts, it is considered unacceptable for talented learners to stand out from their peers (see, for example, Tsui 1995). Such learners fear that they will be resented for breaking acceptable cultural norms by outperforming their peers.

Allwright and Bailey (1991) ask why *language* learners should be particularly prone to suffering anxiety. They point to the possibility that banishing the use of the first language in the classroom diminishes learners as human beings because it deprives them of their normal means of communication:

> . . . learners report that one of their major worries is that when forced to use the language they are learning they constantly feel that they are representing themselves badly, showing only some of their real personality, only some of their real intelligence. Anecdotal evidence suggest that this sort of deprivation seems apt to breed anxiety about communicating with others and just the sort of anxiety that will get in the way of doing well both in the class and out of it, since it could inhibit the learners' use of the target language and thus deprive them of the potential profit to be obtained from practising what has been learned. (Allwright & Bailey 1991: 173)

The notion that banishing the use of the first language is a major factor in the creation of anxiety is plausible, although, as Allwright and Bailey admit, the evidence is anecdotal. If it is a factor, it creates a dilemma, because, as we saw in Chapter 3, allowing or attempting to ban the first language carry both costs and benefits in terms of learning and the management of the learning process. Using the first language can greatly facilitate setting up group work, explaining unfamiliar structures and vocabulary, disciplining students effectively and so on. On the other hand, speaking proficiency will hardly be enhanced if teacher and students spend inordinate amounts of time using the first language. In the final analysis, those teachers who decide to allow the use of the first language will have to exercise judgment as to the extent to which it will be allowed and the functions and purposes for which it will be used.

Summary and conclusions

Affective factors feature strongly in all aspects of classroom management. Although they feature in other parts of this book, we have given them a special focus in this chapter because of their centrality to the essential concerns of the book. We have seen that, although they are notoriously difficult to pin down, concepts such as motivation, aptitude, attitude and anxiety are critical to effective language learning. The challenge for the teacher is to find methods to enhance motivation and decrease anxiety in ways that facilitate the learning process. As we saw in the body of the chapter, meeting this challenge is by no means straightforward, as well-meaning attempts can have the opposite effect from what was intended.

In addition, in dealing with affective factors such as motivation, anxiety and learner attitude, we have to deal with the fact that our classrooms are not isolated islands detached from the mainland of the educational institution to which they belong. Events beyond our classroom, in the institution and beyond, will impinge on learners and therefore on our classrooms in many different ways. If students come into our classrooms after a long and tiring day at work, or, indeed, if they come into our class after a long and tiring day in subject classrooms, their attention, interest, and motivation are going to be affected. The important thing is for us to be aware of the possible influences on our students and deal with these factors. For examples, if your students are tired from work or previous study, you should not subject them to lengthy activities that take up a great deal of time. Interest and motivation can generally be enhanced in such situations by creating a series of short activities and the inclusion, if necessary, of class breaks, even though these may not have been officially scheduled. The basic point we wish to make here is that any teaching and learning situation will be affected by factors beyond the four walls of the classroom. These factors will have a bearing on the motivation of the students, their attitude toward you and your classes, and the effort they are prepared to make to achieve the goals that you and, it is hoped, they have set. It is surprising to us that this rather obvious fact is rarely acknowledged by those who write on affective factors in language education. In the final analysis you need to decide which factors are within your power to change and which are beyond your control.

PROJECT 1

Aim To suggest reasons for behavioral problems and to suggest possible ways of dealing with these.

Procedure

1. Analyze the following situations, and fill in the missing information.
    a. Behavior: Student never does homework.
       Possible reason: _____
       Possible remedy: _____
    b. Behavior: _____
       Possible reason: Students have a hostile attitude toward
                          foreign language classes.
       Possible remedy: _____

c. Behavior: Students lack motivation.
   Possible reason: _____
   Possible remedy: _____
d. Behavior: Student doesn't like to work with class-
                    mates who make mistakes.
   Possible reason: _____
   Possible remedy: _____
e. Behavior: _____
   Possible reason: _____
   Possible remedy: Teacher says that student doesn't need
                    to understand everything.
f. Behavior: _____
   Possible reason: _____
   Possible remedy: Teachers asked to plan challenging ac-
                    tivities for 10–15 minutes.
g. Behavior: Teacher corrects students infrequently.
   Possible reason: _____
   Possible remedy: _____
h. Behavior: _____
   Possible reason: _____
   Possible remedy: Teacher has to prepare classes more
                    effectively.
i. Behavior: Students only told what they are to do,
                    not why.
   Possible reason: _____
   Possible remedy: _____

2. In what ways is each situation related to motivation?

PROJECT 2

Aim To evaluate the role of "affect" in language learning.

Procedure

1. The following questionnaire has been adapted from Lawrence and Andrich (1987). From it, select and adapt those items that are relevant to your own situation and create a questionnaire.
2. Administer the questionnaire to a group of learners and analyze the results.
3. Did the survey confirm your feelings about the students you surveyed? Was there anything surprising in the results?
4. What assumptions are implicit in the survey?

Data

1. If I had known what this country was really like, I wouldn't have come here.
   strongly disagree   disagree   agree   strongly agree   undecided

2. People here don't speak English properly.
   strongly disagree   disagree   agree   strongly agree   undecided

3. If you work hard, you can make a good life here.
   strongly disagree   disagree   agree   strongly agree   undecided

4. People here are relaxed and easygoing.
   strongly disagree   disagree   agree   strongly agree   undecided

5. People here don't look after their parents properly.
   strongly disagree   disagree   agree   strongly agree   undecided

6. All nationalities mix easily here.
   strongly disagree   disagree   agree   strongly agree   undecided

7. This is one of the best places in the world in which to raise children.
   strongly disagree   disagree   agree   strongly agree   undecided

8. There's not much culture here.
   strongly disagree   disagree   agree   strongly agree   undecided

9. People here don't look after their children.
   strongly disagree   disagree   agree   strongly agree   undecided

10. The good thing about Australia is the mix of races, nationalities and cultures.
    strongly disagree   disagree   agree   strongly agree   undecided

11. People here don't want immigrants to have good jobs.
    strongly disagree   disagree   agree   strongly agree   undecided

12. I would like to mix more with Australians.
    strongly disagree   disagree   agree   strongly agree   undecided

13. I would be happy if my children married someone from this country.
    strongly disagree   disagree   agree   strongly agree   undecided

14. People here don't like immigrants from my country.
    strongly disagree   disagree   agree   strongly agree   undecided

15. If I traveled abroad I would be proud to say that I am from here.
    strongly disagree   disagree   agree   strongly agree   undecided

16. I prefer to speak to my children in English rather than my own language.
    strongly disagree   disagree   agree   strongly agree   undecided

17. This is a truly democratic country.
strongly disagree   disagree   agree   strongly agree   undecided

18. Most native speakers here are not cultured or refined.
strongly disagree   disagree   agree   strongly agree   undecided

19. I would not want to live in a street where all of the people were born in this country.
strongly disagree   disagree   agree   strongly agree   undecided

20. It makes me sad that my children are going to grow up as natives of this country.
strongly disagree   disagree   agree   strongly agree   undecided

21. There is nothing about people here that I like or admire.
strongly disagree   disagree   agree   strongly agree   undecided

22. I plan to leave this country as soon as I have enough money.
strongly disagree   disagree   agree   strongly agree   undecided

23. I prefer to mix with my own national group.
strongly disagree   disagree   agree   strongly agree   undecided

24. The teachers don't teach us what we really need to learn.
strongly disagree   disagree   agree   strongly agree   undecided

25. In this country you can be what you want to be.
strongly disagree   disagree   agree   strongly agree   undecided

26. If it weren't for the problems back in my country I wouldn't be here.
strongly disagree   disagree   agree   strongly agree   undecided

27. Most English classes are very useful.
strongly disagree   disagree   agree   strongly agree   undecided

28. If I were an employer, I would not employ a native of this country.
strongly disagree   disagree   agree   strongly agree   undecided

29. People here aren't worried about social class or background.
strongly disagree   disagree   agree   strongly agree   undecided

30. People here do not mix with people from my country.
strongly disagree   disagree   agree   strongly agree   undecided

31. People here are good to work with.
strongly disagree   disagree   agree   strongly agree   undecided

PROJECT 3

Aim To evaluate the role of motivation in language learning.

Procedure

1. The following questionnaire has been adapted from Lawrence and Andrich (1987). From it, select and adapt those items that are relevant to your own situation and create a questionnaire.
2. Administer the questionnaire to a group of learners and analyze the results.
3. Did the survey confirm your feelings about the students you surveyed? Was there anything surprising in the results?
4. What assumptions are implicit in the survey?

Data

Motivational Questionnaire

I. Motivational intensity

Scoring

key	
	1. I actively think about what I have learned in my language class.
3	a. Very frequently
1	b. Hardly ever
2	c. Once in a while
	2. If it were impossible for me to attend English classes at my school, I would:
2	a. Try and pick the language up out of class (e.g., read English books and newspapers, find people to have conversations with).
1	b. Not bother learning English at all.
3	c. Try to get English lessons somewhere else.
	3. When I have a problem understanding something we are learning in class, I:
3	a. Immediately ask the teacher for help.
2	b. Only seek help just before the examination.
1	c. Just forget about it.
	4. When it comes to studying and doing homework out of class, I:
2	a. Put some effort into it, but not as much as I could.
3	b. Work very carefully, making sure I understand everything.
1	c. Just forget about it.
	5. When I think about how I study English, I can honestly say that I:
2	a. Do just enough work to get along.
1	b. Will pass my exams on the basis of luck or intelligence, not because of the amount of work that I do.
3	c. Really try to learn English.

    6. If my teacher wanted someone to do an extra assignment, I would:

1   a. Definitely not volunteer.
3   b. Definitely volunteer.
2   c. Only do it if the teacher asked me directly.

    7. After I get my assignments back, I:

3   a. Always rewrite them, correcting my mistakes.
1   b. Put them away and forget them.
2   c. Look them over, but not bother correcting the mistakes.

    8. When I am in class, I:

3   a. Volunteer answers as much as possible.
2   b. Answer only the easier questions.
1   c. Never say anything.

    9. If there are movies in English on TV or at the cinema, I:

1   a. Never watch them.
2   b. Watch them occasionally.
3   c. Try to watch them as often as possible.

  10. When I hear a song in English, I:

2   a. Listen to the music, paying attention only to the easy words.
3   b. Listen carefully and try to understand all the words.
1   c. Turn to music off.

                (Adapted from Gardner 1985: 180–181)

II. Learning preference orientation

Scoring
key 1. At the beginning of a lesson or unit of work, I:
1   a. Immediately want to get on with language practice.
2   b. Like the teacher to explain what I am going to learn.

    2. During the lesson, I like:
1   a. The teacher to tell me what to do at all times.
2   b. To make choices between different tasks from time to time.

    3. Outside of the language classroom, I:
1   a. Am not interested in using the language.
2   b. Try to find opportunities to practice English.

    4. In class, I:
1   a. Am not really bothered about how tasks help me learn, as long as they work.
2   b. Like the teacher to explain to me how the tasks help me to learn.

    5. In class, I like to spend some time:
2   a. Discovering how the rules of English work.
1   b. Being told how the rules of English work.

    6. During a course, I:
2   a. Like to assess my own progress occasionally.
1   b. Am not interested in assessing my own progress.

7. During a lesson, I prefer to:
2   a. Practice using the language.
1   b. Listen to the teacher talking about the language.
8. During a lesson, I like opportunities to:
1   a. Listen to language that is specially produced for language classrooms.
2   b. Listen to native speakers using the language.
9. During a lesson I:
1   a. Prefer to work with the whole class.
2   b. Like opportunities to do pair and small group work.
10. I would:
2   a. Like to set my own learning goals eventually.
1   b. Not be interested in setting my own goals.

III. Concept differential scale

The purpose of this questionnaire is to find out your ideas and impressions about your English course. How strongly do you feel about the following aspects of your course? Put an "X" in the spaces provided.

Examples:
If the word "meaningful" very strongly describes your feelings toward the course.
meaningful __X__ ____ ____ ____ ____ ____ ____ meaningless

If the word "meaningful" somewhat describes your feelings toward the course
meaningful ____ __X__ ____ ____ ____ ____ ____ meaningless

If the word "meaningful" only slightly describes your feelings toward the course.
meaningful ____ ____ __X__ ____ ____ ____ ____ meaningless

If the word at either end of the scale doesn't seem to be at all related to your ideas about the course.
meaningful ____ ____ ____ __X__ ____ ____ ____ meaningless

If the word "meaningless" only slightly describes your feelings toward the course.
meaningful ____ ____ ____ ____ __X__ ____ ____ meaningless

If the word "meaningless" somewhat describes your feelings toward the course.
meaningful ____ ____ ____ ____ ____ __X__ ____ meaningless

If the word "meaningless" strongly describes your feelings toward the course.
meaningful ____ ____ ____ ____ ____ ____ __X__ meaningless

My English Course

meaningful	___	___	___	___	___	___	___	meaningless
enjoyable	___	___	___	___	___	___	___	unenjoyable
monotonous	___	___	___	___	___	___	___	absorbing
effortless	___	___	___	___	___	___	___	hard
awful	___	___	___	___	___	___	___	nice
interesting	___	___	___	___	___	___	___	boring
good	___	___	___	___	___	___	___	bad
simple	___	___	___	___	___	___	___	complicated
disgreeable	___	___	___	___	___	___	___	agreeable
fascinating	___	___	___	___	___	___	___	tedious
worthless	___	___	___	___	___	___	___	valuable
necessary	___	___	___	___	___	___	___	unnecessary
appealing	___	___	___	___	___	___	___	unappealing
useless	___	___	___	___	___	___	___	useful
elementary	___	___	___	___	___	___	___	complex
pleasurable	___	___	___	___	___	___	___	painful
educational	___	___	___	___	___	___	___	noneducational
unrewarding	___	___	___	___	___	___	___	rewarding
difficult	___	___	___	___	___	___	___	easy
satisfying	___	___	___	___	___	___	___	unsatisfying
unimportant	___	___	___	___	___	___	___	important
exciting	___	___	___	___	___	___	___	dull
clear	___	___	___	___	___	___	___	confusing
colorful	___	___	___	___	___	___	___	uncolorful

(Adapted from Gardner 1985: 183–184)

8 Monitoring and evaluation

Introduction

Monitoring and evaluation are essential and integral parts of everyday life. We monitor ourselves and others as we carry out the many tasks of everyday life – shopping, riding the subway to work, looking after our kids in the park, watching television and so on. Without constant monitoring and evaluation (much of which, of course, is conducted below the level of consciousness), we would be unable to carry out these everyday tasks efficiently and effectively. We have included this as the culminating chapter in the book, because, in one way or another, most of what we had to say in the preceding chapters has an evaluative dimension.

In classroom contexts, formal and informal evaluation are integral to the effective management of learning. As Reay-Dickins and Germaine point out, although evaluation contributes to good management of teaching and learning, it, too, must be well managed. In this chapter, we shall look more closely at the role of monitoring and evaluation in the management of learning, although, as we have indicated, much of what we have already written has an evaluative dimension.

Concept map of Chapter 8

This final chapter covers the following concepts and issues:

- *Formal evaluation* defining evaluation, purposes for evaluation, evaluation and assessment: a sample, tool for doing evaluations
- *Informal evaluation* evaluation and the management of learning
- *Self-evaluation* techniques for self-evaluation, self-evaluation questions and answers, focused evaluations: the case of grammar teaching
- *Evaluation by others* reacting to an observer in your classroom, peer observation: a case study, student evaluation

Formal evaluation

In this section we look at formal evaluation, and in the one that follows, we discuss informal evaluation. However, we would like to point out that the distinction between formal and informal evaluation is often one of emphasis. The concepts exist on a continuum rather than in conceptually distinct boxes. Informal evaluation is usually initiated by teachers themselves for the more effective management of their own classrooms. Formal evaluations on the other hand are more likely to involve outside parties, and the purposes, while ultimately aimed at improving the effectiveness of individual classrooms, are generally aimed beyond individual classrooms. Such purposes might include one or more of the following:

- To demonstrate the effectiveness of a curricular innovation such as a new teaching method or way of grouping learners
- To provide evidence to funding authorities that their money has been well spent
- To determine whether additional resources (or fewer resources) are needed in a particular school district
- To act as a basis for the reorganization of an institution or educational organization

Evaluation involves the collection and interpretation of information about teaching and learning for decision-making purposes. Information collected for formal evaluations is invariably written down in some shape or form. Informal evaluations, although they will generally involve written data, may very well utilize data that do not appear in written records.

The term "evaluation" is sometimes used interchangeably with "assessment," as the following quote shows:

Evaluation may be defined as a systematic process of determining the extent to which instructional objectives are achieved by pupils. There are two important aspects of this definition. First, note that evaluation implies a systematic process, which omits casual, uncontrolled observation of pupils. Second, evaluation assumes that instructional objectives have been previously identified. Without previously determined objectives it is difficult to judge clearly the nature and extent of pupil learning. (Gronlund 1981: 5–6)

It would seem, in this quote by Gronlund, that evaluation is the systematic attempt to measure what students can do in relation to what curricular objectives say they ought to be able to do. When talking about what students can and cannot do, we prefer to use the term "assessment." We would also extend the concept beyond the matching of student outcomes and program objectives. There are times when we want to estimate what students can do without reference to program objectives. For example, when a student enrolls in an institution for the very first time, the institution may wish to find out what the student can or cannot do. This assessment, which we can call diagnostic assessment, is designed to place the students in programs that are appropriate to their current proficiency level.

Evaluation involves the collection of information for the purposes of deciding what works and what does not work. This information is used to decide what aspects of an educational program should be left alone and what should be changed. A good evaluation will also offer advice on how changes might be brought about. From this thumbnail sketch, it can be seen that evaluation goes beyond assessment. Identifying what students can or cannot do is only a first step. We also need to know why they succeeded at some things and failed at others and what might be done to improve things in the future.

To illustrate the relationship between assessment and evaluation, imagine that you are teaching a course in oral skills development to pre-intermediate-level students. Two of the goals set for the students are:

1. To exchange personal information relating to age, nationality, occupation, and place of abode
2. To express degrees of certainty and belief

The end of course test reveals that most students have adequately mastered the first objective, and that few have been successful with the second to the degree that you had hoped. A review of lesson notes, pedagogical materials, and an audiotape of a lesson recorded during the course reveals that modals have not been adequately dealt with. You therefore decide to strengthen this aspect of the course the next time you teach it by including a video and supplementary oral practice material dealing with the language features in question. In this example, assessing what students could and could not do was only the first step in the evaluation process. It was necessary to go beyond the initial assessment, to interpret the information that was gathered and to deal with it in some way. This step is evaluation.

It is possible to carry out formal evaluations at any stage in the curriculum process, from the initial planning stage, through to program implementation. Formal evaluations can be greatly enhanced by the inclusion of classroom data of one sort or another. We have found that raw, undigested classroom data in the form of lesson transcripts are of limited usefulness for formal evaluations. If a teacher is comparing two or more classrooms, it is useful to have some sort of external checklist. In recent years, numerous checklists have appeared in the educational marketplace whose functions are to present classroom interactions in a summary form so that patterns are evident and comparisons can be made. One of the more comprehensive of these checklists is the Communicative Orientation of Language Teaching (COLT). Unfortunately, because it is so comprehensive, the COLT is not immediately usable by the non-researcher. Because of its complexity, Nunan (1992a) derived a series of evaluative questions, based on the COLT scheme, to be used by classroom teachers who wished to analyze their classes for comparative or evaluative purposes. These questions, which are reproduced in Table 1, can be used for focused evaluations of language classes, either individually or collaboratively. In either case, it is a good idea to work from a videotape rather than rely on live observation alone, as some of the interactions need to be revisited several times for the question to be answered satisfactorily.

TASK

Aim   To evaluate the COLT questionnaire in relation to your own teaching situation.

Data   The COLT questionnaire in Table 1.

Procedure   Brainstorm ways in which the questionnaire in Table 1 might be used for monitoring, evaluation and professional development in your own situation, or a situation with which you are familiar.

Informal evaluation

In the preceding section, we dealt with some of the factors which need to be taken into consideration in conducting relatively formal evaluations, although, as we were quick to point out, the distinction between formal and informal evaluation is not always clear-cut. The concepts exist on a continuum rather than being categorically distinct.

The close relationship between evaluation and the management of learning is spelled out in an excellent book on evaluation by Reay-Dickins and Germaine:

What does "the teacher as manager" mean? For some people it means directing learners towards getting a task done effectively or guiding them towards personal learning strategies. But the expression can mean other things. For example, in schools, and more specifically in classrooms, good management includes dealing with financial, material, and physical, as well as human resources. . . . Good management of teaching and learning includes evaluation. You cannot manage properly if you do not monitor. For example, if you set up a group discussion you need to evaluate its effectiveness while it is happening and you may decide to intervene to keep the discussion on course. Or you may decide to evaluate the activity and performance later in the context of the whole class with a view to improving your own planning. Running a class without evaluating its effectiveness is bad management practice. (Reay-Dickins & Germaine 1992: 14–15)

Table 1 Questions relating to the principal features of the COLT scheme

Feature	Questions
Part A Classroom activities	
1a. Activity type	What is the activity type – e.g., drill, role play, dictation?
2a. Participant organization	Is the teacher working with the whole class or not?
	Are students in groups or individual seat work?
	If group work, how is it organized?
3a. Content	Is the focus on classroom management, language (form, function, discourse, sociolinguistics), or other?
	Is the range of topics broad or narrow?
	Who selects the topic, teacher, students or both?
4a. Student modality	Are students involved in listening, speaking, reading, writing, or combinations of these?
5a. Materials	What types of materials are used?
	How long is the text?
	What is the source/purpose of the materials?
	How controlled is their use?
Part B Classroom interaction	
1b. Use of target language	To what extent is the target language used?
2b. Information gap	To what extent is requested information predictable in advance?
3b. Sustained speech	Is discourse extended or restricted to a single sentence, clause or word?
4b. Reaction to code or message	Does the interlocutor react to code or message?
5b. Incorporation of preceding utterance	Does the speaker incorporate the preceding utterance into the contribution?
6b. Discourse initiation	Do learners have opportunities to initiate discourse?
7b. Relative restriction of linguistic form	Does the teacher expect a specific form, or is there no expectation of a particular linguistic form?

Source: Nunan 1992a: 99. Used by permission.

In this quote, we see that the effective management of the learning process (one of the major subthemes of this book) is closely tied to evaluation. But it is not a form of evaluation imposed from outside. Rather, it is integral to the individual teacher as a self-directed professional (the key subtheme of the book.) In the next section, we look at taking this one step further when we turn to the issue of self-evaluation.

Self-evaluation

Ultimately, teaching will probably only improve through self-analysis and self-evaluation (Pak 1986). We have found that an essential element in self-evaluation is some form of observation. The value of self-observation and analysis comes through quite clearly in the following letter, which we received from a teacher trainer in Brazil.

I started working with some teachers on class observation, so that they could analyze their own teaching better, and understand that lesson observation not only helps teachers analyze all aspects of their teaching, but also makes students more aware of their learning process. Nevertheless, teacher's opinions on being observed vary greatly. Questions raised by the teachers included: What features can be pinpointed in observing lessons? What is the role of observation? Do all observers observe the same thing?

I drew up a set of features to observe, and visited a number of teachers. I started doing this alone, since I was the coordinator of the school, and after some time I designed an outline (working initially with three teachers) so that they could work collaboratively on planning, delivering and evaluating their lessons. The observation sheet contained items to be observed, and each of these was rated on a scale of 1–4 (1 = excellent). After working with the teachers for two semesters, I started analyzing the results.

Having identified the items causing most problems for most teachers, the teachers were invited to pinpoint two aspects of their teaching that they wanted to work on. Their next task was to devise activities/procedures for analysis (the objective here was to reflect on the nature of classroom observation and the strengths and weaknesses of the chosen items). I was careful to make clear to teachers that there were no assumptions about the right way to teach, and that, in fact, it would defeat the purpose of the exercise if model lessons which had been carefully worked out and rehearsed were to be used.

The next steps was to conduct a workshop in which questions from Nunan's chapter in the book *Second Language Teacher Education* were used. Teachers reviewed issues and sample investigative questions for teachers, and aspects of learner behavior which might be investigated in the classroom. Later, in groups, teachers were asked to think about and come up with responses to the following questions.

1. What teacher attitudes would make your students unhappy?
2. When does teacher talk become unnecessary?
3. What makes a teacher a good classroom manager?

4. What is not an ideal lesson structure?
5. How effectively are materials exploited?
6. How and when do we give instructions?
7. How can we encourage students to use the target language throughout a lesson?

The teachers came up with the following results:

1. What teacher attitudes would make your students unhappy?
   - A threatening attitude, especially towards students' mistakes.
   - The teacher being too demanding.
   - The teacher is not involved.
   - The teacher corrects too much.
   - The teacher pays attention only to the good students.
   - The teacher lacks enthusiasm.
   - The teacher doesn't encourage the students.
   - The teacher is inflexible.
   - The teacher is not punctual.

2. When does teacher talk become unnecessary?
   - The teacher repeats/paraphrases instructions long after the students have understood.
   - The teacher gives long grammatical explanations.
   - The teacher gets nervous if there is a silence.
   - The teacher asks all the questions and says all the interesting things.
   - The teacher gives more instructions after the students have begun working.
   - The teacher answers his/her own question when students themselves can provide the answers.
   - The teacher echoes answers from the students.
   - The teacher persists in explaining, when additional explanations won't make any difference.
   - The teacher talks about his/her own life and interests all the time.

3. What makes a teacher a good classroom manager?
   - The teacher justifies the use of pair work.
   - Time on task is maximized.
   - The teacher interacts well with the students.
   - The teacher has clear objectives.
   - The teacher is flexible.
   - The teacher shows a capacity to deal with the unexpected.
   - The teacher exploits the learners' likes, needs, and differences.

4. What is not an ideal lesson structure?
   - Good presentation but poor practice.
   - Students do not know what they are doing an activity for.
   - Certain activities/techniques are overused.
   - The teacher deviates from the plan.
   - Students needs are not taken into consideration.
   - Aims and objectives are not clear to the students.
   - The lesson is not well paced.
   - Instructions are not clear and brief.

    – Teacher talking time is maximized and students' minimized.
    – Practice in different language skills is not provided.
5. How effectively are materials exploited?
    – Do not let students get "stuck" to the book.
    – There are clear objectives for listening activities.
    – New activities are shared with all teachers.
    – Use of video is supported with well prepared activities.
6. How and when do we give instructions?
    – The teacher gives short, objective instructions.
    – The teacher writes an outline of instructions on the board.
    – The teacher sets a time limit.
    – The teacher gives instructions before students begin working.
7. How can we encourage students to use the target language throughout a
    lesson?
    – Teach useful language.
    – The teacher should try to speak English whenever possible.
    – Make students recognize classroom activities as genuine classroom tasks.
    – Give students opportunities to negotiate instructions in the book.

In addition to carrying out global evaluations, it is possible to target specific aspects of teaching for closer examination and evaluation. Once again, questionnaires and checklists can help to externalize the teaching process and to provide "objective" data on the teaching and learning process. In the following task, a checklist is presented for evaluating grammar teaching practices.

TASK

Aim: To evaluate a self-observation inventory for evaluating grammatical instructions.

Procedure

1. How useful is the following inventory for self-evaluation of grammar teaching?
2. What modifications would you make to the inventory if you were to use it in your own context and situation?
3. How would you use it?
4. How would you use the information you obtained?

Data

This inventory asks you to identify how many times you used a given teaching practice in a particular class in a given week. Please use the key in responding to the following statements relating to different aspects of grammar presentation.

Key
0 = Never   This is something I did not do in this particular
                   class this week.
1 = Infrequently   This is something that I did once this week in the
                   class.
2 = Sometimes   This is something I did two or three times a week
                   in this class.
3 = Regularly   This is something that I did four or five times this
                   week in this class.

In presenting a grammar teaching point for the first time, I:

_____ 1. Presented the teaching point both orally and with visual
              aids
_____ 2. Used pictures and diagrams to convey the meaning of
              the teaching point
_____ 3. Presented the teaching point indirectly in the context of
              spoken language, but did not formally teach it
_____ 4. Presented the teaching point indirectly in the context of
              written language, but did not formally teach it
_____ 5. Presented the teaching point indirectly in the context of
              spoken language, and pointed it out to the students
_____ 6. Presented the teaching point indirectly in the context of
              written language and pointed it out to the students
_____ 7. Presented the teaching point only using the target lan-
              guage
_____ 8. Reviewed with the students relevant, previously pre-
              sented grammatical structures
_____ 9. Gave the students several examples of the teaching
              point and guided them in discovering the grammatical
              rule
_____ 10. Gave the students several examples of the teaching
              point before supplying them with the grammatical rule
_____ 11. Translated examples of the teaching point to be certain
              that the students understood
_____ 12. Assisted the students in participating in a target lan-
              guage conversation, then drew the teaching point from
              the language that the students themselves had gener-
              ated
_____ 13. Spoke only in the target language, but modified the
              structure, vocabulary and speed so that the students
              could understand easily
_____ 14. Did not focus on grammar in the teaching of the lan-
              guage

——— 15. Based new teaching points on previously presented grammatical structures

——— 16. Gave only one example of the teaching point and did it orally

——— 17. Embedded the teaching point in a command designed to elicit a non-verbal response from the students

——— 18. Relied on gestures and mime to convey the meaning of the teaching point

——— 19. Drew the teaching point from dialogues that the students had memorized

——— 20. Explained the teaching point in English

——— 21. Conducted oral drill on the teaching point before presenting it orally

——— 22. Wrote the grammatical rule on the board or overhead before beginning to explain it

——— 23. Gave the students the general grammatical rule, then wrote examples of the rule on the board or overhead

——— 24. Allowed students to look at the explanation in their textbook while I presented the teaching point

——— 25. Had the students read a grammar explanation in their texts before I presented it in class

(Adapted from Koziol & Call 1988)

Working either alone, or collaboratively with others, develop a similar inventory for evaluating some other aspect of teaching (e.g., teaching vocabulary or pronunciation, teaching the macroskills, error correction, or feedback).

Checklists such as that created by Koziol and Call can be extremely useful for the microanalysis of specific aspects of one's teaching. One of the benefits of such an inventory is that it allows for much greater precision in the documentation and analysis of the teaching process than the rather vague impressions one often comes away with. They also provide a useful means for making decisions about follow-up actions that one might take. In teaching grammar, for instance, the preceding inventory might reveal to us, not only how limited our current practice is, but ways in which we can extend this aspect of our teaching.

Evaluation by others

In addition to self-evaluation, teachers should take the opportunity of being evaluated by others from time to time. For many teachers, external supervision and evaluation are mandatory aspects of their terms of employment. Others are never evaluated (not in a formal sense, at least). External evaluation, particularly when it is for purposes of certification or continued employment can be extremely threatening. In fact, it may well be the most anxiety-creating situation the teacher is ever likely to face.

For those teachers who have the courage, as well as the opportunity, to invite evaluation by others, the experience can be rewarding and can be a valuable opportunity for professional growth. The value of the exercise will be enhanced if the evaluator or critical friend has skills and experience, not only as a language teacher, but also as a supervisor. Such a person should also be aware (or be made aware) that to be useful an evaluation, the process should indicate what the teacher is doing well, as well as pointing out areas where there is room for improvement.

TASK

Aim To provide a personal response to a critical incident involving the observation and criticism of your teaching.

Procedure How would you react if you were the teacher in the following situation?

I had taken a part time job in a well-known language school, and as part of that job I was expected to be open to being supervised. One day a person I had never seen before walked in and sat down as I was in the process of teaching a reading lesson. I was trying out a few new ideas and wanted to see the consequences of not going over vocabulary before having the students read. Instead of presenting vocabulary, I was having the students read a story several times, each working on a different task, such as underlining words which described the person in the story or crossing out words they did not know. The supervisor sat in the back of the room taking notes, and I became nervous. After about fifteen minutes of silence the supervisor came over to me. She smiled and whispered that she would like to meet with me in her office after class. She opened the meeting by leaning over, touching my arm and saying, "I hope you don't mind. I'm not one to beat around the bush." I sank a little further into my chair. She proceeded to tell me that I should always write difficult vocabulary on the board and go over it before the students read, the students should read aloud to help them with pronunciation, and that in every class there should be a discussion so that students have the chance to practice new vocabulary. (Gebhard 1990: 157)

Gebhard's experience is, unfortunately, not unique. It demonstrates lack of planning, foresight, and collaboration on the part of the supervisor. It also demonstrates that the supervisor was evaluating Gebhard against a subjective set of criteria which were neither explicit nor defensible. As Gebhard later reported:

At the time, I wondered what made the supervisor's way of teaching more effective than what I had wanted to do. Now I know that it was not more "effective." It was simply different. It nevertheless appears that most people, including teachers, supervisors, school administrators, the owner of the neighborhood hang out, and the person on the street, believe that they can identify good teaching when they see it. It is probably not, however, good teaching that these people see. It is, more likely, their *idea* of what good teaching should be. (ibid.)

Gebhard's story illustrates the fact that supervisory evaluation should be carefully planned. The planning process should include one or more preliminary meetings between the teacher and the supervisor in which the objectives of the evaluation are negotiated and mutually agreed. Observation reports such as the one included in the next task are invaluable in facilitating collaborative agreement on what should be looked for and how it should be recorded and reported.

Peer observation

We have found that peer observation, in which two teachers observe each other, can be an excellent stimulus for professional development, both for the observer and the observed. However, it is important for both of the teachers to observe each other so that a climate of mutual support and trust is developed.

Peer observation involves the following steps:

1. *Pre-observation discussion*   The lesson plan is discussed as well as the focus of the observation. (Observation is generally more useful if it is focused, rather than the observer trying to note everything.)
2. *Observation*   The observer makes notes on the steps in the lesson, recording such things as departures from the lesson plan. Particular note is made of the aspects of the lesson on which the teacher wants feedback.
3. *Post-lesson discussion*   Both the teacher and observer report their impressions of the lesson, and discuss any differences of interpretation. The teacher may ask for ideas on improving some aspect of the teaching.
4. *Follow up*   The teacher tries out any new ideas or suggestions that arise and reports back to the observer.

The following reports* provide an excellent illustration of the benefits of peer observation. The reports were written by two members of a peer observation interest group that was set up within a language school in Japan.

---

*We would like to thank Paul Kelly and Robert West from the KANDA Institute of Foreign Language for permission to reproduce these two reports. Thanks also to KANDA Curriculum Renewal Project, which facilitated the development of the peer observation project.

TO: Peer Observation members
FROM: Paul Kelly/Robert West
RE: Summary of Observation
DATE: May 19, 19—

Pre-observation
We agreed that I would observe Bob in an SL second year blue class. The focus of the lesson was two exercises using the present progressive tense, one from the text and one original material. We also agreed that I would do a general ethnography of the lesson observing many different aspects of Teacher, student interaction.

    We decided that the observation would last twenty minutes.

Observation
The students were arranged in pairs, three pairs on the left, two pairs on the right of the classroom.

    The teacher moved from each pair to check their answers and understanding of the exercise. Teacher also gave students prompts, such as "ask her."

    There was a high use of Japanese and "chit chat" by pairs not in contact with teacher.

    Teacher frequently praised pairs for completion of task.

    Two pairs made frequent use of classroom English to clarify teacher instructions, "Is this correct?" and "Could you help me?"

    The second exercise began with a handout and teacher directions. Teacher explained and walked to the board to write an example.

    Students wrote their answers before practicing the forms in pairs.

    Teacher assistance followed the same form as Exercise 1, moving from pair to pair while students passed each other answers using English and Japanese.

Post-observation Session
I asked Bob his impressions of the lesson, and he indicated that the students completed the tasks to his satisfaction; however, he expressed his frustration with the high usage of Japanese during the exercise. Bob then asked for suggestions on ways to improve the direction phase of the lesson. I suggested that he model the exercise and refrain from turning his back on the class while walking to the board and writing on the board. I also suggested that he put the students' desks face to face rather than the traditional "back to the wall" position in order to maximize English language usage during pair work. Bob seemed to be receptive to these suggestions and further stated that the students were familiar with today's material from previous lessons and that Exercise 2 was his own material because the text did not provide enough on the use of the present progressive.

Follow up on observation
Bob indicated that he tried the suggested desk arrangement in his next SL class and that the results were immediately observable. He said the students practiced the activities for longer periods when sitting face to face. He also stated that he makes a conscious effort to not turn his back on the class when speaking.

TO: Peer Observation Members
FROM: Robert West
RE: Observation of Paul Kelly
DATE: May 25, 19—

Pre-Observation
We decided that this observation would take place in Paul's second year red SL class. The observation would last 30 minutes. The focus of the lesson was speaking about past events and chronology. We agreed that I would do a general ethnography.

Observation
The class consisted of eight students. They were seated along opposite walls of the classroom. The room was of a narrow enough size to warrant this seating arrangement. For this particular lesson a communication activity in the form of a detective game, "Witness," was utilized to provide speaking practice with the target structures.

The teacher began the class with a brief warm up consisting of small talk. He then introduced the observer to the students and in turn had the students introduce themselves.

The teacher introduced and briefly explained the game. During this time he also elicited vocabulary definitions relevant to the game. The game materials were numerous and took some time to distribute. The teacher used light humorous banter to put the students as ease while handing out the materials. After all materials were distributed, the teacher proceeded to explain the rules, as well as the object, of the game in detail. During this phase he continuously checked comprehension and elicited further relevant vocabulary definitions. The words elicited seemed chosen to arouse student interest in the game.

As the game started, the students were instructed to get up from their desks and move around the room to gather the necessary information from their classmates. They appeared interested in the game and seemed eager to collect their information. Most remembered to speak English with only occasional lapses into Japanese.

During this time the teacher circulated throughout the room answering questions and giving encouragement. There appeared to be a good teacher-student rapport and the complexity of the game seemed suited to the level of the class.

Post-observation discussion

In our post-observation discussion I stated to Paul that I thought the class was well planned, organized, and carried out. I asked him for his own thoughts on how the class went. He agreed that it went well, but pointed out that the number of maps required for the game wasn't adequate and he should have realized that it would have been better if students had their own individual maps. He also expressed concern that only four of the eight students present actually got the correct answer to the game, but thought the ultimate class objectives were met in that all the students satisfactorily used the target structures.

I suggested that if this were my class I would have given the students a little more time to read their roll cards before starting the game, since I perceived some slight confusion about the rules at the start. Paul agreed with this recommendation and further suggested that individual comprehension checks would be desirable as Japanese students are often reluctant to ask questions or show lack of knowledge in front of a group.

Follow-up analysis

In my own classroom I have implemented Paul's suggestion of rearranging the students' desks for pair work activities so that they face each other. I have found that this simple but effective technique has resulted in much greater student interaction. This interaction is evidenced by the increased concentration and interest of the students in what they are saying. There has also been a resulting increase in the length of actual speaking time.

I feel that the use of this seating arrangement creates a much more intimate atmosphere for pair work activities with a subsequent increase in meaningful communication. With this arrangement the students are not just sitting side by side, as I formally had them, looking out across the classroom and awkwardly looking sideways at each other, but rather, naturally facing each other as they would in a real life situation.

Additionally, I am also appreciative of Paul's other observation, namely that I was inadvertently turning my back to the class while writing and referring to the board. I am now very conscious of this oversight and make every effort to rectify it.

Advice and suggestions like these from experienced teachers are of particular interest to me and are what I had hoped to derive from the Peer Observation Program. As we are all adults and professionals we should always be open to constructive comments and should accept them in the light in which they are given, namely the enhancement of our teaching skills and self-confidence. These types of suggestions not only benefit ourselves as teachers, but also the quality of education at school in general. I look forward to and hope to get as much out of future observations.

As we can see from these reports, peer observation can be an excellent way of identifying problems and finding solutions to such problems. It is therefore a useful way of improving the quality of teaching. However, it is not without its problems. One problem reported by several teachers who have taken part in such peer observation exercises is what to do when they observe colleagues doing something which the observer feels is inappropriate or ineffective. To criticize openly would jeopardize the level of trust that is needed in exercises of this sort. One solution to this problem is for the observer and teacher to negotiate beforehand and agree that the observers will identify three aspects of the teaching which they would do the same, and three things that they would do differently. In this non-judgmental way, the observer can raise problematic issues that the teachers themselves may simply not have noticed.

Student evaluation

Being evaluated by students can be a frightening prospect for some teachers. It can also be considered culturally inappropriate in many contexts and situations. However, we believe that if you are teaching students of an appropriate age and level of maturity, in a context in which it is not considered culturally inappropriate, that you should, from time to time, seek feedback from students on your performance. This is not always easy, as most learners feel that it is somehow improper for a student to pass judgment on the teacher. Despite this problem, data from students can be extremely illuminating.

There are several rules to follow if you do solicit evaluative feedback from your students. First, the data should be confidential. Confidentiality makes it easier for the students themselves to be honest in what they say about you and your teaching. Unless your students are highly proficient, it is probably best to allow them do the evaluation in their first language. If you do not speak their language, then stick to quantitative feedback such as in Part A of the student evaluation form contained in Project 2 at the end of the chapter. You can then collate the responses without necessarily knowing the language. The evaluation should also be relatively short and straightforward. In fact, it probably should not be any longer than the sample form. (You will note that Part III is made up of a question that the lecturer has selected from an item bank. This part gives the person being evaluated an opportunity to have some control over what is to be evaluated.)

If direct feedback from students is not feasible, then it may be better to attempt to gather the information indirectly. One technique that we have used successfully is the "action meeting." Action meetings are conducted by members of the class without the teacher being present. They can either be conducted in the first or target language, although with higher-proficiency learners there are obvious advantages to learners using the target language. The purpose of the meeting is for the students to review the progress of their course, to record what they liked as well as what they were not happy with, and to make recommendations about what they would like more of in future. The meetings should cover both content and methodology. Properly conducted, such meetings can furnish invaluable information to teachers about their performance in a way that is less threatening than more direct feedback.

An important consideration with this form, as with other forms of evaluative feedback, has to do with the timing of the feedback. If the data are collected at the end of the course, there is often very little one can do with it, and the evaluation exercise will probably be at most of therapeutic value to the students. Some comments, for example, "the teacher spoke too quickly," might be of value beyond the course in question. Others, such as "some individuals didn't participate much," might be peculiar to the course in question and will not be applicable to other courses.

Summary and conclusions

In a sense, this entire book is an exercise in evaluation. It is therefore fitting that it should culminate in a chapter on evaluation. We suggested that evaluation is a process of collecting and interpreting information for decision-making purposes. It can either be formal or informal, mandatory or voluntary, and can involve a number of players in the educational drama. In our professional lives we are constantly monitoring and evaluating ourselves and our students. Every time we check that students are paying attention, we are evaluating. It is a normal and necessary part of being a teacher.

In this chapter we tried to provide ideas on how these monitoring processes, whether they be formal or informal, can be made more systematic. We also tried to give ideas on how colleagues and students can be involved in evaluation.

PROJECT 1

Aim To evaluate yourself in the course of teaching a lesson.

Procedure

1. Complete the first part of the following self-evaluation form for a lesson you are about to teach.
2. Teach the lesson and complete the rest of the form.
3. If possible have one or more colleagues do the task, and compare results.

4. What modifications, if any, would you make to the form to make a more suitable self-evaluation instrument?

Data

Teacher Self-Evaluation Form

What do I teach? How do I teach? Why do I teach what I teach?

Planning

1. What are my objectives in this lesson?

_____

_____

2. What have I taken into consideration?

_____

_____

Implementation

1. What is the relationship between the lesson I planned and what actually happened in the class?

_____

_____

2. What events in the class made me deviate from my plans?

_____

_____

3. Am I responsible in any way for discipline problems students might have?

_____

_____

Classroom management

1. What aspects of learner behavior do I respond to?

_____

_____

2. How efficient/effective am I at setting up group work?

_____

_____

3. How much talking do I do in class? (Too little, too much, or just enough?) _____
What happens when I vary the amount?

_____

4. How clear and/or useful are the explanations I give to students?

_____

_____

PROJECT 2

Aim To familiarize yourself with a teacher observation/evaluation report.

Procedure Examine the following observation report from Lozano and Vickers (1990).

1. What assumptions about the nature of language and learning under-lie the report?
2. What modifications would you like to see made to the form before it were used to evaluate you?

Data

Teacher Observation/Evaluation Report

Name of teacher: _____ Section: _____
Name of observer: _____ Date: _____

I. The visit was announced/unannounced.

II. Was there a pre-observation conference? Yes _____ No _____

Summary of pre-observation conference, if any: _____
_____
_____
_____

III. Observer's checklist
To the observer: For each of the criteria below, check the appropriate column (*Yes* or *No*). Leave blank if not applicable or if there is not enough evidence for evaluation.

	Yes	No
A. Planning		
1. There was evidence of effective lesson planning and preparation.	____	____
2. The lesson was logically sequenced.	____	____
3. The activities were suitable for the age and level of the group.	____	____
4. The activities were directly related to the aims and objectives of the lesson.	____	____
5. The class contained a variety of activities appropriate for different learning styles (visual-receptive, audio-receptive, motor-receptive).	____	____
6. Practice in different language skills was provided.	____	____

B. Presentation and development

   7. The teacher made the aims and objectives of the lesson clear to the students.   _____   _____

   8. The lesson was well-paced.   _____   _____

   9. Instructions were brief and clear.   _____   _____

  10. Supplementary materials were effectively integrated into the class.   _____   _____

  11. Student talk was maximized and teacher talk was minimized.   _____   _____

  12. The inquiry process was encouraged through elicitation of input from the students (questions, examples, definitions, explanations, comments, etc.).   _____   _____

  13. Student errors were monitored and corrected effectively.   _____   _____

  14. Student performance was monitored throughout the class to ensure that the lesson objectives were being reached.   _____   _____

  15. The teacher spoke clearly and loudly enough for all to hear.   _____   _____

  16. The teacher used correct English grammar and pronunciation.   _____   _____

  17. The teacher spoke in the target language as much as possible.   _____   _____

  18. The teacher developed the students' awareness of the L2 culture.   _____   _____

  19. The textbook and the materials were used effectively and appropriately.   _____   _____

C. Interpersonal dynamics

  20. Genuine communicative interaction took place.   _____   _____

  21. The teacher demonstrated awareness of individual students' learning needs and strategies.   _____   _____

  22. The teacher made a conscious effort to pay attention to all students equally.   _____   _____

  23. The teacher praised and encouraged the students.   _____   _____

  24. The teacher used gestures, body language, and/or humor to enliven the class.   _____   _____

D. Class management

  25. The class started on time.   _____   _____

26. The class ended on time. ———— ————
27. The seating arrangement was appropri- ———— ————
ate for each activity and allowed acces-
sibility to the teacher.
28. The writing on the chalkboard was legi- ———— ————
ble and the information presented was
well-organized.
29. Audiovisual aids were used effectively ———— ————
and were visible/audible to all students.
30. The teacher maintained a class atmo- ———— ————
sphere that was conducive to learning.

IV. Observer's recommendations

A. Teacher should take ———————————————
B. Teacher should visit [Course(s)] ———————— taught by ————————
C. Teacher should read ———————————————————————

V. Post-observation conference   Date: ————————————

A. Teacher's summary
1. Comment on your strengths and weaknesses in the above
lesson.
———————————————————————————————
———————————————————————————————

2. Write down three things you might focus on for improvement.
———————————————————————————————
———————————————————————————————
———————————————————————————————

3. How do you plan to reach your improvement goals?
———————————————————————————————
———————————————————————————————

B. Teacher's comments: ———————————————————————
———————————————————————————————
———————————————————————————————

C. Teacher's signature:
————————————————————————

Observer's signature:
————————————————————————

Academic director:
————————————————————————

Assistant academic director:
————————————————————————

Executive director:
————————————————————— Date: ————————————

(Developed by F. Lozano & M. Vickers 1990)

PROJECT 3

Aim To familiarize yourself with a student evaluation form and to consider how you might modify and use such a form in your own situation

Procedure Study the following student evaluation form. What modifications would you make to this form in your own situation? Which items would you select for inclusion in an evaluation of your own teaching?

Data

Macquarie University
Centre for Higher Education and Professional Development
Student Evaluation of Teaching and Subjects

Student evaluation of teaching and subjects is one way for staff to get feedback on their teaching and subject and to monitor teaching standards in the university. The questionnaire will be processed in the CHEPD. We ask you therefore to fill in the questionnaire and to make thoughtful comments on the back page. We are using the term 'lecturer' for all staff, whether tutor or professor, and regardless of whether this is a lecture, tutorial, lab or other class. The first fifteen items are a standard part of all questionnaires. For each statement you are asked to indicate the extent to which you agree with it in relation to the teaching in this subject by the lecturer, or to the subject, by inserting the appropriate number.

The scale is:

Strongly agree	*Agree*	*Neutral*	*Strongly disagree*	*Not applicable*
1	2	3	4	5

I. Teacher: _____ *(Insert lecturer's name)* _____

1. Made clear the objectives for each session   [ ]
2. Was able to explain concepts clearly   [ ]
3. Seemed well prepared for each session   [ ]
4. Taught the subject matter in a way that helped me understand it   [ ]
5. Tried to make the subject interesting   [ ]
6. Demonstrated the relevance of the subject to the whole course   [ ]
7. Made opportunities to ask questions   [ ]
8. Was available for consultation   [ ]
9. Made clear the criteria used to assess students' work   [ ]
10. Gave adequate feedback on assignments and other prescribed work   [ ]

11. All things considered, how would you rate the teaching of
_____ in this subject? Circle one of the numbers 1–7.

Excellent = 1	Satisfactory = 4	Poor = 6
Very good = 2	Not quite satisfactory = 5	Very poor = 7
Good = 3		

II. The subject: _____ *(Insert name and code)* _____

12. The subject covered what the subject description said it would   [ ]

13. Assessment tasks set and/or exams were related to subject goals   [ ]

14. Assessment tasks allowed me to demonstrate what I had learnt   [ ]

15. The workload was comparable to other subjects at this level   [ ]

III. Feedback items chosen by this lecturer or school

16. I have developed interest in this subject   [ ]
17. The lecturer is professional in attitude   [ ]
18. The lecturer presents material in an interesting way   [ ]
19. The lecturer seems to know the subject matter well   [ ]
20. The lecturer appears confident   [ ]
21. The lecturer communicates enthusiasm for the subject   [ ]
22. The prescribed textbook is useful   [ ]
23. Study guides assisted my learning   [ ]
24. I find this subject interesting   [ ]

Appendix
Language learning in action

Lesson 1

The following lesson transcript has been included for use by readers who wish to do the tasks in the body of the book requiring classroom data, but who do not have ready access to second or foreign language classrooms. The class was conducted with a group of young adults who were undertaking an intensive English class in an English language institute. This was the students' very first class. It was also the first time that the teacher and students had met each other.

After the class had been recorded and transcribed, the teacher reviewed the lesson transcript and provided a commentary on what had happened. This part of the appendix therefore provides the reader, not only with the raw data, in the form of a transcript, but also an interpretive commentary by one of the principal actors of what went on during the lesson.

Lesson transcript

T: Well, good morning. Because this is the very first class that we're having, um, we're going to be doing some things this morning that involve exchanging personal information and talking about ourselves and describing ourselves. OK. And the first thing I'd like you to do – if you open your book on page two. Open up to page two, you'll see in the warm-up section the very first task asks you to think about the language you already know and to think about how well you can do the things we're going to practice this morning. So what I'd like you to do is to take your pen or your pencil and look at each of these things that we're going to be practicing, and put a circle around the words "yes," or "a little" or "not yet." Think about how well you can do these things. "Exchange personal information." OK? So, "My name is Derek. What's your name?" Can you do this very well, or a little bit, or not at all? Put a circle around the words that describe how well you can do these things. So one of the things we're going to practice this morning is "Exchange personal information."
"My name is Derek. What's your name? Where are you from? I'm from Boston. You're from. . . ?

S: From Tokyo.

T: From Tokyo. Um. What about the next thing we're

Teacher's commentary

I always try and start my class making it clear to the learners what the goals of the lesson are. The pilot materials made this easy, because the goals are set out at the beginning of the unit.

I talked more than I usually do, because this was the very first lesson, and I hadn't met the students before. Also, I knew that as Japanese students, they were likely to be very passive, and would need time to relax, to get to know me, and to become familiar with new tasks. I knew they wouldn't have done any learning-how-to-learn, self-checking and self-evaluation tasks before.

254

going to practice? To describe yourself and others? "I'm twenty-three." Well, I'm not

Ss: [Laughter.]

T: . . . I'm twenty-four.

Ss: [Laughter.]

T: Um, "I'm twenty-three, I have dark hair." How well can you do that? "Yes," "a little" or "No."

[Ss complete task, talking quietly among themselves.]

T: How well can you describe yourself? OK? And, the the third thing we're going to practice is "Introducing people." "This is Yoko."

Ss: [Laughter.]

S: That her name.

T: OK, just compare what you've written with the person you're working with. OK? With your partner. Just check what you've circled and compare. You all done the same thing or something different?

[T circulates and check Ss responses.]

T: So some people feel that they can exchange personal information, but they're not very sure about describing themselves and others. All right, before, before we actually, before I ask you to do some talking, I'm going to ask you to listen to somebody else talking. And you're going to hear a number of people talking, and something happens in the

I said these things without thinking, but it was OK. I'm glad they laughed – it helped to break the ice.

I was pleased that they were able to do the task, and that there was a variety of responses from them.

It was pure chance that I happened to hit upon the student's real name as I hadn't learned any names at that stage. I like to jump right into the language work, and then learn the names as I go along. Also I didn't want them all knowing each other's names at the beginning because that was something they were going to be practicing later in the unit.

conversation. And the conversation takes place . . . [points to book] . . . somewhere. Look at the pictures in task number two. Can you see those pictures? What do you think is happening in those pictures? Can anybody guess what's happening? In those pictures? Where do you think those pictures are taking place?

S: At airport.

T: At an airport? OK. How do you know it's an airport? You're right, but how do you know? Because of the big, because of the big airplane in the background?

Ss: [Laughter.]

S: The sign of "arrival."

T: Arrivals. Yes. Arrivals. That gives us the clue. We can see some bags there as well. OK. Now I'm going to play this tape and you'll hear three short conversations, and after I've played the tape I'm going to ask you to give me some information. I want to know who's talking, and I want to know what's happened. OK?

Tape

A: *Can I help you, Sir?*

This was supposed to be a picture matching exercise, but I discovered to my horror just before the lesson started that there was a mismatch between the pictures and the tape in the pilot materials, so I couldn't do the task I'd planned.

Another little joke! Once again, it was good to find them responding.

The tape is reasonably naturalistic, and spoken at normal speed, and I knew this was the first time that they would have encountered such materials, so I was anxious to see how they would respond.

B: Yes. I lost my bag.

A: Where?

B: I don't know!

A: What was in it?

B: My passport, money, ticket, credit cards, driver's license - everything.

A: All right, now I'd just like to ask you some questions.

B: Certainly officer.

A: Last name?

B: Frota.

A: How do you spell that?

B: F–R–O–T–A

A: Are you Mike Frota?

B: That's right.

A: Good news, Mr. Frota. We've got your bag back for you.

B: Great! Where did you find it?

A: You left it in the men's rest room.

T: OK. How many people did you hear talking? How many different people?

S: Three.

S: Four.

T: Four different people. OK. Um, the conversation took place in an airport. What happened? What happened?

257

S: Lost bag.

T: The man lost his bag. Do you know the man's name?

Ss: Roul, Froul. . . ?

T: Frota. That's his, that's his last name, that's his last name. Yes. Did you hear what his first name was? [Pause.] Never mind. OK. So he lost his bag. Why was he worried? What was in the bag?

Ss: Passport, passport, credit card.

T: OK. Passport, credit card, everything. And . . . did he get his bag back?

Ss: Yes. Yes.

T: Yes, he did. Yes he did. Where did he leave it?

Ss: Men's room. Men's rest room. [Laughter.]

T: In the men's room. OK. One of the other things . . . in a minute we'll hear, we'll hear some more conversation from Mr. Frota, but before that we'll also in this unit . . . we'll look at, we'll listen to how people describe themselves - words for describing themselves. In the United States, when people describe themselves they talk about things like how big they are, the size, color of hair, color of eyes, but in different cultures, different culture use have different ways to describe themselves. What about in Japan? How do you describe yourself? How do people describe each other in Japan? Color of hair? [Laughter.] Color of eyes? [Laughter.]

I knew they wouldn't get his last name, but, apart from that, I was pleased by their responses.

Once, again, I was pleased by their animation.

Describing people is an interesting

cross-cultural issue. I knew that different cultures have different ways of describing themselves, and I thought it would be good to raise the cross-cultural issue, because it's an important part of the learning.

A friend of mine who works in Japan told me this, but they denied it. In fact, they thought it was rather funny.

Ss: No.

S: Hair style.

T: Hair style? Yeah? If you were describing a friend, or an interesting person you met, to your friends, how would you describe her? Or him?

S: Tall.

T: So.

S: Tall.

T: OK.

S: How tall she is.

T: OK. Somebody told me Japanese people also describe each other by the shape of the nose. Is this true?

Ss: [Laughter.] No. No.

T: No? [Laughs.]

S: Never do that.

T: You never do that? OK. Have a look at task four on page three. You'll see some words. Two lists of words that're used for describing people. Just look through them, and just put a check mark next to the words you know as I read them through. [T reads list as Ss check words they know.] OK, just, just compare with your partner to see if there are any words that you didn't know there.

Ss: [Inaudible.]

T: Very difficult, eh? [Laughter.] OK, the next task, the next task is slightly more difficult. One of the things, er, we practice in this course . . . is . . . or some of the things we practice are learning strategies. And one of the learning strategies that will help you learn new words is the learning strategy of "classifying." Do you know what "classifying" means?

Ss: No, no.

T: Have you heard this word before?

Ss: No.

T: Classifying means putting things that are similar together in groups. OK? So if I said, er, I want all the girls to go down to that corner of the room and all the boys to go into this corner of the room, I would be classifying the class according to their sex or their gender. What I'd like you to do now in task five is to classify some of the words from the list in task four. OK?

[Ss carry out task as T writes headings on board.]

T: Finished.

Ss: Yes.

T: OK. Someone like to call out the color words for me, please.

S: Dark.

T: Yeah, interesting. Is "dark" a color?

One of the key aspects of the course I was using is teaching students a range of learning strategies. Classifying was the focus of this lesson. Once again, I knew that the idea of focusing on the learning process as well as on the language would be a new idea for them, so I spent a little time focusing on it. They seemed to get the idea OK.

As they were doing the task, I realized that the issue of whether

260

Ss: [Inaudible.]

T: Is dark a color?

S: [Inaudible.]

T: Let's put it in anyway. [Writes on board.] OK. Next one?

Ss: White, white.

T: [Writes on board.] Next one?

Ss: Blue.

T: [Writes on board.] And?

Ss: Blond.

T: Blond. [Writes on board.] What about the "age" words?

S: Eld . . .

T: How do you say that word? How do you pronounce that word?

Ss: Elderly.

T: Next one?

Ss: [Inaudible.]

T: [Writes on board.] Next one?

ss: Old.

T: [Writes on board.] Next one?

Ss: Middle-aged.

T: [Writes on board.] And the last one?

Ss: Teenage.

T: [Writes on board.] OK. And the last list? Size. Big?

Ss: Short.

"dark" was a color or not would come up. I was going to accept it without comment, but then decided that I should let them know that it was an issue, and that I wasn't certain. I think it's important for them to be aware that everything's not cut and dried.

I solicited responses from around the room to get some idea of the overall level of skills in the group. You can get a false idea if you just get responses from the more outspoken students.

261

T: Uh-huh.

Ss: Tall.

T: Uh-huh.

Ss: Small.

T: Right. What's the difference between this word [points to "elderly"] and this word [points to "old"]? Elderly and old? Does anybody know the difference?

S: I know in Japanese.

T: You can't explain in Japanese, because I wouldn't understand.

Ss: [Laughter.]

T: If I said that, um, that Mr. Smith was elderly, but Mr. Jones was old, I think that probably I would imagine that old, someone who's old, is slightly older than someone who is elderly. Elderly also is is slightly more polite. To say that someone is elderly it doesn't sound quite as, quite as direct as if you say that somebody is old. . . . Although I'm not sure. I'd have to check with some other native speakers. [Laughter.] How would you describe yourself? How would you describe yourself? I would say that I'm, well in my culture, I guess I'm short. I'm fairly short. I used to like living in Asia because I was very big there. I was tall 'cause most people in are about that tall. [Gestures]

Ss: [Laughter.]

I knew as soon as I opened my mouth that I'd made a mistake, and that I wasn't certain what the answer was. This can happen if you just raise issues off the top of your head without having planned to teach the item.

I knew they wouldn't understand this, but I felt I had to go ahead with it anyway. In any case, I think it's healthy to make them aware from the beginning that you don't know every thing. I've seen some teachers get into terrible situations pretending that they do know everything, because sooner or later a student is going to ask you something you haven't got a clue about.

The stuff about height and age was probably unnecessary, although,

T: I wouldn't say I was elderly. I guess I'm middle aged. I used to have blond hair, but now it's gone a kind of dirty brown and is going grey. OK. Over the page then. These are some of the things we're going to be practicing this morning. I'm going to ask you to listen to another conversation now. And I'm going to play the conversation three or four times. The first time, I just want you to listen and to check off the words in task 1 when you hear them. OK? Just listen for these words and I'm going to ask you if you actually hear these words, "cause they may not all be on the tape. So the first time you listen I just want you to check off these words. Do you know the meaning of all these words? "last name," "first name," "address," "telephone number," "date of birth," "occupation," and "marital status." Do you know the meaning of all of those words?

S: What word is "occupation"?

T: Sorry?

S: What is "occupation"?

T: Occupation. Can anybody tell, explain what "occupation" is?

S: Work.

S: [Inaudible.]

T: Sorry?

Ss: [Inaudible] Work.

Commentary:

once again, they seemed to be paying attention and they laughed in the right places.

I knew they wouldn't know "marital status," and I wasn't sure about occupation.

If possible, I try to get other students to respond. This makes the class more learner-centered, and also helps me get an idea of who knows what.

263

T: Yes. What sort of job that someone does. What sort of job. Or what work that somebody does. What about "marital status"? Do you know that word? That phrase?

Ss: No, no.

T: That simply means are you married or single or divorced or widowed. OK. Do you have a husband or wife? Or are you single? Or are you divorced? So if somebody asks you your marital status. So if somebody asks you "What's your marital status?" You would say "I'm . . . ? . . . single. I'm single. OK, let's listen to the next conversation.

Tape

A: *All right, now I'd just like to get some information.*

B: *Certainly, officer.*

A: *What's the date today? March fifth, isn't it?*

B: *That's right.*

A: *OK, then, last name?*

B: *Frota.*

A: *How do you spell that?*

B: *F–R–O–T–A.*

A: *First name?*

B: *Mike.*

A: *What's your address, Mr. Frota?*

B: *I'm staying at the Settler's Guest House, 24 Smith Street, North Beach.*

One thing I *did* know was that they were all single.

This is another challenging listening – quite fast. I was anxious to see how well they'd do.

264

A: Telephone?

B: Let's see – 712-3847.

A: Thanks. And what's your date of birth?

B: November eleventh, 1975.

A: OK. And what's your occupation?

B: I'm a student.

A: A student. Right. Now, you lost a bag.

B: Yes, a black travel bag.

T: Did you hear all the words on the list, or not?

Ss: No, no.

T: Did you hear "last name"?

Ss: Yes, yes.

T: Check off "last name"? "First name"?

Ss: Yes, yes.

T: "Address"?

Ss: Yes, yes.

T: "Telephone number"?

Ss: Yes, yes.

T: Did you? I didn't hear "telephone number." I didn't hear "telephone number."

S: Mmm?

T: Mmm.

S: Just telephone.

T: Just telephone. Very good. Yes. He doesn't say

I thought that I would catch some of them out on that one, but I wanted to impress on them the importance of listening carefully for the key words. One of my major aims in listening is to get through to them that they needn't understand every word for listening to be successful. I was "telephone number," he says "telephone?"

Ss: Ahh.

T: Did you hear "date of birth"?

Ss: Yes, yes.

T: Did you hear "occupation"?

Ss: Yes, yes.

T: Did you hear "marital status"?

Ss: No, no.

T: No, neither did I. OK. I'm going to play the conversation again this time I want you to fill in the form in task two. I want you to fill in the information as you hear it. [Plays the conversation again, pausing the tape a certain points, and replaying as students fill in the form.] Do you want me to, do you want me to play that again? Can you see where you put that information? The date. Can you see "date" on the form? It's in a strange place. Just listen again. [Replays tape.] OK. Did you hear that?

Ss: [Inaudible.]

T: Well, we'll check in a minute. Let's just listen, listen for the rest of the information. [Ss complete rest of task.]

T: Now, I want you to work with another student and compare your responses.

[Ss spend five minutes checking each other's work as the teacher circulates and checks.]

pleased that at least one student had heard correctly.

I was also pleased with the response here, because, in fact, marital "status" is not on the tape.

Because of the speed of the tape, I paused the tape at a critical point to give them time to process the information and write it down. I also replayed key sections several times so they could process the information.

I was pleased at how quickly they had adapted to working in pairs,

T: Now, someone who doesn't know Mike is meeting him, and she sent a postcard to Mike before she left, and she put in the postcard a description of herself, and also of him. If you look at task three you'll see the postcard and the message to Mike. Look through and with with the person . . . with your partner, I want you to put a circle around all of the words that describe the woman who's coming to meet him, and also the words that describe Mike. OK?

[Students read postcard and identify description words.]

T: OK. Have you found any, any . . . [pauses and writes the following on the board].

Marcia: _____

Mike: _____

T: Finished.

Ss: Yes, yes.

T: OK. What words describe Marcia?

Ss: Twenty years old.

T: OK. [Writes on board.] What else?

Ss: Short, short.

T: Short.

S: Red hair.

T: [Writes on board.] Do any people in Japan have red hair?

S: [Inaudible.]

T: Sorry? In Japan, do people have red hair?

and also the fact that they were all speaking in English.

Once again, this was a spontaneous question that might have gotten me into trouble. But I remembered

267

seeing these redhead guys in downtown Tokyo and being struck by how weird it looked.

S: [Laughter.] No, no.
T: I saw saw somebody. I've seen some people with red hair, but I don't if they, maybe they have it dyed red, to look different.
S: Yeah.
T: When I was in Tokyo, when I was in Tokyo last month, I saw some young people with red hair . . .
Ss: [Laughter.]
T: . . . and I thought [pulls face]
Ss: [Laughter.]
T: How do you, how, how is Mike described?
Ss: Tall.
T: Tall. [Writes on board.]
Ss: Dark hair, dark hair, blue eyes, blue eyes.
[T writes on board].
T: OK. Turn over to page six. Mike has finally managed to leave the airport, he has his bag and he goes to a party for new students.

Tape
A: *Hello. Are you Mike?*
B: *Yes, I am. Sorry I'm late.*
A: *That's OK. I'm John.*
B: *Nice to meet you John.*
A: *And this is Anna.*

B: *Hello, Anna – good to meet you.*

C: *Hi!*

A: *And this is Maggie.*

B: *Pleased to meet you, Maggie.*

D: *Hi, Mike – come and have a drink and tell us what happened to you.*

B: *Well, I lost my bag at the airport. . . .*

T: OK. What does John, How does John introduce Anna?

Ss: This is Anna.

T: This is Anna. And, what does Mike say to Anna?

S: [Inaudible].

T: What does he say?

Ss: Good to meet you.

T: Good to meet you. Good to meet you. And then John says?

Ss: This is Maggie.

T: This is Maggie. This is Maggie. OK. So these are some of the ways that we can introduce ourselves and other people and what we say when we greet people. Have a look on page seven at task four.

I wondered how they would do on this task, but they coped quite well. It was important for them all to get this, because later they would be practicing these forms.

Extract from Students' Book:

Task 4

a) Groupwork. Read and discuss the following box.

How do single men and women meet each other?		
	% of men	*% of women*
Through friends	30	36
At parties	22	18
At bars, discos	24	18
At singles parties/dances	14	18
At work	10	9
Through newspaper ads	1	1
Don't remember	1	2

These are some of the ways single people meet each other in the United States. Do you understand all of the words here?

[Ss spend several minutes studying the table.]

S: What is "singles parties"?

T: Singles parties are special parties for people who are single, they can go to meet. At work. Through newspaper ads. And don't remember. [Laughter.] OK, that's what I'm going to ask you to do now. I want you to work with your partner and to, er, to look through the information in Part b, and to do the task.

I'd anticipated that they'd have trouble with "singles parties." They were really interested in the data. I find that most students like this kind of real stuff. Also the topic of "relationships," how people meet and so on fascinates most students.

270

Extract from Students' Book (continued):

b) Groupwork. Where can you meet new people?

	Yes	No
At school	_____	_____
At a party	_____	_____
At the movies	_____	_____
At a shopping center	_____	_____
At a sports event	_____	_____
At a concert	_____	_____
At a friend's home	_____	_____
_____	_____	_____
_____	_____	_____

Add to the list and ask some other students.

[Ss in pairs begin to do the task. The teacher circulates, answering queries such as the following.]

S: What is sports event?
T: Maybe at a tennis match, or at football or hockey.
S: Playing or watching.
T: Yeah, just watching. Um. Oh, it could be either. Could be either.
[T circulates and stops by one pair.]

They were all animated, and communicated well in English.

Most students had questions, and it was good to find that they were prepared to ask. Not all Japanese students are like this.
I didn't know the answer to this question so I said, "either." It didn't really matter to the task.

271

T: What kind of sports do you have, do you play? Do you play sports?

S: [Inaudible.]

T: What else did you come up with?

S: Part-time job.

T: Oh, that's a good one, yeah. [T reproduces table on whiteboard.]

T: That's interesting — everybody's put part-time job. Do you have a part-time job?

S: Yes. I was kindergarten teacher when I was in Japan.

T: Oh, really?

T: Most people have managed to find extra things. . . .

T: OK, let's check your responses. At school?

Ss: Yes, yes.

T: At a party.

Ss: Yes.

S: No.

T: Never been to a party? Oh you poor thing. [Laughter.] At the movies?

Ss: No, no.

T: No. why not?

Ss: [Inaudible, laughter.]

T: What about at a shopping center?

Ss: No.

I was particularly pleased at their own ideas for meeting people. If you can get this sort of information from students early in a course, it gives useful information on their needs and interests. The student who volunteered that she had been a kindergarten student in Japan is a case in point.

T: Sports event?

Ss: Yes. No.

S: Why?

S: Not at sports event. [Discussion ensues between students.]

S: What sports event?

S: Baseball game. Stadium.

S: Stadium, stadium, yes.

S: You mean watching.

S: Watching, yeah.

S: Or playing tennis.

Ss: Confusion.

T: OK, difference of opinion there. What about at a concert?

Ss: No.

T: No?

Ss: [Inaudible laughter.]

T: What about at a friend's home?

S: Yes, yes.

S: No. [Laughter.]

T: No, as well. You don't have any friends either. [Laughter.]

S: I didn't meet new people.

T: New people. OK. What other, what other places can you meet?

S: Part-time job.

T: Part-time job.

When there was disagreement within the group, I tried to push them to say why, to get discussion going.

This was the student who had said "no" to "at a party." It's interesting how personalities begin to emerge during the course of the first lesson.

273

Ss: Oh! oh!

T: Yeah! Good one. Yeah. Any more?   This item intrigued those students
                                      who hadn't thought of it.

S: Church.

T: Church.

S: [Inaudible, laughter.]

S: Travel, travel, traveling.

T: Traveling.

S: Some people meet new people at beach or, er, swimming pool.

T: OK.

[Laughter and teasing of S making last remark.]

T: Is this where you meet new people? [Laughter.]

S: Huh?

T: Is this where you meet new people?

S: Yeah. [Laughter.]

T: Any others?

S: At, er, organizations.

T: Organizations. What kind?

S: Oh, like, er, environment group or . . .

T: Environmental groups — that's good. OK. I think I'll have   I wasn't sure that I had heard
to put some of these on my list because they're very   correctly, or where this was likely
                                                               to lead. As it happened, this was an
                                                               interesting contribution.

interesting. . . . What, what sort of language do you use if you're meeting people in an English-speaking, er, place such as you are now? What kind of language do you use? Let's just listen to the next conversation. And I'm going to ask you to listen to the conversation and then practice it. But I want you to use, I want you to use language that is true for you. So use your own name, where you're from, and so on.

Tape
A: *Hi! I'm Yongsue. What's your name?*
B: *Vera.*
A: *Where are you from?*
B: *Chicago. What about you?*
A: *I'm from Seoul, Korea. What do you do?*
B: *I'm a student. What do you do?*
A: *I'm a student, too.*

T: OK, I want you to practice that conversation with your partner. But, use your own name, use where you're from, and say what you do. OK?

Ss: Mm.

T: Off you go.
[Ss mill around practicing the conversation for several minutes. T circulates and monitors.]

T: When you've finished I want to you to practice the questions in number 3, the questions and answers. And you'll get

Once again, I was really pleased with the general level of animation, and the cooperation they showed.

the answers from the box. OK. Practice with your partner. "What's Mike's last name?" "His last name is Frota." OK? Off you go.

[Ss practice in pairs. T circulates and monitors.]

T: [Leans over one student and points to an error.] OK, look you've left out. . . . I want you to see what you've left out here. OK? Just check in the [grammar] box to see which words you've left out here.

T: OK, then where is Mike from?

Ss: From Chicago.

T: He's from Chicago. And where is he now? Is he in Chicago now? Where is he now?

S: San Francisco.

T: San Francisco.

T: Now I want you practice all the language we learned in this unit. Work in pairs, say who you are, where you're from, what you do, then introduce your partner to another pair.

[Ss complete task. T circulates and monitors.]

This is a language focus exercise. The students misunderstood my instructions. I had wanted them to do the task orally, but they began writing the answers out. I let them go on with it, because they'd done quite a lot of speaking, so it was a nice change of pace. I also gave me an opportunity to check their written work, and to self-check for errors.

The culmination of the lesson was another speaking task, in which the students practiced all of the language items that had been introduced during the lesson.

Lesson 2

Context

There were seven students in class, arranged in an "L" figure. The class consisted of adult students, average age 20. They come from different parts of the world, such as Brazil, France, Japan, Korea, Thailand. There were two boys and five girls.

Transcript

T: Let's check Exercise four. How do you feel about four, was that strange?
Number four, ah, page one hundred fifty-four. Was it difficult? How did you feel?

S1:   It was easy! We did that!

T: Ah, no, people, Pat turned off the tape recorder by pushing the stop button. We didn't do that. No, we didn't.

S1:   No?

T: No.

S1:   Ah!

T: How about that kind of pattern, how did you feel about that? Have you used that one before?

Ss: No.

T: Does it look easy?

S2:   I use the wrong way. I . . .

T: You used the wrong way. How was it?

S2:   I . . . how is it? . . . I got the meaning. With reading I get the meaning of this word with reading the dictionary, I got the meaning of this word.

T: By reading the dictionary. By reading the dictionary you got the meaning of this word? OK. Well this is a verb, this is ah.

S3:   [Inaudible.]

T: That's right, you can keep it, [name]. This is ah, this is just a short activity to show you when you want to describe how something is done. When you want to describe how something is done, that's how you do it. all right, so ah, Pat turned off the tape recorder. So here she's going to describe how. How she turned off the tape recorder. By pushing the stop button. This is a "how" answer. How you do it. Ah, we show people we are happy by smiling. How do we show people we are happy?

T and Ss: By smiling.

T: We decided who should get the last piece of pie by flipping a coin. Do you know that one?

        [A student makes the gesture.]

S4:   Flipping a coin?

T: Yeah. Flipping a coin. OK. How about four? How about the next one. We satisfy our hunger.

S1:   We satisfy our hunger by going to MacDonald's

T: By going to MacDonald's [Laughs].

S3:   By eating.

T: By eating. Anything else?

S2:   We quench our thirsty by drinking water.

T: Fine. Anything else? Anything different?

S5:   By drinking beer [Laughs].

T: By drinking beer [Laughs]. I drink a lot, especially on a hot day. Wow, beer is great!

S4:   I found out what "quench" means by just satisfying by drinking.

T: No, but how did you find out what it means?

S4:   By drinking . . .

T: Nope. That's the word you don't know. How do you learn the meaning of the words that you don't know?

S4:   Ah, by looking in the dictionary.

T: By looking it up in the dictionary. Ah, I found out what "quench" means. When a word is impressive to you, it means it's an unknown word. Or words we don't know. So, I found out what "quench" means by looking it up in the dictionary.

S4:   Is it incorrect if I use checking to the dictionary?

T: By checking the dictionary? Yes, and that's the what the sentence means. The sentence means I learned the meaning of a new word by looking it up in the dictionary. Yes. And you looked it up. That's why they used that word. To trick you. OK. And what's the other one?

S6:   Tony improved his listening comprehension by listening radio.

T: Listening to?

S6:   To.

T: Listening to the radio. Or?

S5:   Watching TV

T: By watching TV. Anything different? By listening to the radio, by watching TV. . . .

S3:   By listening cartoons.

T: By what?

S3:   Listening cartoons.

T: Oh, you mean listening to . . . ?

S4:   How about dictating?

T:	Ummm . . . I'd say listening to dictation. If you're speaking, you're not improving listening comprehension. But if you listen, by listening to dictation, that would help. How about by having a conversation with Americans? Or by talking to Americans, talking to native speakers. Gungwan, for number seven, what do you have?
S5:	By watching CNN.
T:	By watching CNN. Eight.
S5:	Alex called my attention by dancing [Laughs].
T:	So, if you want to call my attention you'll start dancing? OK, I'll remember that. OK, another way I can get your attention.
S2:	Coughing?
T:	By coughing? Good. [Teacher makes the sound to explain what coughing means.] OK, another way.
S3:	Yelling.
T:	By yelling.
S1:	What is by yelling?
T:	Hey! Hey! [Loud voice.] That's yelling. What's another way to get someone's attention?
S4:	By singing.
T:	Singing.
S4:	If you sing beautifully.
T:	How about by snapping your fingers?
S2:	I can't!
T:	I can't, either. Can you use your left hand?
Ss:	I can't.
T:	My four-year-old is learning. He's very good in the bath tub, in the water? The sounds comes out very loud. Gungwan, the next?
S5:	They got rid of the rats in the building by scattering rat poison.
T:	By scattering rat poison. What else?
S3:	By putting out traps.
T:	By putting out traps.
S1:	By using chemical products.
T:	By using chemical products. Anything else? Kattel?
S1:	My dog shows me she is happy by wagging her tail.
T:	Wagging her tail.
S5:	How about shaking, shaking her tail?
T:	It's shaking her tail but wagging is the more technical word for what tails do. Tails wag. But sometimes dogs lick your body, you know, they get all excited when they are happy. OK, what are some of the other things dogs do when they are happy? What are other ways to show they're happy?
S2:	By jumping up and down. By barking.

T: By barking . . . Aha. By licking my hand. Lots of ways.

S3:   Lick?

T: Lick [Makes the gesture]. Well, probably actually the face. Dogs lick the face. The next?

S3:   Sometimes teenagers get into trouble with their parents by addicting drugs.

T: By getting addicted to drugs, by becoming addicted to drugs.

S5:   By misunderstanding.

T: By misunderstanding what they want you to do. OK.

S3:   Not going to school?

T: By not going to school. Exactly. Perfect place for the negative. The negative goes right in front of the verb with *-ing*. By not going to school. He accidentally electrocuted himself by what, what did he do?

S1:   By putting his finger in the plug.

T: Yeah, by putting his finger in the plug. What, accidentally? What's another way you can electrocute yourself? By touching the cord with wet hands. Dropping the hair drier in the bath tub?

Ss: Yeah.

T: Can you give me a sentence of your own, anything? What do you do, give me an example of what you do by doing something. I prepare for class by drinking five cups of coffee.

S1:   I come to the school by walking every day?

T: Yeah, no. I prepare for the marathon by running ten miles a day. I get ready for school by washing my hair.

S3:   He traveled around the world by riding his bike.

T: He traveled around the world . . . ah, he . . . he made a world tour. And enjoyed seeing the world by traveling by bike. How do you do something? Anything. How do you improve your English, how do you get a car, how do you find a girlfriend?

S6:   I call for my parents by using AT&T.

T: How do you get money from your parents? What's your technique?

S6:   I don't have a technique.

T: By asking nicely, by crying?

S6:   Yes.

T: I show my parents I love them by calling them once a month. So, in this case "by" is not the method for transportation, it's not exactly the method of calling by a company, it's how you do a job, how you do a task, how you get money, how you show your family you love them, how you prepare for the TOEFL.

S6:   I keep good health by talking a walk in the morning.

T: Yeah, great! How, how do you prepare for the TOEFL?

S2:	By studying a lot.
T:	By studying a lot.
S3:	By cheating [Laughs].
T:	Oh, I don't believe it, show me our shoe bottoms. How do you learn, ahm, how do you improve your English?
S4:	By making sentences in my head.
T:	By making sentences in your head. Right.
S1:	By speaking English with native speakers.
T:	By speaking English with native speakers.
S6:	By reading paperback?
T:	By reading paperback books?
S5:	By listening radio.
T:	By listening to the radio. OK, that's good. Sometimes I hear my students say "I enjoy to play tennis." "I enjoy to walk."
S3:	I enjoy playing?
T:	Playing, yes. I enjoy to drink coffee with my friends. [Pause.] I enjoy drinking coffee. There are some verbs that you are gonna see at the bottom of this page that are followed by a gerund. "Enjoy" is one of them. Because these words are used with an object. So, if you enjoy, what? I enjoy playing tennis. You quit something. You quit smoking. These are the verbs: "enjoy," "appreciate," īnd," "quit," "finish," "stop," "avoid," "postpone," "delay." And you can see the two-word verbs, they are the more casual form of these verbs. So "put off" means postpone. "Delay," "keep," "consider," "think about," "discuss," "talk about," "mention," "suggest." Are there any words that you don't know? [Pause.] If I say, "I don't mind doing my homework," what does that mean?
S1:	I don't care.
T:	I don't care.
S4:	Delay.
T:	Delay, delay. What does "delay" mean?
S2:	Similar to "postpone"?
T:	Similar to "postpone." Ahm, but not. If you are in traffic and they say there will be a ten-minute delay, it means the traffic will continue, but you will have to wait. So "delay" is equal to "wait." "Postpone" is to change the time to another time. So if I have an appointment at three o'clock and they call me and say let's postpone it until tomorrow, they changed the time or canceled it until another time. But "delay" just means you have to wait. "Delay" for you is a part of your travel plans. There might be one-hour delay at the airport. Or a two-hour delay at the train station. But if the flight has been postponed, that means the

flight has been canceled. That's a little bit different from "delay." You are on the same flight, but you will have to wait. OK? All right? So now, just turn to your partner, and let's just try to work on page one hundred fifty-five.

Further reading

The following books are particularly recommended as excellent follow-up reading to the issues dealt with in this book. We found them to be indispensable in the planning and writing of our own volume.

Allwright, D. and K. Bailey. 1991. *Focus on the Language Classroom*. Cambridge: Cambridge University Press.
  This book provides teachers and teachers in preparation with principles and techniques for the systematic study of the language classroom. It describes classroom research, looks at the principles behind successful research practice and provides practical ideas and guidance for doing research.

Legutke, M. and H. Thomas. 1991. *Process and Experience in the Language Classroom*. London: Longman.
  This book provides a detailed rationale for communicative language teaching as an experiential and task-driven learning process. The authors set out the theoretical underpinnings for communicative language teaching and give many detailed examples of how communicative approaches might be achieved in practice.

Nunan, D. 1989. *Understanding Language Classrooms*. London: Prentice-Hall.
  The aim of this book is to encourage teachers to explore processes of teaching and learning through observation and action research in their classrooms. The book provides an introduction to classroom research for those who do not have specialist training in research methods.

Parrott, M. 1993. *Tasks for Language Teachers*. Cambridge: Cambridge University Press.
  This book contains an excellent series of tasks for small-scale action research projects.

Reay-Dickins, P. and K. Germaine. 1992. *Evaluation*. Oxford: Oxford University Press.
  This book provides a readable and teacher-oriented account of evaluation. It contains many practical examples, tools and techniques that the teacher

can use to monitor and evaluate various aspects of teaching and learning in their own context.

Richards, J. and C. Lockhart. 1993. *Reflective Teaching in Second Language Classrooms.* New York: Cambridge University Press.

This book introduces teachers and teachers-in-training to a reflective approach to teaching. In a sense, it represents a companion volume to our own, and many of the ideas contained in it could quite happily have found a home here.

Richards, J. and D. Nunan (eds.). 1990. *Second Language Teacher Education.* New York: Cambridge University Press.

This book covers several areas of relevance to the management of the learning process, including observation, supervision, action research and reflective teaching. In addition to the papers in the collection, it also contains end of section questions and tasks for applying and contesting ideas in different classroom contexts.

Wajnryb, R. 1992. *Classroom Observation Tasks.* Cambridge: Cambridge University Press.

This resource book provides a range of observation tasks to guide the user through the processes of observing, analyzing and reflecting on teaching and learning. It is directed at teachers, trainee teachers, trainers, people involved in school-based support (e.g., coordinators, senior teachers, heads of school) and people involved in trainer training.

References

Allan, M. 1985. *Teaching English with Video.* London: Longman.

Allwright, D. and K. Bailey. 1991. *Focus on the Language Classroom.* Cambridge: Cambridge University Press.

Bailey, K. 1983. Competitiveness and anxiety in adult second language acquisition: Looking *at* and *through* the diary studies. In H. W. Seliger and M. H. Long (eds.), *Classroom Oriented Research in Second Language Acquisition.* Rowley, MA: Newbury House.

Baker, N. 1990. Teacher explanation of unplanned vocabulary. In G. Brindley (ed.), *The Second Language Curriculum in Action.* Sydney: NCELTR.

Bartlett, L. 1990. Teacher development through reflective teaching. In J. C. Richards and D. Nunan (eds.) *Second Language Teacher Education.* New York: Cambridge University Press.

Bartram, M. and R. Walton. 1991. *Correction.* Hove U.K.: Language Teaching Publications.

Bell, J. 1991. *Teaching Multilevel Classes in ESL.* San Diego, CA: Dominie Press.

Biggs, J. and R. Telfer. 1987. *The Process of Learning.* 2nd edition. Sydney: Prentice-Hall.

Block, D. 1994. A day in the life of a class: Teacher/learner perceptions of task purpose in conflict. System, 22, 4, 473–486.

Block, D. Forthcoming. A window on the classroom: Classroom events viewed from different angles. In K. Bailey and D. Nunan (eds.), *Voices from the Language Classroom: Qualitative Research in Second Language Education.* New York: Cambridge University Press.

Blum, R. 1984. *Effective Schooling Practices: A Research Synthesis.* Portland, Oregon: Northwest Regional Educational Laboratory.

Borg, W., M. Kelley, P. Langer and M. Gall. 1970. *The Mini-course: A Microteaching Approach to Teacher Education.* Beverly Hills, CA: Macmillan Educational Services.

Breen, M. and C. N. Candlin. 1987. Which materials? A consumer's and designer's guide. In L. Sheldon (ed.), *ELT Textbooks and Materials: Problems in Evaluation and Development.* ELT Document 126. London: Modern English Publications.

Brindley, G. 1984. *Needs Analysis and Objective Setting in the Adult Migrant Education Program.* Sydney: NSW Adult Migrant Education Service.

Brindley, G. 1989. *Assessing Achievement in a Learner-Centred Curriculum.* Sydney: NCELTR.

Brock, C. 1986. The effects of referential questions on ESL classroom discourse. *TESOL Quarterly,* 20, 1, 47–59.

Brophy, J. and T. Good. 1986. Teacher behavior and student achievement. In M. Wittrock (ed.), *Handbook of Research on Teaching.* 3rd edition. New York: Macmillan.

Brown, H. D. 1992. Toward a new understanding of the role of motivation in your English language classroom. In Kral, T., L. Morkpring, S. Tanewong, A. Wongsorn, S. Tiancharoen, D. Chulasai and P. Navarat (eds.), *Exploitations and Innovations in ELT Methodology.* Bangkok: Chulalonghorn University Language Institute.

Brown, R. 1989. Classroom pedagogics: A syllabus for the interactive stage? *The Teacher Trainer,* 2, 2, 13–17; 3, 8–9.

Cathcart, R. and J. Olsen. 1976. Teachers' and students' preferences for correction of classroom conversation errors. In J. Fanselow and R. Crymes (eds.), *On TESOL 1976.* Washington, D.C.: TESOL.

Cazden, C. 1988. *Classroom Discourse: The Language of Teaching and Learning.* Portsmouth, NH: Heinemann.

Chaix, P. and C. O'Neil. 1978. A Critical Analysis of Forms of Autonomous Learning (Autodidaxy and Semi-autonomy) in the Field of Foreign Language Learning: Final Report, UNESCO Doc Ed 78/WS/58.

Chaudron, C. 1988. *Second Language Classrooms: Research on Teaching and Learning.* New York: Cambridge University Press.

Clark, C. M. and R. L. Yinger. 1979. Teachers' thinking. In P. Peterson and H.J. Walberg (eds.) *Research on Teaching.* Berkley, CA: McCutchen.

Cole, K. 1994. Error correction: Teacher behaviors and student responses, unpublished monograph.

Coleman, H. 1989a. Large Classes in Nigeria, Project Report No. 6. Leeds: Lancaster-Leeds Language Learning in Large Classes Research Project.

Coleman, H. 1989b. How Large Are Large Classes? Project Report No. 4. Leeds: Lancaster-Leeds Language Learning in Large Classes Research Project.

Crichton, J. 1990. Crisis points in error correction. In G. Brindley (ed.), *The Second Language Curriculum in Action.* Sydney: NCELTR.

Dewey, J. 1963. *Experience and Education.* New York: Macmillan.

Dickinson, L. 1987. *Self-instruction in Language Learning.* Cambridge: Cambridge University Press.

Doyle, W. 1986. Classroom organization and management. In M. Wittrock (ed.) *Handbook of Research on Teaching.* 3rd edition. New York: Macmillan.

Duppenthaler, P. 1991. Suggestions for language classes. *Guidelines,* 13, 1, 64–73.

Emmer, E., C. Evertson and L. Anderson. 1980. Effective classroom management at the beginning of the school year. *Elementary School Journal,* 80, 219–231.

Estaire, S. and J. Zanón. 1994. *Planning Classwork: A Task Based Approach.* Oxford: Heinemann.

Everard, K. 1986. *Developing Management in Schools.* Oxford: Blackwell.

Everard, K. and G. Morris. 1990. *Effective School Management.* London: Paul Chapman Publishing.

Evertson, C. 1985. Training teachers in classroom management: An experimental study in secondary school classrooms. *Journal of Educational Research,* 79, 51–58.

Evertson, C., E. Emmer, J. Sanford and B. Clemments. 1983. Improving classroom management: An experiment in elementary school classrooms. *Elementary School Journal,* 84, 173–188.

Franke, F. 1884. *Die Praktische Spracherlernung auf Grund der Psychologie und der Physiologie der Sprache dargestellt.* Leipzig: O. R. Reisland.

Gardner, R. 1985. *Social Psychology and Second Language Learning: The Role of Attitudes and Motivation.* London: Arnold.

Gardner, R. and W. E. Lambert. 1972. *Attitudes and Motivation in Second Language Learning.* Rowley, MA.: Newbury House.

Gebhard, J. 1990. Models of supervision: Choices. In J. C. Richards and D. Nunan (eds.), *Second Language Teacher Evaluation.* New York: Cambridge University Press.

Good, T. and J. Brophy. 1987. *Looking in Classrooms.* New York: Harper & Row.

Gronlund, N. 1981. *Measurement and Evaluation in Education.* New York: Macmillan.

Grosse, C. U. 1991. The TESOL methods course. *TESOL* Quarterly, 25, 1, 29–49.

Hadfield, J. 1992. *Classroom Dynamics.* Oxford: Oxford University Press.

Hammond, J., A. Burns, H. Joyce, D. Brosnan and L. Gerot. 1992. *English for Social Purposes: A Handbook for Teachers of Adult Literacy.* Sydney: NCELTR.

Hardisty, D. and S. Windeatt. 1989. *CALL.* Oxford: Oxford University Press.

Harmer, J. 1991. *The Practice of English Language Teaching.* London: Longman.

Higgins, J. and T. Johns. 1984. *Computers in Language Learning.* London: Collins.

Holley, F. and J. King. 1971. Imitation and correction in foreign language learning. *Modern Language Journal,* 55, 494–498.

Honeyfield, J. 1991. The formation of small groups in the language classroom. *Guidelines,* 13, 1, 11–18.

Horvitz, E. and D. Young. (eds.), 1989. *Language Anxiety: From Theory and Research to Classroom Implications*. Englewood Cliffs, NJ: Prentice-Hall.

Hunkins, F. 1980. *Curriculum Development: Program Improvement*. Columbus, Ohio: Charles Merrill Publishing Co.

Jackson, P. and H. Lahaderne. 1967. Inequalities of teacher-pupil contacts. *Psychology in the Schools*, 4, 204–208.

Johnson, K. 1992. Learning to teach: Instructional actions and decisions of preservice ESL teachers. *TESOL Quarterly*, 26, 507–535.

Johnson, K. 1994. The emerging beliefs and instructional practices of preservice English as a second language teachers. *Teaching and Teacher Education*, 10, 4, 439–452.

Joyce, B. and M. Weil. 1986. *Models of Teaching*. Englewood Cliffs, NJ: Prentice-Hall.

Kohonen, V. 1992. Experiential language learning: Second language learning as cooperative learner education. In D. Nunan (ed.), *Collaborative Language Learning and Teaching*. Cambridge: Cambridge University Press.

Kolb, D. 1984. *Experiential Learning: Experience as the Source of Learning and Development*. Englewood Cliffs, NJ: Prentice-Hall.

Kounin, J. 1970. *Discipline and Group Management in Schools*. New York: Holt, Rinehart and Winston.

Koziol, S. and M. Call. 1988. Constructing and Using Teacher Self-Report Inventories. Workshop presented at the 22nd Annual TESOL Convention, Chicago, March 1988.

Lampert, M. 1985. How do teachers manage to teach? Perspectives on problems in practice. *Harvard Educational Review*, 55, 2, 178–194.

Lawrence, M. and D. Andrich. 1987. The Affective Domain Study, Report to the Department of Immigration and Ethnic Affairs: Canberra, Australia.

Legutke, M. and H. Thomas. 1991. *Process and Experience in the Language Classroom*. London: Longman.

Long, M. and G. Crookes. 1986. Intervention points in second language classroom processes. In B. B. Das (ed.), *Patterns of Classroom Interaction in Southeast Asia*. Singapore: RELC.

Lozano, F. and M. Vickers. 1990. Teacher Observation/Evaluation Report, Instituto Mexicano de Relaciones Culturales, A.C. Hamburgo 115, 06600 Mexico, D.F.

McPherson, K. 1992. Responses to Correction of Spoken Errors in Beginner and Advanced Adult Learners, unpublished M.Ed. (TESOL) dissertation, University of South Australia.

Malamah-Thomas, A. 1987. *Classroom Interaction*. Oxford: Oxford University Press.

Malcolm, I. 1991. "All right then, if you don't want to do that. . .": Strategy and counterstrategy in classroom discourse management. Guidelines, 13, 2, 1–17.

Marland, P. 1977. A study of teachers' interactive thoughts. Unpublished manuscript, University of Alberta, Canada.

Munby, H. 1982. The place of teachers' beliefs in research on teacher thinking and decision making, and an alternative methodology. *Instructional Science,* 11, 201–225.

Murphey, T. 1991. *Teaching One to One.* London: Longman.

Nolasco, R. and L. Arthur. 1988. *Large Classes.* London: Macmillan.

Nunan, D. 1987. Communicative language teaching: Making it work. *ELT Journal,* 41, 2, 136–45.

Nunan, D. 1988. *The Learner Centred Curriculum.* Cambridge: Cambridge University Press.

Nunan, D. 1989a. *Designing Tasks for the Communicative Classroom.* Cambridge: Cambridge University Press.

Nunan, D. 1989b. *Understanding Language Classrooms.* London: Prentice-Hall.

Nunan, D. 1990. Action research in the language classroom. In J. Richards and D. Nunan (eds.), *Second Language Teacher Education.* New York: Cambridge University Press.

Nunan, D. 1991. Language teachers' thoughts, judgments and decisions, plenary presentation, International Conference on Second Language Teacher Education, City Polytechnic of Hong Kong, Hong Kong, April 1991.

Nunan, D. 1992a. *Research Methods in Language Learning.* New York: Cambridge University Press.

Nunan, D. 1992b. Understanding classroom interaction, plenary presentation, BrazTESOL, São Paulo, July 1992.

Nunan, D. (ed.) 1992c. *Collaborative Language Learning and Teaching.* Cambridge: Cambridge University Press.

Nunan, D. 1995a. *ATLAS: Learning-Centered Communication.* Boston: Heinle & Heinle.

Nunan, D. 1995b. Closing the gap between learning and instruction. *TESOL Quarterly,* Spring 1995.

Nunan, D. Forthcoming. Hidden voices: Insiders' views on teaching and learning. In K. Bailey and D. Nunan (eds.) *Voices from the Language Classroom: Qualitative Research in Second Language Education.* New York: Cambridge University Press.

Nunan, D. and G. Brindley. 1986. The learner-centred curriculum in theory and practice, paper presented at the Annual TESOL Convention, Anaheim, April 1986.

Nunan, D., J. Lockwood and S. Hood. 1993. *The Australian English Course.* Cambridge: Cambridge University Press.

Pajares, M. 1992. Teachers' beliefs and educational research: Cleaning up a messy construct. *Review of Educational Research,* 62, 307–332.

Pak, J. 1986. *Find Out How You Teach.* Adelaide: National Curriculum Resource Centre.

Parrott, M. 1993. *Tasks for Language Teachers.* Cambridge: Cambridge University Press.

Peterson, P., R. Marx and C. M. Clark. 1978. Teacher planning, teacher behavior, and student achievement. *American Educational Research Journal,* 15, 417–432.

Reay-Dickins, P. and K. Germaine. 1992. *Evaluation.* Oxford: Oxford University Press.

Richards, J. 1993. Beyond the text book: The role of commercial materials in language teaching. *RELC Journal,* 24, 1, 1–14.

Richards, J. C. and D. Nunan. (eds.) 1990. *Second Language Teacher Education.* New York: Cambridge University Press.

Richards, J. C. and C. Lockhart. 1994. *Reflective Teaching in Second Language Classrooms.* New York: Cambridge University Press.

Richards, J. and T. Rodgers. 1986. *Approaches and Methods in Language Teaching.* New York: Cambridge University Press.

Richards, J., P. Tung and P. Ng. 1992. The Culture of the English Language Teacher, City Polytechnic of Hong Kong, Department of English, Research Report No. 6.

Rowe, M. 1974. Wait-time and rewards as instructional variables, their influence on language, logic and fate control: Part I – Wait-time. *Journal of Research on Science Teaching,* 11, 81–94.

Rowe, M. 1986. Wait time: Slowing down may be a way of speeding up. Journal of Teacher Education, 37, 43–50.

Scarino, A., D. Vale, P. McKay and J. Clark. 1988. *Australian Language Levels Guidelines.* Canberra: Curriculum Development Centre.

Scott, M. and S. Murison-Bowie. 1993. *MicroConcord Manual: An Introduction to the Practices and Principles of Concordancing in Language Teaching.* Oxford: Oxford University Press.

Scovel, T. 1978. The effect of affect on foreign language learning: A review of the anxiety research. *Language Learning,* 28, 129–142.

Shamin, F. (forthcoming) In and out of the action zone: Location as a feature of interaction in large classes in Pakistan. In K. Bailey and D. Nunan (eds.), *Voices from the Language Classroom: Qualitative Research in Second Language Education.* New York: Cambridge University Press.

Shrum, J. and V. Tech. 1985. Wait-time and the use of target or native languages. *Foreign Language Annals,* 18, 304–313.

Shulman, L. 1987. Knowledge and teaching: Foundations of the new reform. Harvard Educational Review, 57, 1, 1–22.

South Australian Education Department. 1990. *ESL Curriculum Guidelines.* Adelaide, SA: Educational Department.

Taylor, P. 1970. *How Teachers Plan Their Courses.* England: National Foundation for the Educational Research in England and Wales.

Tribble, C. and G. Jones. 1990. *Concordances in the Classroom.* London: Longman.

Tsui, A. 1995. *Introducing Classroom Interaction.* London: Penguin.

Tyler, R. 1949. *Principles of Curriculum and Instruction.* New York: Harcourt Brace.

Underhill, A. 1989. Process in humanistic education. *English Language Teaching Journal,* 43, 250–256.

van Lier, L. 1988. *The Classroom and the Language Learner.* London: Longman.

van Lier, L. 1989. *The Classroom and the Language Learner.* London: Longman.

Wajnryb, R. 1992. *Classroom Observation Tasks.* Cambridge: Cambridge University Press.

White, P. 1961. *The Tree of Man.* London: Penguin.

Wiberg, P. 1987. *One-to-One: A Teacher's Handbook.* Brighton: Language Teaching Publications.

Willing, K. 1988. *Learning Styles in Adult Migrant Education.* Adelaide: National Curriculum Resource Centre.

Wong, A. K. C., Y. C. Au-Yeung and J. A. G. McClelland. 1992. *Classroom Management.* Hong Kong: Longman.

Woods, D. 1993. Processes in ESL teaching: A study of the role of planning and interpretive processes in the practice of teaching english as a second language. *Carleton Papers in Applied Language Studies.* Occasional Papers, 3.

Woods, D. 1993. *Processes in ESL Teaching: A Study of the Role of Planning and Interpretive Processes in the Practice of Teaching English as a Second Language.* Ottawa, Canada: Centre for Applied Language Studies.

Wright, T. 1987. *Roles of Teachers and Learners.* Oxford: Oxford University Press.

Yorkey, R. 1970. *Study Skills for Students of English as a Second Language.* New York: McGraw–Hill.

Zahoric, J. 1986. Acquiring teaching skills. *Journal of Teacher Education,* 27, 5, 21–25.

Author index

Subject index